HOW TO HELP
CHILDREN AND
YOUNG PEOPLE
WITH COMPLEX
BEHAVIOURAL
DIFFICULTIES

of related interest

Promoting Emotional Education
Engaging Children and Young People with Social, Emotional and
Behavioural Difficulties
Edited by Carmel Cefai and Paul Cooper
Part of the Innovative Learning for All series
ISBN 978 1 84310 996 9

Working with Young Women
Activities for Exploring Personal, Social and Emotional Issues
2nd edition
Vanessa Rogers
ISBN 978 1 84905 095 1

Working with Young Men
Activities for Exploring Personal, Social and Emotional Issues
2nd edition
Vanessa Rogers
ISBN 978 1 84905 101 9

Help your Child or Teen Get Back On Track
What Parents and Professionals Can Do for Childhood Emotional and
Behavioral Problems
Kenneth H. Talan, M.D.
ISBN hardback 978 1 84310 870 2
ISBN paperback 978 1 84310 914 3

**Children with Emotional and Behavioural Difficulties and
Communication Problems**
There is always a reason
Melanie Cross
ISBN 978 1 84310 135 2

HOW TO HELP CHILDREN AND YOUNG PEOPLE WITH COMPLEX BEHAVIOURAL DIFFICULTIES:

A Guide for Practitioners Working in Educational Settings

Ted Cole and
Barbara Knowles

Foreword by
Joan Pritchard

sebda
Working together for children

Jessica Kingsley *Publishers*
London and Philadelphia

First published in 2011
by Jessica Kingsley Publishers
116 Pentonville Road
London N1 9JB, UK
and
400 Market Street, Suite 400
Philadelphia, PA 19106, USA

www.jkp.com

Library of Congress Cataloging in Publication Data
A CIP catalog record for this book is available from the Library of Congress

British Library Cataloguing in Publication Data
A CIP catalogue record for this book is available from the British Library

ISBN 978 1 84905 049 4

Printed and bound in Great Britain by MPG Books Group

CONTENTS

List of Abbreviations 9

Foreword... 11

CHAPTER 1
Introduction

.... 13

The need for this book 13
Case studies 14; How the English government sees BESD 16;
Terminology: Why 'BESD' rather than 'SEBD' or 'EBD'? 18; The
extent of BESD 19; Are BESDs in children getting more frequent
and worse? 22; The content of the book 23; People rather than
places matter 24

PART 1: UNDERSTANDING BESD

CHAPTER 2
The Past, the Present and Patterns of Educational
Provision 29

Problems of definition and placement 30; Debates and themes:
c.1850–1950 30; Providing for 'the maladjusted': 1950–1975 31;
Provision for young offenders and other children 'at risk' 33; The
national survey of provision for maladjusted children, 1975–
1978 34; 'Emotional and behavioural difficulties': 1980s into
the new century 35; Developments in the early 21st century 38;
Patterns of provision for children with BESD 43; Review 44

CHAPTER 3
Child Development and BESD...................... 46

Genetic inheritance: The nature/nurture debate 48; The
development of the brain 48; Attachment 52; Bonding and
'claiming' 56; Meeting the needs of children 57; Parenting
style 58; Development of self-concept and self-esteem 58; Internal
working models 60; 'Fixed' and 'growth' mindsets 61; Ages and
stages of development 62; Play 64; Risk and resilience factors
in childhood 65; Separation and loss 67; Parental separation and
divorce 69; Defining well-being, mental health and mental-health
problems 71; ADHD 71; Anxiety 72; Depression 72; Self-harm
and suicide 74; Eating disorders and obesity 76; Review:The
iceberg of behaviour 78

CHAPTER 4
Further Theory Underpinning Effective Interventions   80

The Psychodynamic Approach 81; The Behaviourist Approach 82;
The Cognitive-Behavioural Approach 86; Mindfulness 88;
Positive Psychology 90; Review 92

PART 2: HELPFUL INTERVENTIONS

CHAPTER 5
Whole-School Influences 95

Inclusive values and ethos 95; Leadership 96; A critical mass
of staff committed to inclusive values 97; Whole-school
learning and behaviour policies 98; Caring, sharing, learning
settings 100; Delivering skilled teaching responsive to
BESD 101; Respecting and listening to pupils with BESD and
encouraging participation 103; SEAL and promoting health and
well-being 104; 'Outward-looking schools' 105; Review 105

CHAPTER 6
Helpful Group Interventions in Class and Around
School... 106

Do we sometimes make BESD worse? 107; Skilled class teaching
and curriculum delivery reduces BESD 108; The positive impact

of established and rehearsed routines 115; Building well-being in the classroom (SEAL) 118; Specific group approaches 123; Checking the behavioural environment: Physical design and layout 126; Your part in lessening BESD 128; Review 129

CHAPTER 7
The Individual Child from an Educational Perspective   130

The teaching and learning intervention cycle 131; Assessment and planning 132; Identifying and responding to special (or 'additional') educational needs 136; Individual support through personalised learning 142; Staff language and communication 144; Rewarding behaviour to encourage a 'growth' mindset 146; Behaviour in and around the classroom 147; Helpful use of support staff 151; Handling transitions to new classes or schools 152; Review 152

CHAPTER 8
Well-being, Mental Health and the Individual Child   154

Factors in creating a helpful relationship with a child with BESD 155; Talking and listening 157; Using art, creative activities and play 158; Sport and exercise 159; The appropriate use of physical contact 160; 'Positive handling' or 'use of force' 162; Safeguarding issues 164; A healing approach to anger management 165; Applying cognitive behavioural principles to practice 169; Mindfulness 171; Solution-focused brief approaches 173; Addressing mental-health difficulties in children with BESD 176; Review 183

CHAPTER 9
Support from Beyond Your Work Setting 185

Behaviour partnerships 185; 'Pastoral Support Programmes': Accessing support from other agencies 187; The Common Assessment Framework 188; Different supporting agencies and their roles 189; Fair expectations of social workers and CAMHS 194; The challenge of confidentiality, information sharing and working together 198; Building links and trust 199; Knowing your local services 199; Review 199

CHAPTER 10
Working with Parents and Carers.................... 201

Government advice and expectations 202; Obstacles to close working with parents and carers 203; How people feel when referred to CAMHS or children's services 204; Strategies for engaging parents 205; Parent training and support programmes 208; Review 209

CHAPTER 11
Review and Conclusions............................ 210

Review of key points 210; Caring for the practitioner 213

Appendix 1
The SEBDA abbreviated policy on inclusion and SEBD (BESD). 219

Appendix 2
Identifying support from local services 220

Recommended Resources.................................... 221

References 224

Subject Index... 235

Author Index... 239

LIST OF ABBREVIATIONS

3MBS	Three Minute Breathing Space ('mini-meditation')
ABC	(behaviourist theory) Antecedents, behaviour and consequences
ADD or AD/HD	Attention deficit disorder or AD/hyperactivity disorder (a DSM category)
AFL	Assessment for Learning (National Strategies' term)
ASD	Autistic spectrum difficulties
BESD	Behavioural, emotional and social difficulties
CAF	Common Assessment Framework (multi-agency procedure)
CAMHS	Child and Adolescent Mental Health Services
CBT	Cognitive Behaviour Therapy
CPD	Continuing professional development
CPN	Community psychiatric nurse
CSIE	Centre for Studies in Inclusive Education
DCSF	Department for Children, Schools and Families
DDA	Disability and Discrimination Act, 1995
DFE/ DFEE/ DfES	Dept for Education/…and Employment/.for Education and Science (old names for DCSF).
DHSS	Department for Health and Social Security
DoH	Department of Health (replaced DHSS)
DSM	*Diagnostic and Statistical Manual*, the American Psychiatric Association
EBD	Emotional and Behavioural Difficulties
ECM	*Every Child Matters* 2003 Green Paper and later policy agenda
EP	Educational psychologist
GCSE	General Certificate of Secondary Education
GP	General practitioner (community-based family doctor)
HMI	Her Majesty's Inspectorate (of schools) – (England)

HMIE	Her Majesty's Inspectorate – Education (Scotland)
IWM	Internal working model (how a child perceives his/her world)
LA/LEA	Local Authority – superseded 'Local Education Authorities' when the 2004 Children Act created unified education and children's social services
LSU	'Learning Support Unit' (special behavioural unit within a mainstream school)
MLD	Moderate learning difficulties (a type of SEN)
OCD	Obsessive compulsive disorder (a DSM category)
ODD	Oppositional defiance disorder (a DSM category)
Ofsted	Office for Standards in Education: Government inspectorate also responsible for inspecting children's homes/services
PRU	'Pupil Referral Unit' (from 2010, called 'short stay school' – off-site special unit for children excluded or otherwise at risk, e.g. pregnant school girls)
PSP	Pastoral support programme (multi-disciplinary plan to try to avoid school exclusion for a pupil)
QCA	Qualifications and Curriculum Authority
QFT	'Quality First Teaching' – National Strategies term for skilled basic teaching.
RPI	'Restrictive physical intervention' ('physical restraint' or 'positive handling')
SATs	Standard assessments tasks/tests
SDQ	'Strengths and Difficulties Questionnaire' (Goodman's)
SEAL	Social and emotional aspects of learning
SEBD	Social, emotional and behavioural difficulties
SEBDA	The Social, Emotional and Behavioural Difficulties Association
SEBS	Social, emotional and behavioural skills
SEN	Special educational needs
SENCo	Special educational needs co-ordinator
SFBA/ SFBT	Solution-focused brief approaches/brief therapy
SLCN	Speech, language and communication needs (type of SEN)
SMART	Small, measurable, achievable, relevant, time-limited targets
YOT	Youth offending team
ZPD	Zone of proximal development (associated with Vygotsky)

FOREWORD

I was very pleased to be asked to write the foreword to this book. It gives me the opportunity to recommend it to what I trust will be a wide range of people at government and local authority level, as well as those working in the field with children and young people who are experiencing social, emotional and behavioural difficulties ('SEBD' – or 'BESD', the descriptor used in this book). It is important for the emotional health and well-being of practitioners that they have access to a textbook to which they can turn for background information and advice on the challenges they face every day.

It is a sad fact that the pressures, obstacles and life situations many children and young people face result in acute and complex difficulties at some point in their childhood. Some experience social, physical and emotional deprivation, which other agencies as well as educational practitioners have to address. It is vital that all practitioners working with these children and young people gain the necessary skills and understanding to guide them to the best possible outcomes. This book will assist in that task.

The book provides some explanation of the history and development of the labels used to describe the difficulties they present. It goes on to explore the wide range of strategies that have been, and continue to be, used to ameliorate these children and young people's difficulties across a range of settings, including mainstream and special schools. All this is set in the context of current legislation and government guidelines and initiatives.

I am confident that all who read this text will be encouraged to continue with the vital role they play in helping children and young people with social, emotional and behavioural difficulties to make educational progress and to achieve a greater degree of happiness and well-being.

Joan Pritchard
Chairman, SEBDA
(Social, Emotional and Behavioural Difficulties Association)

CHAPTER 1

INTRODUCTION

THE NEED FOR THIS BOOK

This book has been written as a response to the intense concerns of teachers and other professionals working in, or supporting, educational settings, about children and young people's complex behaviour difficulties. Pupils with 'BESD', i.e. behavioural, emotional and social difficulties (or 'SEBD' or 'EBD' – see below), often cause highly challenging disruption in lessons, at break-times or in the residential provision attached to some special schools. A single child's actions can cause extreme and long-lasting stress to staff, inducing feelings of inadequacy, anger and, at times, despair. There are other girls and boys, sometimes quiet and withdrawn, who also have BESD but can be overlooked. They, too, need our support.

We shall talk about children,[1] most commonly males, who could be of any ethnic heritage but will most frequently be white, who present contrasting behavioural traits and come from varied home backgrounds. They could be in a range of educational settings – mainstream schools, special schools (sometimes residential) or 'short stay schools' (also known as 'pupil referral units' or 'PRUs'). If in their teenage years, these children could be in other forms of alternative educational provision or attending further education colleges.

Despite the best efforts of professionals involved in assessing children, there can be practical difficulties in the way of matching pupils with BESD to the educational settings most appropriate to their needs. History warns against assuming that special schools (particularly those with residential places) necessarily provide for the children with the most complex and challenging of needs, or that mainstream and day schools only cope with children with mild forms of BESD (see, e.g., Cole, Daniels and Visser 2003; Laslett 1977). Most pupils with BESD attend their local primary school or comprehensive.

CASE STUDIES

You might be working, or will work, with children who resemble the five fictional pupils described below:

Cameron, six years of age, has just started his second year of schooling. He is very anxious, rarely smiles and is reluctant to speak. He has no friends, tends to be teased and often bursts into tears. He does not have the resilience of normal children and can be knocked back by the slightest event. He reacts badly to comments, however mild, about his behaviour. His mother has always appeared distant from her son and has serious mental-health problems. His father is in prison (although his teacher does not know this). Cameron has a problem with speech and language (speaking and writing are very difficult for him) and uses limited speech. He seems increasingly to be in 'a different place' – not finishing work – and lacks confidence to try new tasks. He is benefiting from spending some of each week in his school's 'nurture group'.

Ashley, ten years of age, is in his final year at primary school. His mother left home without warning when he was six. He lives with his over 'physical' father and partner, who just tolerates Ashley. He has been on his school's special educational needs' register for two years at the 'school action plus' stage of the Special Educational Needs (SEN) Code of Practice (DfEE 2001a). He clearly has mild to moderate learning difficulties, reading only haltingly. He is falling further and further behind in class and his behaviour difficulties are increasing. In class, he frequently talks out of turn, hinders other children and finds difficulty in staying on his chair. He can be defiant and argumentative. He is often in trouble in the playground or in the corridors. He is embarrassed by having a support worker in class. He is helped by clear, small-step learning. He is suspicious of all adults, who find it hard to relate to him. Sometimes a violent side appears and he attacks his peers. He has frightening, angry outbursts, which take a long time to subside. He is very worried about moving to secondary school at the end of the school year.

Ryan, twelve years of age, in his second year at secondary school, has been on the school's SEN register for BESD since late primary school. He lives with his unmarried mother and her boyfriend, whom Ryan hates and who fathered his half-brother. Ryan feels that he is 'in the way' at home. At school, he displays a short attention span, has limited skills in language and basic skills. He feels bad about the fact that he operates at the level of an eight or nine year old. He is easily upset by others and has anger issues. He is unpopular and tends to spoil offered friendships. He has had two fixed-term exclusions for physical attacks on peers. However, at times he smiles a lot and responds to humour, clear routines, structures and staff attention and supervision.

Cheryl, fourteen years of age, is now in her second year at a 'short-stay school' (formerly known as a 'pupil referral unit' or 'PRU'). Attempts to find her a place at a special school have failed and the local mainstream schools have found reasons not to admit her because of her record of highly disruptive, sometimes sexualised, and, at times, violent behaviour in the two mainstream schools from which she was excluded. She lives with her mother and step-father. She has run away from home more than once but now appears more settled. She is responding quite well to the highly personalised, small-group educational setting in which she has developed a good relationship with staff, who can make some allowance for her swearing and intransigence. She is working towards a limited range of accredited examinations.

Stephen, fifteen years of age, was long ago 'statemented' for BESD and is 'looked after' ('in care'[2]). His alcoholic mother was suspected of abuse and neglect. There was never a firm attachment between mother and son. He rarely sees her and does not know his father. He has had a succession of failed foster placements. He did quite well at a primary special school before 'transferring at eleven to a mainstream secondary school, where his hyperactivity and behaviour are regarded as the root causes of his difficulties. However dyslexia contributes to his frustration and failure in class. When he resists his medication, his hyperactive behaviour, inability to follow social conventions and violence mean that the school are considering a transfer to a 'short stay school' (or PRU), but there are no vacancies there at present. Stephen has been warned by police for minor offences. Recently his half-hearted attempt to cut his wrists and depressed mood led to a social worker involving Child and Adolescent Mental Health Services (CAMHS).

These five case studies suggest that the permutations of BESD are legion. BESDs are a mixture of social, emotional/psychological and biological/ genetic/physical factors shifting in constant interaction with each other and with the environment in which a child lives. Major influences are the quality of nurturing and other aspects of parenting (or substitute care) that the child experiences from the moment of his or her conception. This blend of factors gives rise to a child's complex psychology and often challenging behaviour. Sometimes the behaviour will be 'acted out' (i.e. externalised for others to experience) and sometimes 'acted in' (i.e. as emotional difficulties that are internalised). Often, like an iceberg, much can be hidden from view.

HOW THE ENGLISH GOVERNMENT SEES BESD

The English government's current guidance in this area (DCSF 2008a) sketches many varied facets of what is called, in its terminology, 'behavioural, emotional and social difficulties'. It refers back to the demand in the Education Act 1996 for more children with special educational needs (SENs) to be educated in mainstream schools. This Act led to the government's guidance, the revised SEN Code of Practice (DfEE 2001a). This Code allowed for 'a very small minority of children' with complex needs to receive 'special educational provision', defined as 'educational provision which is additional to, or otherwise different from, the educational provision made generally for children of their age in schools maintained by the LEA, other than special schools'. Local authorities were to make effective arrangements for SEN by ensuring that the needs of children and young people with SEN were identified and assessed quickly and matched by appropriate provision. BESD was identified as a type of SEN.

Quoting from the SEN Code of Practice, the 2008 guidance says that BESD are:

> a learning difficulty where children and young people demonstrate features of emotional and behavioural difficulties such as: being withdrawn or isolated, disruptive and disturbing; being hyperactive and lacking concentration; having immature social skills; or presenting challenging behaviours arising from other complex special needs. (DCSF 2008a paragraph 49)

Indicating the links between BESD and mental health, the guidance makes reference to DfE (2001b), an excellent document which we commend to readers. Paragraph 54 says that the term BESD can include mental-health conditions such as 'conduct disorders', attention deficit hyperactivity disorder

(ADHD), school phobia, self-harm or depression. Mention is also made of related disorders with a probable biological causation (paragraph 58):

> There need not be a medical diagnosis for a child or young person to be identified as having BESD. However, children and young people with a medical diagnosis, including emotional disorders such as depression and eating disorders; conduct disorders such as oppositional defiance disorder (ODD); hyperkinetic disorders including attention deficit disorder or attention deficit hyperactivity disorder (ADD/ADHD); and syndromes such as Tourette's, are all likely to have BESD, as defined in the SEN Code of Practice.

The guidance considers the relationship between disability and BESD (paragraph 51), saying that many children and young people with BESD are also covered by the Disability Discrimination Act 1995 (DDA). The DDA says: 'someone has a disability if they have "a mental or physical impairment that has a long-term and substantial adverse effect on their ability to carry out normal day-to-day activities". The terms "long-term" and "substantial" provide a relatively low threshold and therefore include a significant group of children within the definition.'

An educational and mental health perspective is also given:

> Pupils with BESD cover the full range of ability...behaviour difficulties may frustrate access to the curriculum, for example if aggressive behaviour leads to exclusion from some classroom activities or from the school. For others, a learning difficulty may lead to or exacerbate behavioural and emotional difficulties... Difficulties in acquiring basic skills can also lead to low self-esteem and even depression. (paragraph 57)

Internalised, 'within child' factors are separated from more obvious externalised ones: 'Underlying reasons for BESD can encompass both "within child" factors and external factors' (paragraph 60).

The guidance stresses the link between BESD and other SENs:

> There is a higher incidence of BESD identified in children with other special educational needs. It is sometimes difficult to discern the main cause of the behavioural or emotional difficulties or to decide whether BESD or another learning difficulty is the primary need. (paragraph 60)

Belatedly, in our view (given their crucial, and arguably overarching, importance), social factors are recognised:

Early childhood experiences can have a major impact on later development, with the lack of a positive attachment to an adult being seen as
particularly detrimental to some children. Parents are the biggest influence on a child's development. Social circumstances can also impact
on development. Children who experience family difficulties, including
parental conflict, separation, neglect, indifference or erratic discipline,
are more likely to develop BESD. (paragraph 61)

The value of residential special education is recognised by the guidance,
although readers are referred to the sections in the previous government
guidance (DFE 1994b) for advice on good practice.

On identification rates (DCSF 2008a, paragraph 60), the guidance claims
that there are higher rates of BESD in socially deprived areas, amongst boys
and amongst Black Caribbean and Mixed White and Black Caribbean pupils and Travellers. It reports that over 60 per cent of pupils attending Pupil
Referral Units (PRUs) have SEN and that many of these children and young
people have BESD.

The guidance offers key advice on how to determine whether or not a
pupil has BESD:

Whether a child or young person is considered to have BESD depends
on a range of factors, including the nature, frequency, persistence, se-
verity and abnormality of the difficulties and their cumulative effect on
the child or young person's behaviour and/or emotional well-being
compared with what might generally be expected for a particular age.
(paragraph 55)

TERMINOLOGY: WHY 'BESD' RATHER THAN 'SEBD' OR 'EBD'?

This book is more likely to be read by practitioners in England than by
those working in other countries. We therefore feel obliged to use the English Government's current ordering of letters, and this term is now in fairly
common parlance and is likely to be used for some years.

For reasons to which we have already alluded, we believe it would be
wiser to draw attention to the *social, emotional* and, at times, *biological/ge-
netic* factors first. This would be in keeping with the English Government's
stress in the first decade of this century on the importance of developing
social and emotional skills through education, using the 'SEAL' (social and
emotional aspects of learning) programmes. It is our sense that putting 'behaviour' first can lead to an over-emphasis on behaviour, which can affect

the way in which professionals perceive the situation and, consequently, how they respond to it. There can be an assumption that the 'behaviour' is usually 'bad', is probably the child's fault and needs 'managing', suppressing or even punishing. Such an attitude can guide practice rather than allowing teachers and support professionals to seek to *understand* the behaviour and to consider more reflective and effective responses to it.

We prefer the term EBD (emotional and behavioural difficulties[3]), which first appeared in the 1950s (Cole 1989; Min. of Ed. 1955) but became commonplace in the 1980s. We would far rather talk – as Scottish educationalists do – of SEBD (Social, Emotional and Behavioural Difficulties).

We also note that BESD is an educational professional's term and that a child assessed by a *medical* professional could be labelled as having a 'conduct disorder', or assessed on checklists by qualified medical professionals (e.g. using the American DSM categories – see APA 2000) and given other labels, such as 'oppositional defiance disorder' (ODD) or OCD (obsessive compulsive disorder). Some of those with BESD could also be assessed as having significant attention and hyperactivity difficulties meriting the label ADHD. McLeod (2010) alludes to the possible 'medicalisation of naughtiness', although Colley (2010) defends psychiatric assessments and believes that some educationalists' criticism of DSM categories can be flawed.

So, for present purposes, we believe it is wise to use BESD. However, we wish to attach our own wording to these letters:

- BESD could either be '**B**ehaviour difficulties mainly caused by disrupted or unusual **E**motional and **S**ocial **D**evelopment'.

- In recognition of big strides made recently in research into neuroscience and the latter's relationship to behaviour – but not likely to be popular with parents – BESD might also be '**B**iological, **E**motional and **S**ocial **D**ifficulties'.

THE EXTENT OF BESD

Whichever label is chosen,[4] we are left with an imprecise concept (Thomas 2005) and a category of special educational need to which children in England are assigned inconsistently. Officially, at the start of 2009 (see Table 1.1), there were over 154,000 pupils said to have substantial BESD (i.e. they were placed on their school's special educational needs register with a 'statement' or at the 'school action plus' stage, with the primary SEN identified as BESD). The majority were attending mainstream schools, but over 13,000 were in special schools. Also, some thousands of the 15,230 pupils in Pupil Referral Units (DCSF 2009a) could have been deemed BESD (see DCSF 2008a and b). Beyond this, there are probably a few thousand children with BESD in independent special schools. In total, about 2 per cent of England's 8 million schoolchildren were categorised as having significant BESD in early 2009.

Table 1.1: Pupils with BESD as their primary SEN at 'school action plus' and 'with statements of SEN' in 2009

[State schools]	School action plus (% of pupils with SENs at school action plus)	With statements (% of pupils with statements for SENs)	Total (% of pupils with SENs)
Primary schools	51,650 (19.8%)	7,290 (12.6%)	58,930 (18.5%)
Secondary schools	72,250 (35.4%)	10,020 (15.4%)	82,270 (30.6%)
Special schools (all types)	330 (19.1%)	12,920 (14.7%)	13,240 (14.8%)
TOTAL	124,230 (26.6%)	30,230 (14.3%)	154,440 (22.8%)

Note: Pupils with BESD in independent special schools, in PRUs or further education colleges are not included in Table 1.1.
(DCSF 2009a)

The percentage of students in BESD schools and PRUs was about 0.3–0.4 per cent of the total number of children of compulsory school age in England, a figure that has remained fairly consistent over the past two decades (see Cole, Visser and Upton 1998). A small and declining percentage of this group are residential at special schools with care facilities. The vast majority of children formally placed in the BESD category are boys.

BESD is the second-most numerous category of SEN, with nearly 23 per cent of those with substantial SENs placed in it. The commonest form is 'moderate learning difficulties' (MLD – 25.3%) and the third-commonest 'speech, language and communication difficulties' (SLCN – 15.4%) (DCSF 2009a).

There are also clearly many thousands of disengaged, often disruptive, pupils, who have not been formally identified as BESD. It is not possible to put an accurate figure on this large group, given the fact that statistics are not kept nationally and recording practice can vary: the merely 'naughty but normal' in one school can be seen as having severely disturbed behaviour in another school. Children may well be seen as having 'behaviour' problems, and the existence of these problems would help to explain why Layard and

Dunn (2009) report that nearly 6 per cent of school children are thought to have a 'conduct disorder'.

In short, it is likely that in England, as has been estimated for the United States (Kauffman 2001), the BESD group will amount to somewhere between 3 per cent and 6 per cent of the school population. The figure might arguably be higher as many troubled children with mental-health problems are not included in the BESD grouping who might be (Cole and Visser 2005). These can be the withdrawn, quiet children, who tend to escape attention. Layard and Dunn (2009, p.115) report that 3.7 per cent of children are thought to have emotional disorders (3.3% anxiety; 0.9% depression); and 0.3 per cent have eating disorders. They repeat the contention of the DCSF/Dept. of Health (2008a) that probably 10 per cent of children between age 5 and 15 have a 'clinically diagnosable mental disorder that is associated with considerable distress and substantial interference with personal functions, such as family and social relationships' (p.20).

Layard and Dunn (2009) also cite medical research suggesting that 1.5 per cent of children have attention deficit hyperactivity disorder (ADHD). DfEE (2001b, p.27) offers a lower figure of 0.5–1 per cent. The government's guidance explains that these children

> find it hard to concentrate and therefore to learn new skills, both academic and practical. Research from the USA suggests that 90% of children with ADHD underachieve at school and 20% have reading difficulties. Children with ADHD are also often rejected and disliked by their peers, because they disrupt their play or damage their possessions.

Some would argue that ADHD is under-diagnosed – others (e.g. Visser and Jehan 2009) that the whole concept of ADHD is challengeable (for a riposte, see Colley 2010).

DfEE (2001b) helps to explain the local differences in the diagnosis of children with ADHD:

- there is no *clinical* test for ADHD (unlike testing a child for diabetes, diagnosis is based on observation perhaps not across a range of situations and, usually, completing a checklist);

- there are other disorders which can present a similar profile of behaviours, e.g. anxiety states, attachment disorders;

- all children have problems with self-control, and it can be hard to decide where to draw the line and give a diagnosis of ADHD; and

- other problems can result in behaviour similar to ADHD, for example language or hearing difficulties, dyslexia, major disruptions in a child's life. Over half of the children with ADHD will have other areas of difficulty, such as these, in addition to ADHD. (DfEE 2001b, p.27)

All in all it is far from easy to determine just how many children have BESD and how many of those with an overlapping and, essentially, medical label should be included in the grouping.

ARE BESDs IN CHILDREN GETTING MORE FREQUENT AND WORSE?

Given the section above, it is to be expected that offering a definitive answer to these questions is not possible. Talking to practitioners we hear comments about the increasingly young age of children who are posing them with the most acute and complex of problems – but firm data are lacking. DCSF/DoH (2008a) was one of many documents reporting an increase in childhood mental-health problems in the last decades of the twentieth century, citing a range of evidence from medical researchers.

The Children's Society's influential *Good Childhood Inquiry* (Layard and Dunn 2009) gave a persuasive overview of many factors at work that seem to contribute to present difficulties, and which perhaps explain more widespread mental-health problems and BESD in children. Expanding on ideas earlier expressed in Postman's (1982) *The Disappearance of Childhood*, James' (2007) *Affluenza* and Palmer's (2007) *Toxic Childhood*, Layard and Dunn highlight stark differences in the experiences of children today compared with those in earlier generations. Gone are the absolute poverty (in most cases at least), mass deaths of parents in world wars or mothers dying in childbirth. In their place, Layard and Dunn (2009, p.3) find extensive 'relative poverty' (where the household's income is less than 60 per cent of average) as well as the following:

> Britain and the US have more broken families than other countries, and our families are less cohesive in the way they live… British children are rougher with each other, and live more riskily in terms of alcohol, drugs and teenage pregnancy.

International studies, e.g. by UNICEF in 2007, claimed to show Britain as faring worse than all of the world's 21 richest countries across a range of measures. For example, for 11–15 year olds, 12 per cent live in step-families (compared with 8% for the rest of Europe) and 16 per cent live in single-parent families. The report (Layard and Dunn 2009) identified 'excessive individualism' as a likely contributor to a changed world. It found that most women now work outside the home, leaving (as Gerhardt 2004 also noted) their young children too often in indifferent, un-nurturing child-care for long hours. A third of 16-year-olds now live apart from their biological fathers. Parents separating leads to confusion, sadness and feelings of betrayal amongst their children. Family members often live many miles apart so the support of grandparents is absent. That children now eat a different and, often unhealthy, diet as well as taking little exercise may also be relevant, although convincing research on this is still lacking.

Young people now tend to have their own money, and so they are subject to sexualised advertising and peer pressures pushing them down a materialistic, consumerist path. Exaggerated media headlines about 'stranger danger' and child abuse have made parents over-protective, denying young children the chance to play outside, as earlier generations did. Fears about traffic and the reduction in green-play areas in towns make this worse. Such factors could also be driving more children into spending hours each day in the virtual world of computer games, DVDs, TV and social network websites – possibly damaging face-to-face interpersonal communications and relationships. Criticising the media, the report (Layard and Dunn 2009) notes 'There is much evidence that exposure to violent images encourages aggressive behaviour' (p.60) and 'it seems likely that the upward trend in media violence is helping to produce the upward trend in violent behaviour – and also the growth of psychological conflict in family relationships' (Layard and Dunn 2009, p.62).

Although there were some criticisms of the methodology of this inquiry (Layard and Dunn 2009) many of its themes are likely to strike a chord with readers of this book, as they view the lives of the children and families with whom they work. Also, some of Layard and Dunn's (2009) proposed remedies will be echoed by the approaches described in later chapters.

But, has a plateau now been reached? It was interesting to note that at least in terms of mental-health disorders, a major study by Green *et al.* (2005) (cited in, and informing, Layard and Dunn (2009)) indicated no deterioration between 1999 and 2004. An article by Cooper and Cefai (2009) on changed adult attitudes to children is also recommended.

THE CONTENT OF THE BOOK

In the chapters that follow we draw together materials found useful in the professional development of hundreds of mainly educational, but also some child-care, professionals over the past decade. We have sought to offer an approachable overview of good practice, informed by wise advice from past and present practitioners and evidence from recent research-based theory.

The content is based on the well-founded premise that *understanding* social, emotional and sometimes biological/genetic factors in child development is an important first step in reducing troublesome behaviour in class, around school and in child-care situations. Where skilled staff are knowledgeable about these factors and focus on addressing the child or young person's needs in these areas, the *behaviour problems* presented at school can lessen in dramatic fashion (even where fundamental and chronic difficulties, e.g. in the child's home, are not resolved). It has been noted by schools inspectors and researchers how settled and peaceful classrooms in 'BESD schools' can sometimes be (see Laslett 1977; the large detailed national study by Cole *et al.* 1998, and the many Ofsted school inspection reports of the past decade indicating good behaviour in many BESD schools). The same can be said for some care situations in residential special schools. Where professionals understand and empathise with the motivation and explanation for children's behaviours, and can apply a range of appropriate helpful interventions, their work can bring very real help that can touch, and sometimes transform, very troubled young lives.

The book gives brief coverage to some 'lessons from history' and explanation for the diverse range of provision now made. It examines key aspects of child development and factors which might help to explain children's BESD. It looks at key theoretical approaches that can usefully underpin practice. It focuses in some depth on practical intervention approaches at wholeschool, class and individual levels. It considers the crucial area of working with parents and carers. The book also looks at how best to retain, train and sustain professionals working in what at times can be highly stressful environments.

PEOPLE RATHER THAN PLACES MATTER

An ongoing commitment to providing well-trained, motivated and supported staff is crucial. Sufficient numbers of skilled practitioners should provide pupils with BESD with a broad, balanced and, wherever possible, 'normal' educational experience, leading to accredited qualifications. Alongside this function, these staff should deliver the key factors that are crucial in easing children's BESD: giving *respite*, helping the children make positive *relationships* and aiding their re-*signification* (Cooper 1993).[5] This last sociological term means helping troubled children to alter often negative patterns of thinking and feeling through experiencing increasing social and educational success as well as emotional stability, thereby coming to see themselves in a more positive light and being able to take a more optimistic view of what they can achieve. By doing this, staff should also be promoters of that crucial fourth 'R' – *resilience.*

We believe that such practitioners are at the heart of effective intervention. Altering local-authority structures, arguing the relative merits of mainstream over special, specialist or academy status, school federation over local-authority supported, State provided over voluntary or independent are all of secondary importance (and have led to much unhelpful and disruptive reorganisation over the past three decades). Where successful work has taken place – as it so often has – it has mainly been down to people not places, nor the details of patterns of organisation. It has happened where practitioners are energised, efficient, expert and empathetic, well led and in control of their settings. Key members of staff have often been in post for some time and provide the security and stability so badly needed by children who have experienced much unpredictability and trauma in their lives.

Operating from the right values, successful practitioners have high expectations of children with BESD. They know that education is very important and an entitlement, but that it must be delivered imaginatively and flexibly, making appropriate allowance for the children's social and emotional difficulties and building where possible on the children's strengths. They are skilled at forging helpful relationships with these young people. As Harris (2007, p.37) suggests

> such relationships gradually enable individuals to emerge from the emotional isolation of their defensiveness, show their true feelings and the experience of the newness of being accepted, affirmed, appreciated for their difference rather than being judged, labelled and ostracised.

We hope that the chapters that follow will inform, provoke thought, reaffirm your existing ways of successful working as well as providing suggestions for improved practice.

NOTES

1. For simplicity's sake we will often use the term 'children' to include babies, pre-schoolers, children and teenagers up to the age of 18. We shall also, in most cases, avoid the long-winded phrase 'children and young people'.

2. In England 'looked after' or 'in care' are terms meaning that the State has taken legal responsibility for the child away from the parent(s), usually placing the child with foster carers or, less frequently, in children's homes, although often seeking to maintain the child's links with his or her family.

3. In the United States the 'D' in 'EBD' generally stands for 'disorders' rather than 'difficulties'.

4. Labels were again proved to be necessary by the failure of the 1981 Education Act's attempt to operate without them. However, the finding of Daniels *et al.* (1999) – that a feature of the best mainstream schools was their reluctance to attach labels to children with BESD – is noteworthy.

5. Cooper (1993) was concerned with residential provision but later work (e.g. by Cole *et al.* (1998)) suggests the applicability of the three 'Rs' to day settings, whether in special or mainstream schooling.

PART 1

UNDERSTANDING BESD

CHAPTER 2

THE PAST, THE PRESENT AND PATTERNS OF EDUCATIONAL PROVISION

A society that forgets its history, the old adage goes, is a society that has lost its memory. It is therefore important, we believe, to take a brief look at key developments and themes from the history of provision for children now said to have BESD – themes that often help to explain the approaches and patterns of provision of today. Kauffman (2001, p.96), writing on the history of 'EBD' provision in the USA, noted, 'Current issues and trends seem only to be a recycling of those that have been with us for well over a century'. Reflections of this observation can be seen in developments in England. History underscores certain intractable dilemmas and warns us against advocates of simplistic or single-perspective solutions. At times, however, history also shows the wisdom of earlier generations being re-affirmed by practitioners and scientists of the present one.

In the final section of this chapter we will sketch the range of provision currently made in this country. Differences in how local authorities respond to BESD will be noted and some deeply held views about school inclusion challenged. Trying to keep all pupils with SENs in 'mainstream' schools is scarcely a new notion, and clearly dates back to early in the nineteenth century in relation to some children with special educational needs (Cole 1989) and certainly the 1950s to children with BESD. Experience and values demand that we keep the promotion of increased inclusion of pupils with SEN in mainstream schools as a goal. However, we do need to recognise that for a proportion of children with BESD, providing an education *outside* mainstream schools can be a better means of giving them a less troubled childhood and a chance of greater social inclusion as adults.

PROBLEMS OF DEFINITION AND PLACEMENT

It has been a matter of debate over generations who the children with BESD are and where they should be placed (Laslett 1983; McLeod 2010; Min. of Ed. 1955; Thomas 2005). In the nineteenth and early twentieth centuries such children and young people were sometimes confused with 'mental defectives' or 'moral imbeciles', or minor delinquents. In the twentieth century, an umbrella term came into usage: 'maladjustment'. In England, this descriptor was in official use by 1930. A legally enshrined category of 'maladjusted children' was instigated by the 1944 Education Act and was to last until the attempted abolition of categories of special educational needs by the 1981 Education Act (Cole 1989).

In 1955, a long-running government inquiry into provision for the maladjusted (the Underwood Report) acknowledged confusion over who they were, finding it necessary to stress that maladjustment should not be equated with bad behaviour, delinquency, oddness or educational subnormality (Min. of Ed. 1955). Laslett (1983, p.6) described 'maladjustment' as 'a kind of catch-all for children showing a wide range of behaviour and learning difficulties'.

Uncertainties over the identification of children with BESD were sometimes accompanied by haphazard placement procedures. Dating back more than a century (Cole 1989), the precursors of the BESD would seem to have been taken under the wing of any one of four government departments – welfare, juvenile justice, education or health. In the nineteenth and early twentieth century many 'at risk' children were placed in Home Office 'industrial' and sometimes 'reformatory schools'. They could also find themselves in early mental-hospital provision or children's homes. In the first half of the twentieth century they could go to early special classes or, occasionally, to pioneer residential schools. Whether the 'problem child' was 'cared for', 'punished', 'educated' or 'treated' was often a matter of chance depending upon which individuals in which agency first took up the case (Cole 2005).

DEBATES AND THEMES: c.1850–1950

Some timeless themes emerge from the historical sources for the century preceding 1950 (see Kauffman 2001, for similarities in the USA):

- *Nurture or nature?* Some pioneers saw the important role of poverty and family influences in behaviour causation as counteracting the influence of believers in the effects of inherited defective genes (Cole 1989).

- *'Rescue' or community care?* Should children be 'rescued' from their families by residential placement or should staff work with the parents while children attended local day units or schools?

- *'Discipline'/group conformity or individualised child-centred approaches?* Too many reformatory and industrial schools, in which thousands of children who would now be said to have BESD were placed, succumbed to punitive institutionalism, which did little to address individual needs (Cole 1989). Yet by 1925 Homer Lane and A.S. Neill had created democratic, liberal regimes that stressed individualised learning (Bridgeland 1971).

- *The danger of 'contamination'.* It was understood that the placing of disturbed and sometimes delinquent children together in institutions could lead to worse behaviour (Millham, Bullock and Cherrett 1975).

- *Education, social work or therapy?* 'The school itself was a therapeutic situation and I would guess that about three-quarters of the children received no other form of therapy'. (R.A. Dewhurst, Head of the Day Maladjusted School, founded 1939, in Oxford (see Bridgeland 1971, p.298)). This educational approach contrasted with the application of therapy and psychoanalysis in some pioneer residential schools (Bridgeland 1971).

PROVIDING FOR 'THE MALADJUSTED': 1950–1975

The Education Act of 1944 required local education authorities (LEAs) to identify and provide for all children in need of 'special educational treatment', including children who should be placed in the new category of 'maladjustment'. Where possible, maladjusted children were to be helped within their local community by:

- transfer to different mainstream schools

- use of foster homes

- living in small hostels and attending local day schools (Cole 1989).

In practice, most development was residential, with many new special schools opening in large, disused country mansions. However, in 1950, 'tutorial classes' (the precursors of the small off-site special units of the 1970s and Pupil Referral Units/'short stay schools' of the present) were started in London. 'Maladjusted' children attended these small centres for a part of the week and their teachers had time allowed for working with the children's families (Cole 1989).

The influential Underwood Report (Min. of Ed. 1955) reflected the theoretical debates of its age, recording 'a considerable difference of opinion about the value of psychodynamic approaches, espoused in a few high-profile pioneer schools and many multi-disciplinary Child Guidance Clinics'. This report saw maladjustment not as 'a medical term diagnosing a medical condition... It is a term describing an individual's relation at a particular time to the people and circumstances which make up his environment' (paras 88 and 89, p.22). Foreshadowing later research (e.g. Cooper 1993; Wilson and Evans 1980), it stressed the importance of fostering positive relationships: maladjusted children were 'insecure and unhappy, and...fail in their personal relationships. Receiving is difficult for them as well as giving, and they appear unable to respond to simple measures of love, comfort and reassurance' (p.22).

In relation to teaching and care approaches, the Report wanted staff to have a grasp of mainstream education and care approaches before training to work specifically with the maladjusted. The Committee believed (foreshadowing the 'positive psychology' of today?): 'Much more can be done for a child who is maladjusted by a teacher who is warm-hearted and loving than by one who approaches maladjustment through the abnormal and broods over him as a problem child' (Min. of Ed. 1955, para.513). It had written of the classroom experience: 'The simple fact of receiving individual attention in a small class in an informal non-competitive atmosphere often enables a boy or girl to make progress and this can help in solving a child's emotional problems' (Min. of Ed. 1955, para.281). However, it recognised the need for approaches that contrasted with the mainstream school experience: toleration of some 'acting out' in class was necessary as the maladjusted 'were not readily capable of improvement by ordinary discipline' (p.22) and, reflecting some psychodynamic pioneers' view, the Committee saw the need to wait until some disturbed children were 'ready' to tackle conventional education. The value of play was also stressed.

On curriculum, the Underwood Report expressed views that could have come from Victorian times (Cole 1989) or the Labour Government in the early 2000s: some children who were 'bright but not bookish' found that as the work became more abstract and formal it did not suit them: 'They cannot cope with the variety of subjects and with the many changes of teacher' (para.133, p.32). This advice was backed by Wilson and Evans' (1980) research but did not find favour with government inspectors (now called Ofsted) advocating the new National Curriculum in the 1990s (see below).

Underwood wrote about the siting of provision (providing food for thought for planners of today?): 'It has often been found better to have the premises of a class quite separate from a school, since school may have unhappy associations for many maladjusted children'. Provision away from mainstream school sites also allowed an alternative regime where perhaps necessary 'acting out' could be tolerated (para.218, p.55). It advocated more day schools to reduce the need for residential placements, which were often distant from the child's home.

Wanting a proactive and preventative approach involving inter-agency working (which foreshadowed DfES (2003b) *Every Child Matters*) the Underwood Report strongly recommended a nation-wide schools psychological service or a national system of multi-disciplinary child guidance clinics (CGCs). The medical professionals in the CGCs were urged to involve themselves in family work and to put down roots on school sites (a plea repeated in the 2000s – see Chapter 9, p.197).

A decade later, and after the opening of more local-authority schools for the maladjusted, the government altered assessment procedures, taking some powers away from school medical officers and passing them to school psychologists (Circular 2/75, DES 1975). Laslett (1983) saw this as a sign of the growing ascendancy of an 'educational' over a 'medical' model.

PROVISION FOR YOUNG OFFENDERS AND OTHER CHILDREN 'AT RISK'

In 1933, the Home Office's industrial and reform schools became 'approved schools' (Cole 1989). The punitive, over-regimented regimes of most of these establishments for offenders and other 'at risk' youth deserved David Wills' (1971) criticism. However, Millham, Bullock and Cherrett (1975) and Hyland (1993) record better practice that would seem to have passed into some later schools for children with BESD. Millham *et al.*'s (1975) important study led them to prefer so-called 'training schools' that stressed education, vocational training, sport and keeping the boys constantly busy. They noted that:

> Boys differ markedly from adults in the sorts of regimes that they enjoy... Some flourish on cross-country runs, maths projects and endless showers, and institutions that provide these should not be viewed as less caring than those which discuss problems at length over cocoa and slices of dripping toast. (p.84)

The 1969 Children and Young Person's Act transferred the approved schools to local social-service departments' jurisdiction and renamed them 'community homes with education' (CHEs). What was seen as a more child-centred approach was advocated, notably through DHSS (1970). However, the hopes of this document were rarely to be realised: in contrast to the approved schools of the 1930s, rates of re-offending among leavers were now very high, and more generous staffing increased costs. Within twenty years most of the CHEs had closed (Hyland 1993). Young people who once could have gone to CHEs tended to enter the expanding special schools for the maladjusted, to which their staff also gravitated (Cole 1989).

THE NATIONAL SURVEY OF PROVISION FOR MALADJUSTED CHILDREN, 1975–1978

Wilson and Evans' (1980) major study found many more day schools and special classes attached to mainstream schools and more residential provision for maladjusted children, as well as a growing number of off-site special 'units' for the 'disruptive'. Most provision paid only limited attention to the psychodynamic ('therapeutic') approach and to behaviour modification, which was now coming into vogue (Wilson and Evans 1980). The majority favoured a humanistic (perhaps cognitive-behaviourist?) standpoint. What mattered was working through close relationships, and reversing a child's expectancy of failure by ensuring that he or she achieved regular success in a range of activities that boosted low self-esteem. Talking and listening to children was crucial. Classroom help targeted on underachievement in basic literacy and numeracy and a general educational approach was seen as important – even a form of therapy. Maladjusted children were also believed, by a clear majority of respondents to Wilson and Evans, to appreciate steady routines and clear structures. The value of residential schools was also underlined. The study thought a basically normal educational experience could, and should, be provided and contributed greatly to the self-esteem of 'disturbed' children. However, they were realists and advised: 'a smaller range of subjects well taught has more value than an ambitious and wide-ranging programme which does not engage the interests of the pupils' (Wilson and Evans 1980, p.170).

'EMOTIONAL AND BEHAVIOURAL DIFFICULTIES': 1980S INTO THE NEW CENTURY

In the latter decades of the twentieth century and the beginning of the twenty-first, themes and approaches already discussed continued to be important but new forces were also at work. As outlined in Chapter 1, the nature of childhood altered in some dramatic ways, probably contributing to more complex behaviour difficulties in children (Layard and Dunn 2009).

The category of maladjustment – seen as stigmatising and unsatisfactory – was abolished by the mildly 'inclusionist' 1981 Education Act. It was soon unofficially replaced by the term 'EBD': some label and grouping was necessary for policy construction and resource allocation. The government's Circular 9/94 contained another vague 'catch-all' definition: 'Children with EBD are on a continuum. Their problems are clearer and greater than sporadic naughtiness or moodiness and yet not so great as to be classed as mental illness' (DFE 1994b, p.4).

This was a period of increasing concern for the promotiom of 'inclusion', reflected in the aims of the Education Act 1996, yet the use of segregated provision for children with BESD was maintained at a similar level in England (Cole *et al.* 2003). Closures of some 'EBD' schools was offset by the rapid expansion of off-site unit provision (under the name of 'Pupil Referral Units') in the 1990s and early 2000s and the opening of some new BESD schools. The continuing usefulness of – indeed, necessity for – such provision was recognised in various government publications (e.g. DFE 1994b; DfES 2003a and 2004b; Ofsted 1999). Realism was aided by media concerns about standards of 'discipline' in mainstream schools and increasing levels of exclusions from schools. In the 1980s these issues led to the Elton Report (DES 1989) and in the 2000s to Ofsted (2005) and the Steer Report (DfES 2005a).

Key 'school improvement' texts, e.g. Rutter *et al.* (1979), were influential. Charlton and David (1993) asserted that 'effectiveness factors', taken from these books and other British and American literature, tended to be present in schools that successfully managed difficult behaviour. These included:

- consultative and collaborative leadership that takes into account pupil and parent opinion
- consistently applied school-wide policies on education and behaviour management
- differentiated curricula
- high, but not unreasonable, academic expectations

- positive behaviour management stressing prevention and offering more rewards than sanctions
- efficient and punctual staff offering skilful, responsive teaching
- supportive and respectful relationships between all adults and pupils
- effective systems of pastoral care.

Research into mainstream and special school EBD provision in England (e.g. Cole *et al*. 1998; Cooper 1993; Daniels *et al*. 1999; Ofsted 1999 and 2003) underlined that such factors were indeed relevant.

School improvement research influenced the English government's advice on coping with difficult behaviour and the education of children with EBD in mainstream and other settings (DFE 1994a; 1994b). However, in the field, the emphasis too often remained on control and management rather than an attempt to understand and prevent perceived unacceptable behaviour. Harris (2007, p.153) said of approaches commonly used: 'Behaviour management may actually exacerbate behaviour problems in schools by creating greater distance between adults and young people whose primary deficit and hence greatest need in life is for love, care and proximity to a caring adult.' The government, influenced by HMI, clearly wanted a 'mainstream' type approach to predominate in special schools and units. For example, staff were advised to 'establish firm boundaries of behaviour for all pupils. Good standards of behaviour should be the norm' (DFE 1994b, Circular 9/94, para.68, p.24).

However, Circular 9/94 also saw the importance of allowing for children's affective and social development. Staff should look at the emotions beneath the surface behaviour and address needs. Education (in the form of remedial help in literacy skills) was seen as building pupils' morale and self-esteem (paragraph 98). Teaching style had to be carefully attuned to pupil learning style and capabilities. The circular said: 'It is important to set short-term targets and goals which will stretch but not overwhelm them, to involve them in the formation of these learning goals and to establish high expectations of their performance' (p.23). A collaborative approach to learning could help pupils to break out of negative cycles of pessimistic thinking about their abilities, into which they were often locked.

The section on residential schooling worried about its high cost but again recognised that boarding could be beneficial where 'EBD' exist and/ or 'where family support is lacking or inadequate, or family influence is damaging' (para.73, p.27). Cole *et al*. (2003) reported a marked reduction in the use of boarding education in the 1990s.

Robert Laslett was an influential practitioner, trainer and writer in this era. His widely read books stressed the importance of 'normal' education in the lives of children with BESD, but saw the personal and social development of such pupils as the primary need, necessarily impacting on what could be achieved in the classroom (Laslett 1977; 1983). Yet, following the 1988 Education Act, a wide range of 'academic' subjects, prescribed in great detail by the National Curriculum, were made compulsory for practitioners working with children with BESD (unless rarely used bureaucratic procedures to exempt a child from particular aspects of the National Curriculum were followed). Providers found it hard to adjust to these new demands. Sometimes as a consequence, inspectors of the new Ofsted delivered critical inspection reports on many special schools (e.g. Ofsted 1995) as the debate about what should and could be achieved in such provision continued (e.g. Marchant 1995).

When a new, detailed national survey of specialist BESD provision took place in the late 1990s (Cole *et al.* 1998), interesting comment was made by school leaders on what was then expected. One said of the National Curriculum: 'There are times in a school day when it appears the least appropriate thing on earth for particular pupils' (Cole *et al.* 1998, p.100). Others complained of the width of subjects; many noted the lack of perceived relevance of some compulsory subjects at that time, notably modern foreign languages and religious education – and, to a substantial but lesser extent, geography, history and music. In the main, however, special school leaders recognised, as the following quote summarises: 'The National Curriculum has certainly forced us to move away from the "sums, worksheets and minibus" curriculum which existed in the past' (Cole *et al.* 1998, p.100).

It was gradually recognised that the early National Curriculum had been over-prescriptive and 'academic'. There followed a partial retreat, which was seen first in the freeing up of Key Stage 4 in the late 1990s, and then in the Labour Government's stress on the need for 'personalised' learning and the requirement for time in the school week to be devoted to the social and emotional aspects of learning (SEAL). It seems that these developments were met with much relief by many practitioners working with children with BESD.

Although research evidence is lacking, it is likely that government policies in the 1990s designed to improve behaviour and to raise academic standards in mainstream, special schools and PRUs did at times impact negatively on the educational experience of the child with BESD. Harris (2007, p.152) recognised the dilemmas that senior staff faced then and now:

Increasing concerns about behaviour and violence in schools put leaders under pressure to find effective ways of controlling the most challenging pupils in order to minimise the negative effects of their behaviour on teaching and learning and the school climate. Fearful of events spiralling out of control, teachers and leaders' efforts to manage such pupils unwittingly compound their underlying problems.

Resulting practice would seem to have contributed in part to the four-fold increase in the numbers of school exclusions in the 1990s. Levels remained high in 2010, indicating that either more children were pushing teachers beyond reasonable limits or that schools had become less tolerant places for pupils labelled 'disruptive'.

The ingredients of BESD 'best practice' for all settings were summarised in Ofsted (1999; 2005) and Cole *et al.* (1998) for special schools. Good provision *was* sometimes made in mainstream schools (Daniels *et al.* 1999; Ofsted 2003). This message was reiterated by Ofsted (2006), which reported that effective provision for children with SEN (including those with BESD) was distributed equally between mainstream and special schools when key factors were securely in place. Furthermore, this report found, in relation to the general SEN population, that more good or outstanding provision existed in resourced mainstream schools than in special schools.

DEVELOPMENTS IN THE EARLY 21ST CENTURY

There seems now to be a slackening in attempts to push forward the inclusion of all children with SEN in mainstream schools (certainly those with behaviour difficulties). DfEE (2003a) saw a secure future for special schools. In the next year, the writers of the government's SEN strategy 'Removing Barriers to Achievement' (RBA) adopted a position that overlapped with the Social, Emotional and Behavioural Difficulties Association's policy on inclusion (see Appendix 1). RBA contained the following: 'Inclusion is about much more than the type of school that children attend: it is about the quality of their experience, how they are helped to learn, achieve and participate fully in the life of the school' (DfES 2004a, p.25). It foresaw a fall in the number of children attending special schools 'as the mainstream becomes more inclusive' but said they still had an important role to play (p.37). In a widely reported move, Lady Warnock, wrongly (see DES 1978) but frequently seen as a major 'architect' of inclusion, looked back in 2005 on the implementation of the inclusionary 1981 Education Act. She regretted that the experience of some children with SEN subsequently educated in mainstream schools had been a painful kind of exclusion (Warnock 2005). Government statistics show overall numbers in special schools remaining constant and the percentage of pupils with significant special needs placed in special schools rising from 32 per cent in 2004 to 35 per cent in 2008. Also, children with SEN educated in special resourced classes in mainstream schools fell from 7.8 per cent in 2004 to 4 per cent in 2008 (DCSF 2009a). Durham, Lincolnshire and Kent were examples of local authorities building new BESD schools.

In recent years, there has been a movement of power to central government as part of its attempt to raise school standards and improve behaviour and attendance (e.g. through the National Strategies). The once rigid National Curriculum is now a flexible shadow of what was promulgated in the early 1990s, probably to the relief of most professionals working with children with BESD. The importance of target setting and testing of achievement through SATs (Standard Assessment Tests) could also be waning.

The reduction in the power of local authorities, the delegation of greater powers to schools, the effects of disruptive reorganisation of local government areas (Cole *et al.* 2003) and the creation of Children's Services after the 2004 Children Act (bringing together separate education and social work departments as part of the *Every Child Matters* agenda, DfES 2003b) were noteworthy developments. These changes will at times have made life easier and at times more difficult for the governing bodies and school leaders as they try to make effective provision for children with BESD.

The implementation of the *Every Child Matters* agenda (DfES 2003b) is ongoing. Can agencies, increasingly under-funded and under-staffed in the massive financial crisis beginning in 2008, alter the habits of generations in order to reach out across the physical and psychological barriers between them? All concerned need to develop understanding and empathy for the values, working practices and priorities of other, previously separate agencies (a point made decades earlier in the major Warnock Report, DES 1978). Mary Warnock (2005) expressed doubts, wondering whether the concept of 'needs' rather than 'disabilities' has actually led to a failure to discriminate between the educationally needy and others, but also between the various *kinds* of need.

The holistic view of children's needs expressed in ECM reflected increased interest in the expanding science around the promotion of well-being, even of happiness, in children and their families. This is an area that influences later content of this book and underpins the government's endorsement of the SEAL programmes in English schools.

Briefly, respected researchers such as Professor Martin Seligman are counteracting many psychologists' and psychiatrists' concentration on identifying and then seeking to fix the mental *deficits* or *disorders* of people. His research, and that of other eminent academics, provides evidence that psychological interventions concentrating on the positive by promoting healthier, more fulfilled and active lives help to ward off unhappiness and build personal resilience (see, for example, Seligman, Steen, Park and Peterson 2005). Living and thinking differently can reduce obsessive rumination over painful past events, which so afflict many with mental-health problems. Sonia Lyubomirsky (2008) gave a list of activities likely to increase levels of happiness. This included: cultivating optimism, practising acts of kindness, taking care of the body, savouring pleasures and nurturing social relationships. Seligman (1993) and Lyubomirsky (2008) describe factors that are within people's voluntary control, which they argue can contribute to up to 40 per cent of a person's emotional health.

Work by Werner and Smith (1992) on resilience supports this positive psychology view. They believe it is possible to build resilience through the provision of protective factors, including the promotion of participation and choice, rather than by concentrating on the identification by risk. The research methods on occasion used by 'positive psychology' investigators are sometimes questioned (e.g. Baylis 2009) but the central messages of positive psychology seem to be supported by substantial research by neuroscientists (see, for instance, Gerhardt 2004).

The indirect influence of 'positive psychology' on English schooling, through the promotion of social and emotional skills through a structured national programme (SEAL) could be substantial. Hard data on the effects of SEAL could remain elusive but the response of many teachers, particularly those working with vulnerable 'at risk' children, suggests the initiative is highly promising, worthy of long-term support and helps to address some of the concerns expressed by Layard and Dunn (2009), outlined in Chapter 1 of this book.

Also making life more demanding and sometimes precarious for professionals working with children with BESD are the consequences of high-profile child abuse cases (e.g. the deaths of Victoria Climbié in 2003 and Baby P in 2007). Such events have led to understandable media obsession and parental concern about safeguarding children, leading to bureaucratic and onerous vetting procedures and methods of investigating allegations of abuse against staff, which can deny the accused adults their basic natural justice (SEBDA 2009). Official government guidance in this area (DCSF 2009b) does not recognise the convincing evidence from teacher associations (e.g. ATL 2009) that there is no substance in more than nine out of ten allegations made against staff.

Concern about discipline in schools has continued to be a highly political issue, even if some evidence indicates that pupils in general are becoming better behaved (Ofsted 2009). Negative perceptions led to the commissioning by government of *Managing Challenging Behaviour* (Ofsted 2005), an important research-based study, and the higher-profile Steer Report (DfES

2005a), although the latter did not include consideration of BESD in its remit. Both reports are recommended to readers. They both reframe ideas and approaches already sketched in this chapter in the light of the politics and some practical developments of recent years (e.g. the impact of information technology on the delivery of teaching and wider educational and social systems). The Steer Report urged the issuing of revised BESD guidance, resulting in DCSF 2008a.

Both reports (*Managing Challenging Behaviour*, Ofsted 2005; the Steer Report, DfES 2005a) stressed the link between behaviour and good teaching and learning. As in earlier key reports, strong leadership was found to be crucial to the effective management of behaviour. With more echoes of the past, adapting the curriculum so that it is perceived as more relevant by children was also seen as being important.

Other factors seen as significantly improving behaviour (and lessening BESD) included:

- consistently applied behaviour policies that reward good behaviour (echoes of the Elton Report, DES 1989, and DFE 1994a and b)
- a strong sense of community
- good links with parents (stressed in so many studies on BESD)
- the use of information systems that track and analyse behaviour
- well-maintained accommodation that fosters a sense of pride in the place of learning
- regular training, focused on classroom practice, and combined with an in-depth appreciation of child and adolescent development.

The reports reiterated the findings of Ofsted's annual reports (e.g. Ofsted 2009) that most schools are characterised by good behaviour, despite media claims to the contrary.

Summarising much of the Ofsted and Steer view is the following comment about secondary school classrooms:

Pupils' attitudes, behaviour, and achievement are best where staff know pupils well and plan lessons which are well matched to their abilities and interests and take account of their different learning styles. In these lessons the transition between activities is managed well. High expectations are constantly reinforced and staff give meaningful praise. Marking is positive and takes learning forward. Pupils assess their work and discuss their progress with staff. (Ofsted 2005, para. 67, p.15)

Relationships, respect of adults for pupils, humour, pace, and responsiveness to pupil learning styles were all seen as being important. This quotation contains advice to which we return in later chapters. The Ofsted and Steer reports also noted that pupils displaying withdrawn, anxious and depressed behaviour were under-identified in all types of setting.

In recent years there has been a rediscovery of the need for flexible curricula that are sensitive to vulnerabilities and that build on pupils' interests and strengths. The government review *2020 Vision* (DfES 2006a) sketched a future in which schools address students' social and emotional needs and make learning 'personalised'. Teaching should be matched to the individual student's learning needs by:

- Projects that cut across national curriculum subject boundaries
- Flexible timetabling
- Developing 'learning how to learn' skills, e.g. oral communication, teamwork, evaluating data, creativity, reliability skills
- Formative assessment/less 'testing'– 'stage not age'
- 'Learning spaces' as well as 'classrooms'
- Flexibility of curriculum, building on the student's present level of learning and understanding, interests and what she/he sees as relevant (DfES 2006a).

The messages of *2020 Vision* and the government's endorsement and promotion of the Social and Emotional Aspects of Learning (SEAL – DCSF 2007d; 2009d) are encouraging. These developments gave grounds for cautious optimism as many of the wishes of school leaders working with children with BESD and speaking to Cole *et al.* (1998) and Daniels *et al.* (1999) had been granted (although a new Ofsted inspection framework, stressing raw examination results, introduced in autumn 2009, produced fresh apprehension). Such developments allowed more for time-honoured and evidence-based good practice with pupils said to have BESD in all educational settings.

Unsurprisingly (given the tenor of this chapter), aspects of *2020 Vision* were scarcely new. In 1939, R.A. Dewhurst said of maladjusted children and the task of his school in Oxford:

> There is something that every child can do well…and we try to find what that something is… When proficiency is found the child acquires a feeling of achievement and projects this feeling towards work of which he was previously afraid. Confidence in his work dispels the child's need of gaining compensation through obtrusive and difficult behaviour, so his energy is now directed into right channels and the behaviour problem clears up. (cited in Cole *et al.* 1998, p.155)

PATTERNS OF PROVISION FOR CHILDREN WITH BESD

Local authorities have a statutory duty to promote high standards of education for all children, including those with SEN. Meeting this obligation requires a varied response, involving different types and locations for intervention. The BESD guidance (DCSF 2008a) outlines an appropriate range of settings (encouraging and facilitating provision in mainstream schools, including the provision of resource bases or 'designated units' and ensuring access to appropriate special schools – see paragraphs 128–136). Placement in residential special schools 'may be appropriate' for a small minority (paragraph 133). LAs are reminded (paragraph 135) that 'Pupil referral units are not planned or designed to be a long-term setting and should not be regarded as part of a local authority's range of planned SEN provision'. This last point alludes to DCSF and Ofsted disapproval of the common practice in the 1990s and early 2000s whereby some LAs clearly used PRUs for long-term placement of pupils with BESD. The range of provision does not have to be maintained by or within their own LA: places can be purchased in schools or services in other LAs, in the private or voluntary sector (childcare organisations such as Barnardo's continue to provide residential BESD schools).

The range of provision is summarised in Figure 2.1. The width of Tiers 1,2 and 3 indicate that they are by far the most common responses (see statistics in Chapter 1, Table 1.1, p.20) and the narrowness of Tier 5 signifies it is now the rarest form of provision. This diagram is not able to include young people with BESD placed in further education colleges at Key Stage 4, a practice that has probably increased over the past decade.

Earlier versions of Figure 2.1 have shown this diagram with arrows at the sides of the triangle (e.g. Topping 1983 and Visser and Rayner 1999). The arrow on the left side pointing downwards from Tier 1 to Tier 5 said 'Move this way only as far as necessary'; and on the right upwards from Tier 5 to Tier 1 saying 'Return this way as rapidly as possible'. These instructions reflect the beliefs that it is desirable and the child's right to be fully included with his or her peers in mainstream schools, if possible spending all their time in mainstream classes. Placement in Tiers 4 or 5 has been portrayed (e.g. by CSIE 2010) as the antithesis of inclusion and as conflicting with human rights. In the light of experience and recent research (e.g. Daniels *et al.* 2003) viewing the placement of all children with BESD outside mainstream schools as a denial of children's rights is admirable as a principle but ill-founded when it comes to a minority of such children. It presupposes that the daily experience of the child with severe BESD in what might be

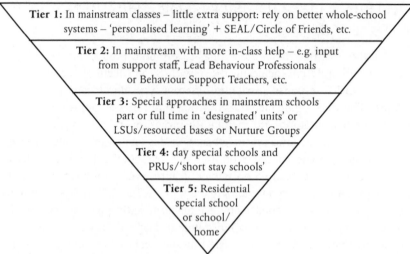

Figure 2.1: The five tiers of provision

an imperfect mainstream setting would be superior and the child's capacity for learning better than if that child went to a well-run, sympathetic and outward-looking special class or special school, PRU or other alternative setting. As has been stated already, we believe that what matters most is the quality of the relationships between the child and its teachers and peers and the quality of educational and social experience the child can actually access. The best provision for a particular child might be at any of the five tiers. Any one of the tiers can open the door to better opportunities and increase the likelihood of social inclusion as an adult.

These observations should not be misinterpreted – we remain fully committed to making mainstream schooling truly inclusive for far more children with BESD than at present and believe that it is possible to achieve this goal.

REVIEW

In this chapter, key events and ideas from the distant and more recent past have been outlined. We have ended with an overview of patterns of provisions long made, and still being made, across this and across most countries.

From our perspective, there *are* helpful *pointers* if not *lessons* from history and these include:

- the quality and commitment of the professionals serving children with BESD matter more than the espousal of any particular conceptual or organisational model
- education, broadly defined, can be a kind of therapy, helping children in difficulties feel 'normal', but the 'E' and 'S' in 'BESD' must also be stressed
- combined children's services, spanning the professions, should be given a real chance to prove themselves
- mainstream schools should, and can, be made inclusive for more pupils with BESD
- running effective special provision is usually a difficult challenge; nevertheless, a range of contrasting forms of provision continues to be essential for some children with BESD.

These messages – and others from this chapter – will be further explored in the chapters that follow.

CHAPTER 3

CHILD DEVELOPMENT AND BESD

The difficult and, at times, poignant backgrounds of Cameron, Ashley, Ryan, Cheryl and Stephen described in Chapter 1 are probably similar to those of children and young people with whom you work. The unusual development histories of nearly all children with BESD will have influenced their thoughts, beliefs, how they interpret the world around them and how they behave.

As we have noted, pupils with BESD are often part of the 10 per cent of all 5–15-year-olds thought to have a diagnosable mental-health disorder (Layard and Dunn 2009) but it would be neither possible nor desirable for us to assume that they should therefore be supported solely by Child and Adolescent Mental Health Services (CAMHS). As the national review of CAMHS in England (DCSF/DoH 2008a) emphasised: promoting better mental health must be a key concern for *all professionals* working with children. Practitioners in educational settings can, and often do, have a significant compensatory effect. Schooling is the second most important factor (after family influences) most able to enhance a child's self-esteem (Thomas 1980). Indeed, neuroscientists' vastly improved understanding of how the brain develops has shown that the damaged or unusually wired brain of the child with severe mental-health difficulties and/or BESD can be adjusted and repaired to an extent through interactions and relationships with caring and skilled adults beyond the child's family (see, for instance, Gerhardt 2004). Positive experiences and interventions, even in the teenage years, can be of immense help. In short, what you do as part of your daily working lives with children with BESD is of crucial importance and often makes a positive difference.

In this chapter, we look at key factors producing good mental health in children or – when absent or lacking in balance – which contribute to BESD. We consider:

- genetic inheritance
- neuroscience and the development of a child's brain

- attachment and bonding
- the needs of children
- parenting style
- development of self-concept and 'internal working models'
- 'fixed' and 'growth' mindsets
- ages and stages of development
- risk and resilience factors in childhood
- separation and loss (including parental separation or divorce)
- mental-health problems or disorders (ADHD; anxiety and depression; self-harm, suicide; eating disorders and obesity).

We, the authors, are committed to the 'bio-psycho-social' theoretical model, seeing this as a useful way of explaining the development of behaviours in a child (Cooper 1999, 2005). BESD are likely to spring from the following factors:

- *bio* e.g. genetic inheritance and imbalances in the body's biochemistry
- *psycho* e.g. distorted thought patterns, tending to expect the worst/ emotional damage caused by abuse or neglect
- *social* e.g. attachment difficulties, parental separation.

Rather than separate one element from the others, we need to think of the continuing interaction between the three elements within the child and with the different environments in which children find themselves. There is constancy in some thoughts, feeling and behaviour traits across settings but much behaviour is affected by, and adjusts to, the nature of the specific context in which children are. It is therefore helpful to take an *ecosystemic* view. Practitioners need to consider children's experience at home, at school, amongst family, peers and professionals and both inside and outside themselves. They need to take into account all the factors that make up the child's world and that influence the other factors, sometimes in a helpful and sometimes in a harmful way (Cooper, Smith and Upton 1994). A key and encouraging feature of this perspective is that if you can bring about positive change in one part of a child's ecosystem, this can have positive effects on other areas.

GENETIC INHERITANCE: THE NATURE/NURTURE DEBATE

Recent research has led scientists to dismiss the old question 'Was it nature [what we were born with]?' or 'Was it nurture [how we are brought up]?' People are clearly products of both nature and nurture in constant interaction. This is particularly important in relation to children with BESD. Just as whether they have brown or blue eyes will be determined by inherited genes, so certain aspects of their temperament, aptitudes and behaviour will, to an extent, be influenced by inherited family traits going back generations. Genes are likely to explain some of a child with BESD's speech, language and communication needs (SLCN) and dyslexia, and could explain ADHD (which are often 'co-morbid', i.e. occur alongside the BESD). However, in the light of recent science, it is clear that nurture *significantly affects and creates* much of our nature clearly making many children more vulnerable – or in other children creating a well of resilience to support them through times of need.

THE DEVELOPMENT OF THE BRAIN

Research into neuroscience demonstrates the extent of nurture's power on a child's brain development. The brain of a baby who receives consistent love and care from a mother or other responsive adult will grow up in a different way to that of the child in a neglectful or threatening setting. Environmental influences are crucial to the brain before birth and in the early years of life, but also remain important through childhood – particularly the teenage years.

Excellent accounts on a fascinating, if complex, topic are given in Gerhardt (2004) and in Sunderland (2007). These accounts include an explanation of how the brain is made up of millions of brain cells called 'neurons', which connect through 'synapses' to form a complex mass of 'neural pathways and networks'. Along these pathways pass messages sent by the brain's natural chemicals called 'neurotransmitters' (types of hormones), nearly all of which are amino-acids. The brain communicates through the nervous system, the blood supply and through lymph systems, to different parts of the body – for example, to the adrenal gland near the kidneys, where cortisol (known as 'the stress hormone') is produced.

There are dozens of neurotransmitters but the following seem particularly important to the study of BESD:

- *oxytocin*: sometimes called 'the love hormone' (Guardian 2009) is released particularly at birth in mother and baby to help them bond

- *dopamine*: this controls arousal levels in many parts of the brain and is vital for giving physical motivation
- *noradrenaline* (also called *norepinephrine*): a chemical that excites, inducing physical and mental arousal and alert mood
- *serotonin*: known as the 'feel good' chemical – when produced in large quantities, it produces feelings of serenity and optimism
- *endorphins*: these are opioids (having a similar effect to morphine), which modulate pain, reduce stress and promote a sensation of calm; they are produced when a child is lovingly touched or held by a parent or other caring person
- *acetylcholine* (ACh): this controls activity in the brain areas connected with attention, learning and memory
- *glutamate*: another 'excitatory' neurotransmitter crucial to forging links between neurons upon which learning and long-term memory are built.

As you may already be aware, there are three parts to the brain. Early in humankind's evolution, our distant ancestors developed in the following way. Our pre-human ancestors (reptiles) developed a 'reptilian brain' to which was added in mammalian descendants the 'mammalian brain'; later homo sapiens developed the upper parts of the brain (cortex) to exist alongside the other two parts of the brain. (Gerhardt 2004; Sunderland 2007).

- First, their **reptilian brain**: this is shared with all other vertebrates. This governs and activates instinctive behaviour related to survival. It controls basic bodily functions including hunger, digestion, breathing, circulation, temperature, movement, territorial instincts and survival responses to escape predators or other danger. The basic functions of this part of the brain are to stimulate *fight, flight* or, where these are not effective, *freeze* ('play dead'), or *flock* together.
- Second, their **mammalian brain**: this is also known as the 'emotional brain', or the 'limbic system' (it includes the amygdala, hippocampus and hypothalamus – see below). This is involved in bonding needs, including emotions linked to attachment. It acts as the brain's 'emotion factory', creating the chemical messages that connect information into a person's memory. It triggers strong feelings that need to be managed well by the rational brain in the neocortex. It also helps fight or flight impulses. It activates rage, fear, separation, distress, caring and nurturing, social bonding, playfulness and explorative urges.

49

- Third, their **higher** or **rational brain** (also known as the 'neo-cortex'). This now forms about 85 per cent of the brain. The cortex, particularly the prefrontal cortex, is concerned with imagination, problem-solving, reasoning and reflections; self-awareness, kindness, empathy and concern. It controls such high-level processes as logic, creative thought, language, and the integration of sensory information.

Human alarm systems lie partly in the mammalian brain, which control emotions. Here in times of stress the amygdala communicates with another part of the brain, called the hypothalamus, which triggers the release of stress hormones, particularly cortisol, which can flood the prefrontal cortex thereby preventing rational thought. As mentioned, there is also another alarm system in the primitive reptilian brain that causes fight, flight or 'freeze' responses (as seen in anger, anxiety or depression) and in some cases the tendency to flock or herd together under perceived attack.

Gerhardt (2004, p.19) saw the newborn baby as an 'external foetus', coming into the world unfinished with its brain ready to be programmed and customised to suit the child's environment, to adapt it to the particular family and social group. Early experience impacts on the amount and nature of the neural pathways formed and on which neurotransmitters are under- or over-produced. Since the baby's brain over-produces synapses the synapses are forced to compete with the 'fittest', or most used, and thus useful synapses are selected. Pathways that are *not* useful are culled, possibly in part while we sleep. A substantial 'pruning' is underway from about two years old, as 90 per cent of the growth of the human brain occurs in the first five years of life. Sunderland (2007, p.21) writes: 'Over these crucial years, millions of brain connections are being formed, unformed, and then re-formed, directly due to the influence of your child's life experiences and in particular his emotional experiences with you [the parent or close carer].'

The prefrontal cortex (which rapidly becomes the 'social brain') develops almost entirely post-natally. Between 6 and 12 months old there is a rapid expansion of synaptic connections in this area (although connections do continue to be made throughout life). Without love and a nurturing social experience (being held, touched, having physical needs met in a warm and affectionate manner, being smiled at, spoken to and comforted) this crucial part of the brain will not develop well, leaving the child over-reacting and stressed for long periods. The hormone serotonin, which usually helps to modulate emotions, could be under-produced while an over-production of the stress hormones cortisol and testosterone could be regularly triggered.

The effects of a negative early experience can cause damage lasting throughout childhood and beyond. This harmful experience can start before birth, for example, a stressed pregnant woman can pass her high levels of cortisol through the placenta into the baby's brain before birth. Once born, the baby's experience of parenting determines whether stress chemicals are strongly activated on a regular basis in later life. If they are, Sunderland (2007) warns that the child can be in a persisting state of hyperarousal, feeling threatened for much of the time – feeling fundamentally unsafe. As a result, the child may conduct his or her life in a chronic state of mistrust either withdrawing from life or 'doing battle' with it (see also Balbernie 2007a).

If parents do not understand their child's need for closeness and, instead, treat the child with frequent criticism or shouting or other abuse – or, indeed, fail to respond to signals of distress at all – then the release of opioids and oxytocin is blocked. If children become focused on a feeling of threat, real or imagined, and are not soothed in any way their bodies move into a state of *hyperarousal*, activating powerful reptilian and mammalian brain aggressive responses. When the baby's crying is regularly ignored for long periods, hypoarousal also results, which leaves the child anxious and often in a 'frozen' state. Over time these responses generalise and become patterns of behaviour that are over-sensitive to the smallest of triggers.

Babies of depressed mothers adjust to low stimulation from their carer and get used to a lack of positive feelings. The more depressed the mother is, the less activity there is in the prefrontal cortex, and with less blood flow in this area of the brain, fewer neurotransmitters like serotonin or noradrenaline are released. Gerhardt (2004) notes how the physiological balances producing depression in the mothers tend to be mirrored in the child's brain and can thus be passed on from generation to generation.

In contrast to the above is the healthy brain development of the child, who has experienced what Gerhardt (2004, p.118) calls a 'blissful protected infancy'. When a mother or other caring adult is attuned and attentive to the baby's needs, when she responds to its physical needs and also looks at, smiles at, touches, caresses, holds and regularly comforts the child, then the prognosis is good. The child will develop a large number of dopamine synapses helping the child to approach experience in a positive way. Gerhardt suggests: 'Dopamine flowing through the orbitofrontal cortex helps it to do its job of evaluating events and adapting to them quickly. It also helps to delay gratification and stop and think about choice of action' (2004, p.119). Lovingly nurtured babies come to expect a world that is responsive to their feelings. Their higher brains (the neo-cortex) quickly become proficient at counteracting unpleasant feelings by releasing hormones (for example, endorphins) that flow through the body, thereby reducing stress and anxiety.

It is difficult to represent the complexities of this topic in a short space and it is not possible to say precisely how the above paragraphs link to children with BESD. However, we do know that many children with BESD will not have experienced a 'blissful protected infancy', toddlerhood or later childhood and it is highly likely that they have unusual levels of hormones, imbalances in how their neurotransmitters function and gaps in their neural networks compared with well-adjusted children. These factors are likely to have an ongoing influence on how these troubled, and sometimes troublesome, children think, feel and behave. Their dopamine and serotonin production levels could be low and their bodies could over-produce cortisol. The end result is that they are likely to have great difficulty in regulating their emotions, leaving them subject to over-reacting, anger and stress, which interferes with these children's ability to think clearly, to concentrate and to find rational solutions (Balbernie 2007a).

However, re-assuring for professionals 'picking up the pieces' in educational settings is the fact that the brain continues to develop after the age of three and that there is a second wave of proliferation and pruning of synapses in the teenage brain, making it receptive to compensatory adult inputs, which can offset some of the effects of early life experience. The brain retains some plasticity – that is, the ability to reshape and adapt (in part to 'rewire') – through to adulthood, and probably up to the age of thirty. Children with BESD can therefore be responsive to and be helped by nurturing or 'Positive Psychology' approaches (see later) provided by skilled, empathetic practitioners in educational settings.

ATTACHMENT

The bio-chemistry of the brain and the rest of the body should be borne in mind as we go on to look at another crucial area – that of attachment theory and practice.

'Attachment theory' is largely associated with the pioneer child-care researcher, John Bowlby (1969). Bowlby realised, before 1950 and before neurotransmitters had been identified, that infants seek attachments to adults for reasons other than a basic instinct to find food. He saw early relationships as being part of an interactive system with key adults in which physical closeness and comfort were important in their own right, and were achieved by behaviours that babies are born with or reach at a very early stage of their lives.

Attachment of a baby to the mother (or other loving and nurturing carer) should be the first and most fundamental relationship that a child makes

– thus helping to establish healthy emotions, thoughts and expectations, and acting as a yardstick for future relationships with others. Growing up with secure attachments to their carers is a crucial protective factor in children against developing emotional and behaviour problems. Secure attachment is also the basis for the healthy socialisation of the child (Elliott and Place 1998; Geddes 2006; Talbot 2002). In contrast, *insecure* attachment patterns are associated with neglectful, inconsistent or abusive parenting and leave a child more likely to develop BESD, poor control of impulses and difficulties in developing social relationships with peers and adults (Talbot 2002).

Attachment is, at its best, an emotional and physical relationship between mother and child, triggering the flow of comforting neurotransmitters in both of them. It leads the infant to seek out his mother's presence and comfort, particularly when the infant is frightened or uncertain, and experiencing the effects of hormones such as cortisol. However, attachment is also about *older* children's need to be valued by and to be able to depend on others (and this is where professionals in education and care settings can contribute). In fact, attachment, when defined as an enduring affectionate bond between two individuals that serves to join them emotionally, is important *throughout* our lives as children who were well attached to their parent or carer in their early years can more easily develop attachments to others in later life.

Unsurprisingly, abused or neglected children are usually found to have insecure and disorganised attachments, which are accompanied by painful or frozen feelings, linking to unhealthy imbalances in their hormones. Gerhardt (2004, p.64) noted that:

> Early experience sets up physiological expectations as to what our 'normal' levels of bio-chemicals are. In this way, they affect our baseline levels of serotonin or cortisol or norepinephrine, and the 'set point' that our body regards as its normal state.

Babies who are ignored when they cry produce high levels of cortisol, which affect the development of their other neurotransmitter systems. Babies of withdrawn mothers have lower noradrenaline and dopamine than other babies. There is a strong link between emotional insecurity and cortisol dysfunction produced by parents' lack of responsiveness and emotional support to their child. Early abuse and neglect leads to the emotional circuits of brain pruning away many of the crucial links between the neo-cortex and the limbic system, lessening the child's capacity to control the urgent fear reactions produced in the amygdala. Such babies can find it unusually difficult to cope with the daily separations that are part of any child's life (see also Balbernie 2007a).

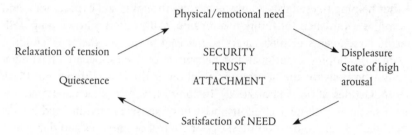

Figure 3.1: The arousal–relaxation cycle
Source: based on Fahlberg 2003. Published by BAAF, 1994 in London.

Moving away from the bio-chemistry associated with attachment, the 'arousal – relaxation cycle' (Fahlberg 2003) can provide a visual representation of aspects of the attachment process (see Figure 3.1). Babies will usually behave in ways that will get them the care they need from attachment figures around them. Small babies cry; soon they learn to smile at loved ones or to use other strategies to gain attention. These 'attachment behaviours' occur when the baby is feeling threatened, because of hunger, pain, fear or because their care giver is unavailable, physically or psychologically. The *degree* of attachment will be affected by the speed and intensity with which the mother (or other carer) responds to the child – also by the extent to which the primary caregiver initiates interactions with the child (Talbot 2002).

In a healthy parent–child situation you get a 'positive interaction cycle' – the parent/carer initiates interaction to get a positive response from the child ('Satisfaction of need', Figure 3.1). This ongoing process starts to build the child's feelings of self-worth and gradually gives the child the confidence to cope with separations and to be more independent. In neglectful or abusive situations, this normal cycle happens infrequently (or perhaps not at all) leaving the child angry, alone or with 'frozen' emotions.

It is now known that while it is best for the birth-mother to be the primary attachment figure, it is not essential that she is. Rutter and Smith (1995) reported that children can, in fact, cope well with having *up to five* adults looking after them provided that:

- it is the same adults over an extended time

- the individuals with whom they have a secure attachment relationship are available at times when the child is tired, distressed or facing challenging circumstances.

The crucial factor is that the child *feels* accepted, valued, understood and has a degree of intimacy with a small number of carers. These could be staff in a care home.

When the child starts school, he or she will show various indicators of secure or insecure attachments. Does the child behave as though she/he likes him/herself? Show pride in achievements? Share with others? Speak about likes and dislikes? Try new tasks? Make eye contact? Show a wide range of emotions? Seem confident when talking to adults? Show pleasure when physically close to parents? Get on well with other people? If the answer is 'yes', then the child is likely to have secure attachments.

If parents have bonded well to their children, they are likely to be responsive and affectionate to their child. They will enjoy his or her company; cope well with the child's expression of negative feelings; provide clear boundaries; comment on positive as well as negative behaviours; show interest in a child's school performance; know what their child likes and dislikes.

At secondary school age, secure attachment is indicated by the young person's showing awareness of their personal strengths and weaknesses, interacting well with peers, and performing satisfactorily in lessons. They are likely to be comfortable with their sexuality, being amenable to normal school rules, staying emotionally close to their parents and having ambitions for the future. The parents of the securely attached child will tend to set appropriate limits, trust the young person, show interest and acceptance in the adolescent's friends, show affection and stand by the young person if in trouble.

It is likely that your observations of many of the children with whom you work will suggest that many of these conditions have not been met. Nonetheless there *will be* repeated opportunities for you to provide useful support to children who have attachment difficulties. Interventions should include work on raising self-esteem, increasing social skills, and emotional literacy, encouraging the formation of relationships and friendships, promoting resilience, building trust and empathy. 'Nurture groups', 'Circles of Friends' and SEAL programmes (see later in this book) can all provide a safe environment and structure in which children with attachment disorders can experience success and develop interpersonal skills.

It is possible that perhaps only two-thirds of children are securely attached to their parents. This leaves about 35 per cent who are not (Layard and Dunn 2009), including many children with severe BESD and mental-health difficulties that can last into adulthood. As parents, young people who have experienced disturbed attachments tend to display poorer parenting practices, and are more likely to maltreat their own children. Since they themselves did not develop secure attachments in childhood, they find it difficult to develop such attachments with their own children – although this is not always the case. Some adults who were not securely attached *do* parent their own children satisfactorily or even very well. The worst prognosis is for children who have experienced inconsistent parenting, leaving 'confused attachment' states.

A minority of the population will have severe attachment disorders, including 'primary attachment disorder' (PAD) – but this could be a significant proportion of the children with whom you work. Children with PAD have often experienced an unsettled early life and/or inadequate parenting and have not developed specific attachments to their carers. They tend to form quick, superficial links with any adults and demand much attention. As they grow up they can show the following signs of disturbance: over-activity, aggression, low tolerance of frustrations, sudden mood changes.

BONDING AND 'CLAIMING'

'Bonding' (an idea from attachment theory) describes the process whereby parents and family, particularly the mother, come to see the child as belonging to them and worthy of their care and love. They 'claim' the child as their own. When the baby is 'difficult' or different the parents might resist what is often assumed to be an innate and natural process.

Balbernie (2007b) refers to the concept of 'intersubjectivity', a theory based around recent discoveries about 'mirror neurons'. The latter function allows one brain to resonate with the goal-centred activity of another. Balbernie describes the process of intersubjectivity as allowing the parent to intuitively accompany their child's development and actively join each other's emotional experience. As a process it creates conditions to allow attachment and bonding to deepen through shared experiences within the mother's and the child's brains.

'Claiming behaviour' is usually positive and starts when a family has its first contact with the new baby and their first look at it. They might:

- explore the baby to see if he or she has any physical disabilities
- examine the baby to see who in the family the child resembles.

If physical similarities are perceived then the parents often feel entitled to 'claim' the child as theirs. 'Claiming' should be a positive process – but it can also be negative if defects are seen or bad comparisons drawn with others. Claiming behaviour continues in families throughout childhood and beyond: for example, a relative saying to the child 'Your hair is the same colour as Aunty Clare's' or 'You have your Grandad's smile'.

MEETING THE NEEDS OF CHILDREN

To ensure the healthy development of children, there are a number of key needs that must consistently be met. Maslow's Hierarchy of Needs (which is more correctly called his 'Theory of Motivation' – see Maslow 1943) gives an enduring view of what these are (see Figure 3.2). Maslow proposed that a series of different levels exist in human need, from basic satisfaction of physical wants (i.e. hunger, thirst, warmth) to achievement of goals and life-challenges (a process that Maslow called 'self-actualisation').

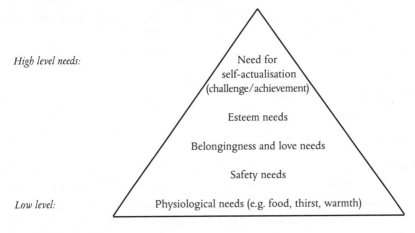

High level needs:

Need for
self-actualisation
(challenge/achievement)

Esteem needs

Belongingness and love needs

Safety needs

Low level:

Physiological needs (e.g. food, thirst, warmth)

Figure 3.2: The Maslow Hierarchy of Needs

These needs are seen as hierarchical, i.e. lower level needs must be satisfied before a person would be concerned about higher level needs. For example, only when a child's physiological needs have been met ('Bodily comfort speaketh the loudest', Maier 1981) and when she/he feels safe, will she/he be concerned about self-esteem and then self-actualisation. However, this notion of 'hierarchy' can be a bit simplistic because, for example, a busy, playing child will forget his or her hunger for a time.

In the influential Green Paper *Every Child Matters* (DfES 2003b) the government gave a view of children's needs, which when met, issue in 'key outcomes'. These needs overlap substantially with – yet are less complete than – the Maslow view. You may be familiar with the text shown in Figure 3.3.

'We want to help all children and young people to:

- **Be healthy:** enjoying good physical and mental health and living a healthy lifestyle;

- **Stay safe:** being protected from harm and neglect and growing up able to look after themselves;

- **Enjoy and achieve:** getting the most out of life and developing broad skills for adulthood;

- **Make a positive contribution:** to the community and to society and not engaging in anti-social or offending behaviour;

- **Achieve economic well-being:** not being prevented by economic disadvantage from achieving their full potential in life.'

Figure 3.3: The *Every Child Matters* Five Key Outcomes
(*Every Child Matters*, para. 3.2, DfES 2003b)

PARENTING STYLE

Clearly the most important and influential provider of children's needs should be at least one caring, dedicated parent who provides structure and boundaries. This parent should give 'unconditional love', meaning that no matter what the child does, the love and commitment of the parent to caring for the child remains. This love should provide the child with stability, security, consistency, a sense of history and basis on which the child can develop his or her own identity.

Successful mothers and fathers achieve 'authoritative parenting', which

- is strong on nurturing
- sets sensible boundaries for the child
- allows for regular and effective two-way communication between adults.

Such parenting is neither too permissive, nor too authoritarian.

DEVELOPMENT OF SELF-CONCEPT AND SELF-ESTEEM

With neurotransmitters functioning well, secure early attachments and 'authoritative parenting' in place, young children develop a good sense of who they are, of their unique identity, of their ability to make good things happen, i.e. they can grow a positive sense of 'self'. They are likely to have the confidence to explore, to be adventurous. They expect to succeed. If they experience setbacks they have the security and support of loving parents/ carers to turn to, to build them up again ready to try again. They have a good self-concept in relation to most areas of their life.

'Self-concept' (usually seen as being identical to self-image) is the view a child takes of him or herself. It contains many related aspects, e.g. a self-concept in relation to maths, French, playing football – and, very importantly, body image. It is heavily influenced by how we think others see us and is sometimes called 'the looking glass theory of self'.

Self-concept can be broken down into two components:

* *perceived self* (how we rate ourselves overall)

* *ideal self* (how we would like to see ourselves).

If the gap between perceived self and ideal self is small then our self-concept (or self-image) is good and we will have good self-esteem.

There could be a big gap between our perceived self and our ideal self in an area that is important to us (and to our peers) and we would then have poor self-esteem in this area. This could be in major areas such as ability to make friends or thinking that we are too fat. The consequences for our global self-esteem, and sometimes our mental health, can then be serious. If the gap is big in an area that is unimportant to us, it is likely to be of little relevance to our mental health. We might hate sport or school – and our friends might share our feelings. When this happens our overall self-esteem will not be affected. Unsurprisingly, the two most important factors in determining a child's global self-esteem are their family, followed by school experience (Thomas 1980). Fortunately self-esteem is not fixed: it can alter according to the people we are with, what we do and the situations in which we find ourselves (Dowling 2010). Long and Fogell (1999, p.32) claimed 'Self-esteem is like oxygen. Children must have a good supply to thrive'.

It is often said that children with BESD have low self-esteem, and such a description can be entered on a child's records, usually without serious attempt beforehand to measure it objectively. However, some recent research suggests that BESD and poor self-image do not necessarily go hand in hand (Swinson 2008) and certainly to enrol the child in self-esteem classes or subject them to an excess of praise may not be the appropriate response. In the view of positive psychologists, overt, head-on efforts to boost self-esteem can result in a child becoming overly self-absorbed and experiencing depression (Centre for Confidence and Well-being 2009; Dweck 2009 – see the later section on 'mindsets' p.62). Dowling (2010) states that self-esteem depends on whether children feel accepted and are seen as worthwhile. A more appropriate response, therefore, may be to value and encourage effort, being aware that it is most commonly through nonverbal cues, e.g. a facial expression – rather than speech – that we communicate our view of others.

INTERNAL WORKING MODELS

The 'internal working model' (IWM) concept can help in understanding the skewed and irrational thinking that often accompanies BESD.

As a baby develops, it starts to interpret and have a view about his or her world, which increasingly influences his or her thoughts and perceptions. This view becomes an 'internal working model' of how the world works, a habitual way of interpreting life and the child's place within it and its sense of self (Bowlby 1969). According to the quality of care received and the nature of communication experienced, the young child comes to interpret life – who to trust, what to expect will happen, what best to do under what circumstances. The child develops 'beliefs' and 'scripts' (series of responses to specific stimuli/events).

In most cases, the child will have experienced love, security, and prompt attention to its physical needs. It will therefore have grown a healthy dependence on reliable and nurturing caregivers. From this healthy dependence, the child has growing confidence to explore its environment and to learn. Those who have experienced good attachments are likely to put positive interpretations on what happens around them, to expect good things to happen, e.g. to trust adults, to be well looked after and to be loved. They will have a healthy, optimistic IWM (Gerhardt 2004).

If early experiences have been largely negative, the young child is likely to have a pessimistic view of the world and a negative perhaps hostile or aggressive IWM. Those who had bad experiences and damaged attachments are likely to see the world as an unhelpful, cold, cruel and, perhaps, dangerous place – and they will anticipate or confront events thinking they can do little to make things better. When past experiences have been painful, important information is often excluded from the child's perceptions (and interpretations) and its IWM can become rigid, does not work properly and precludes the usual mental searching for less negative explanations or alternatives. Attachment-related events such as loss and abuse lead to modifications for the worse in these internal representations and can affect the child's strategies for processing thoughts and feelings. Distorted and often pessimistic, self-critical thinking can start young and is closely connected to the child's early experience. IWMs have usually taken root by the age of five.

Helen Bee wrote 'We notice and remember experiences that fit our model or forget experiences that don't match' (Bee 2000, p.328). In summary, an IWM enables the individual to

- construct and evaluate several alternative explanations and perceptions
- explore mentally the probable effects of alternate responses
- select and implement a logically coherent response.

An IWM reduces the time and effort needed to scan perpetually the state of the environment and to formulate responses to it.

'FIXED' AND 'GROWTH' MINDSETS

Of a similar nature to IWMs are 'mindsets'. These are not our temporary passing moods or physical states that might mean we find it difficult to concentrate on a particular task at a given time or remember the instructions that our partner has just given us (being in the wrong 'frame of mind') but, rather, are entrenched ways we have of looking at whether we can or cannot improve, whether we will stick at tasks even after setbacks and failure – or whether we just give up because we think more effort would be wasted.

The research of Carol Dweck and colleagues over recent decades has led to this idea of 'mindset'. Her studies suggest that children can develop one of two basic mindsets, 'fixed' or 'growth', which often persist into adulthood (although they can be changed). Those with 'fixed mindsets' believe that their achievements are based on innate abilities – for example, their amount of intelligence is seen as a fixed trait: you have what you have and it cannot be altered. As a result, these people are reluctant to take on challenges that might make them feel or look stupid. In contrast, children and adults with 'growth mindsets' believe that they can learn, change, and develop needed skills. They are better at handling setbacks, accepting constructive advice and believe that hard work can help them achieve goals. Unsurprisingly, Dweck (2006, 2009) finds that neuroscience research supports the notion that intelligence can be enhanced through learning and 'stickability'.

We will return in a later chapter to Dweck's view of mindset and its practical implications – for example, how we can alter children's mindsets through the type of praise we use and through formative assessment.

AGES AND STAGES OF DEVELOPMENT

It is worth reflecting on the 'normal' developments (beyond babyhood) that generally produce social and emotionally stable children and then comparing these developments to the experience of children with BESD, who are well known to you:

The toddler years: 12–36 months

Along with physical growth, the baby starts to form his or her own identity, with a growing awareness of 'self' accompanied by a growing awareness of being separate psychologically from the primary carer. The baby develops language that is functional, that is, helping to express and satisfy his or her needs. Through developing social interactions/connections to the parent or other primary carers, the toddler's emotions develop.

At this stage the parent or other carers should help the child:

- to feel more capable, e.g. by putting a stool at the sink so the child can reach to wash his or her own hands
- through giving encouragement
- through considering the safety aspects for the exploring child
- by establishing routines (without being over-rigid).

Pre-school: 3–4 or 5 years

The child should be proficient and confident within his or her family, feeling safe, encouraged, valued and loved – perhaps benefiting from living with siblings. There could be increasing and regular social interactions with a growing number of other children and some adults, for example, through play groups, visits to the homes of friends of the family or shopping trips with mother or extended family.

Key to continuing healthy social and emotional development is the freedom and encouragement to explore the expanding world around the child through play. Play is also used to solve early psychological conflicts. At this stage it is important for play to be used to explain the difference between 'big' and 'little' and 'bad' and 'good'. The child needs to experience these conflicting states and integrate them, e.g. pre-schoolers often play at being babies as well as the parental role (i.e. being strong and in charge).

The primary school years: 5–10 or 11 years

Children who have experienced good emotional and social care in their early years, usually display the following:

- confidence in/mastery of an increasing range of social situations outside the family
- steady physical growth and robust health
- respond well to teaching, and learn at school
- rewarding social interaction with their peers
- a strong sense of fair play
- early reflections of their family's values
- the beginnings of a conscience
- awareness of their (and others') strengths and weaknesses.

As children move through the final years of Key Stage 2, parents need to facilitate an expanding world for their child, creating opportunities for him or her to spend time with friends. They should allow their child to have personal likes and dislikes. Clear messages on family values further help the child's development of conscience.

Adolescence

For many young people, adolescence is a time filled with excitement, challenge and change but mixed with uncertainty. Given the absence of 'resilience-building' factors (explained later on in this chapter) in the lives of so many young people with BESD, many of the children you work with could experience great 'adolescent turmoil' perhaps characterised by more 'acting out', fighting, self-consciousness or loss of confidence.

During their secondary school education, young people undergo profound physical change as they acquire adult bodies. There is a new flowering of neural pathways and it is not until late adolescence that the prefrontal cortex of the brain, and the competences of control and consequence, are fully developed (Gerhardt 2004). Rapid hormone changes accompanying sexualisation are also experienced. Teenagers can be moody and unreliable one minute and reliable the next.

Adolescence is a time when development tends to exaggerate psychological traits – for example, some teenagers compulsively need to check that lights are switched off. Some will withdraw into themselves, rarely volunteering information. Questions will often be met with 'Don't know' (Elliott and Place 1998). Adolescents often transfer their psychological and social investment from their parents to their peers. They might oppose family rules, values and expectations and be over-compliant with peers. Teenagers internalise new models to copy: sometimes teachers, peers or heroes. They move from the external controls of their parents and adults to their own internal controls, self-control and independence.

In adolescence, the prevalence of mental-health problems rises, with the pattern of disorders changing to be more like that in the adult population. Rates of depression increase, particularly amongst young women, and early onset of psychotic illnesses begins to appear. In a minority of young people serious 'disturbance' may be shown through bullying, early pregnancy, prostitution or sexual abuse; depressive illness or anxiety, neurosis, eating disorder or self-harm.

At this time, having parents who can provide positive family role models is clearly beneficial. They should encourage their children to take more responsibility for their own behaviour, but if there are 'issues' the parents should make their views known, sometimes saying 'No' firmly – and meaning it.

PLAY

It is important to enlarge on one particular childhood need that is crucial to healthy social and emotional development and cognitive learning – play. Indeed, it might be said that in normal circumstances 'play is what children do!' Children play to:

- have fun
- learn
- experiment
- make relationships
- belong
- develop their sense of self
- experience success
- handle frustrations
- exercise/develop their bodies.

Play should be stimulated and encouraged by the companionship of parents and other family members in the early years. Where this has not happened, it is particularly important for workers in child-care and educational settings to provide opportunities for it. As the child grows older, play should be more dependent on peer group activities. Play needs objects, space, time and companions. Children use their imagination to fill many gaps in equipment and creativity. They are stimulated as they exchange ideas. Play helps to strengthen the body, improve the mind and develop the personality, and gives opportunities for developing physical, social and creative skills and competence.

RISK AND RESILIENCE FACTORS IN CHILDHOOD

BESD commonly develop in children who are subject to harmful 'risk factors'. Such children also 'lack resilience' – that is, the usual capacity to 'bounce back' from stress and adversity. Key individual resilience factors include secure attachments, communication skills in the child and caring parenting. We can help to build resilience by having high expectations of children and involving them in the learning process and through providing them with relationships and encouragement.

Below is a summary of risk factors based on wide research (DCSF/DoH 2008a).

The presence of two factors more than *doubles* the impact on a child; the presence of three risk factors more than *quadruples* the bad effects (Talbot 2002). As you will know from your work, children with BESD often have *many* different risk factors in their lives.

COMMUNITY OR ENVIRONMENTAL FACTORS:

- socio-economic disadvantage, i.e. poverty
- poor housing or homelessness
- ongoing and serious discrimination.

FAMILY FACTORS:

- frequent, open and serious conflict between parents/partners
- family breakdown
- inconsistent, unclear 'discipline'
- neglect or a *laissez-faire* approach to child-care
- hostile and rejecting relationships
- failure to adapt to the child's changing development needs
- abuse – physical, sexual and/or emotional
- severe parental mental-health problems
- parental criminality or substance addiction

- death and loss – including loss of friendships
- other traumatic life events.

Key factors that help to protect and to develop the resilience of children can be placed in three groups (DCSF/DoH 2008a):

WITHIN-CHILD PROTECTIVE/RESILIENCE FACTORS

- gender (being female)
- higher intelligence
- an easy temperament when an infant
- secure attachment to parent(s), carer and/or others
- positive attitude, problem-solving approach
- good communication skills
- planner, belief in control
- sense of humour
- religious faith
- capacity to reflect.

WITHIN-FAMILY PROTECTIVE/RESILIENCE FACTORS

- at least one good parent– child relationship
- affection
- authoritative discipline/parenting
- parental support for education
- supportive parental relationship/absence of severe discord
- supportive extended family.

COMMUNITY/ENVIRONMENTAL PROTECTIVE/RESILIENCE FACTORS

- wide supportive network around the family and child
- good housing
- high standard of living
- good schooling with strong pastoral and academic sides
- range of sport and leisure activities.

We would suggest Cefai's (2008) book on resilience as recommended reading on this topic.

SEPARATION AND LOSS

It is likely that we will be working and sharing our lives with some children with BESD who are experiencing intense pain and mental-health problems that result from separation from, or loss of, adults they love or would liked to have loved. It is important to reflect on the different *types* of separation and loss that could be contributing powerfully to a child's BESD.

The many types of separation and loss include:

- death through illness or accidents of parent(s)or other carer or sibling to whom a child is very close

- being fostered

- transition from one foster carer to another or to adoptive parents

- divorce leading to loss of contact with a parent

- separation of parents

- loss of affection, following break-up of teenage relationship

- loss of house through parents' financial problems

- loss of friends when changing school

- loss of property after break-in/burglary – and the lost feelings of security attached to this

- loss of security and/or self-esteem that is associated with being attacked and/or raped.

Long and Fogell (1999, p.76) used the phrase 'little deaths', explaining that these were the common losses experienced in childhood (such as losing a good friend when the family moves, losing a favourite teacher or the death of a pet). Such losses precipitate emotional reactions. They argue that how children respond to these 'little deaths' will influence how they deal with major ones. However, they believe that parents and staff should not over-protect children from such events as that could make them more vulnerable.

Actual bereavement will sometimes be a feature of children with BESDs' lives, whether through a tragic suicide of a child at school or sometimes the suicide, or even murder, of a family member (see Daniels *et al.* 2003). Bereavements can give rise to powerful emotions, can be very confusing and can be linked to mental-health difficulties, sometimes showing up in behaviour difficulties. However, if dealt with in a sensitive way, children – including those with BESD – can undergo grieving 'successfully' (see Chapter 8).

Children of different ages and stages of development tend to see death in different ways:

- **Pre-school** – 'Dead' is similar to 'going away': the very young think that dead people will return. Their emotional distress is like that of separation. There will be little understanding. Children can be egocentric and have feelings of guilt and anger, perhaps 'Aunty died because I did not visit her'.

- **Aged 5–9s** – Infants and young junior-school children generally understand the finality of death, while finding difficulty in dealing with the fear and anxiety this produces.

- **After age 9** – Older children and adolescents accept that death is universal and irreversible. They tend to use their personal beliefs and values to make sense of it.

- **'Stuck children'** – Some children are 'stuck' at stages of development earlier than their chronological age. They are likely to therefore 're-act' in ways expected of a younger child. This can cause carers and practitioners confusion, but staff need to try to observe and work with the immature way in which the child is behaving.

Whatever the age, we need to watch out for those children who suppress their grief and appear to be coping. Children of all ages can hide their true feelings under a veneer of apparent indifference.

Abnormal responses to grief may be displayed in:

- somatic (e.g. wetting themselves) and other behavioural problems in under 5s

- primary-school children displaying challenging behaviour

- older children/adolescents displaying some of a range of behaviours: withdrawal; sleeping problems; regressive behaviour; attention seeking; eating difficulties; denial (e.g. 'We weren't that close anyway!'); anger; apparent apathy; unusually deep immersion in their usual activities.

We should also be aware of the danger of re-activation. The mourning process might not reach the final stage of full acceptance and so readjustment and grief might be reactivated later in the child's life (even in adulthood) by related experiences of separation and loss.

Particular attention should be paid to children who are 'looked after' ('in care'), who have lost family and who have experienced a succession of carers. These children could be experiencing multiple grieving, with a number of unresolved grief issues (Fletcher 2005).

Readers are recommended to look at Long and Fogell (1999) and Cowie *et al.* (2004) for a more detailed consideration of separation and loss.

PARENTAL SEPARATION AND DIVORCE

Given the fact that nowadays one in three marriages end in divorce and that unmarried co-habiting couples tend to break up more easily than married ones, you will almost certainly have worked with children who have experienced long-lasting damage resulting from such break-ups. Parental separation trebles the chances of a child developing mental-health problems and can exacerbate BESD. There are often extended and damaging aftermaths to parental separations. However, if separation and divorce are well managed, the children can emerge with reasonable, sometimes good, mental health and we professionals can assist in lessening their pain.

There is, commonly, a pattern to separations and their effects. In the majority of cases there will have been a long and hurtful lead-up period to the actual separation. During this the child could have experienced his or her parents' bitter rows, which can seriously damage the well-being of the child.

There are usually three phases following a separation:

1. The acute phase

This is a highly emotional period with much conflict between parents and with one, or both, developing depression and perhaps becoming suicidal. It is usually a fairly brief phase but it can last for several years if one or more of the following happens:

- there are protracted legal battles
- there is personal recrimination
- attempts are made to get the parents back together again/rebuild the relationship.

2. The transitional phase

The parents begin to distance themselves from each other and build new relationships – this is a time of uncertainty but excitement.

3. The settlement phase

New patterns of living are established and the emotional bonds between the former couple diminish substantially or cease altogether.

There are likely to be some common effects of a separation:

- **Practical:** Changes to income and therefore lifestyle; change of school and possibly home.

- **Quality of parenting:** this can deteriorate in the lead up to and after the separation as the parents are wrapped up in their own difficulties.

- **The child might be used as a prop** by the parent looking after the child, with (usually) the mother relying too much on him/her, interrupting the child's own normal development pattern.

- **Competition for affection** and allegiance leads to suffering for the child. This causes major stress for the child who does not want to upset the parent who looks after him/her, knowing that liking the other parent will be seen as disloyalty (Elliott and Place 1998).

How children respond also tends to relate to their stage of development:

- **Infants:** These will worry about whether the parent who has left will continue to care for them. The children will demonstrate grief at the separation and, not understanding the complexities, they will often try to re-unite their parents.

- **Pre-schoolers:** These resist separation, become more demanding, cry frequently, get out of usual routines/lose acquired skills. They may have problems sleeping. They may have toileting problems or wet the bed (enuresis).

- **Junior school/early secondary school children:** These might react by anger at the 'bad' parent who is seen to have caused the separation and an intense commitment to the 'hurt' one. Friendships, peer relationships and schoolwork often suffer.

- **Age and gender responses:** Until adolescence, it tends to be boys who react the worst and suffer most. Long and Fogell (1999) suggest this is because they hide their feelings and can act out in negative ways that tend not to gain sympathy. They often lose their father, their male role model, and might have to act as 'the man in the house'. Girls express their feelings more and tend to evoke more understanding and sympathy.

- **Adolescents:** The additional stresses of separation intensify the emotional 'storms' of adolescence, perhaps displayed in acting-out behaviour, depression or even suicidal feelings. Girls tend to fare worse in adolescence. Peer groups can act as a major source of support.

The practical effects on the children could be severe, including possible changes to income, lifestyle, school, house and, perhaps, a worse quality of parenting, with the parent wrapped up in her or his own concerns.

DEFINING WELL-BEING, MENTAL HEALTH AND MENTAL-HEALTH PROBLEMS

The national CAMHS review team (DCSF/DoH 2008a, p.15) cited a World Health Organisation definition of mental health, which saw it as

> a state of well-being in which the individual realises his or her own abilities, can cope with the normal stresses of life, can work productively and fruitfully, and is able to make a contribution to his or her community.

They stressed that mental health was the foundation of well-being and effective functioning and that 'any child or young person who is not in this state of well-being is at risk of poor mental health' (paragraph 1.7, p.15).

A definition from the Mental Health Foundation (1999, p.6) starts from a different perspective: a mental health problem can be seen as a

> disturbance in functioning in one area of relationships, mood, behaviour or development... When a problem is particularly severe or persistent over time, or when a number of these difficulties are experienced at the same time a child is said to have a mental-health disorder.

Clearly many children with BESD have mental-health problems and some have other disorders. These might take the form of school phobia; obsessive compulsive disorder (OCD); oppositional defiance disorder (ODD); schizophrenia; bi-polar disorders (all beyond the scope of this book) and/or conduct disorders; or − as will be sketched in the sections that follow below − ADHD, anxiety, depression and eating disorders.

ADHD

Attention deficit/hyperactivity disorder (ADHD) is a huge topic that has been covered in other recent accessible publications (e.g. Kutscher 2008; NICE 2008) and which might involve a child being on medication (e.g. methylphenidate, which is the basis of the well-known drug 'Ritalin'). It is likely that you have encountered the restless and often highly disruptive behaviour of children given this label. You will possibly have experienced the highs and lows of what happens when a child in your care has not taken, or is being given inappropriate, medication. ADHD is also seen as a disability, bringing in a social and financial perspective to diagnosis. Brief advice on managing children with ADHD is given in Chapter 7.

ANXIETY

Anxiety is a normal reaction to abnormal circumstances. A threat is perceived that makes us feel anxious, whether adult or child. The caring adult will seek to reduce the threat, often by comforting the child and seeking to reduce the factors that are causing the stress.

Socially allowable and normal anxieties include those arising from: physical threat, aggression, loud noises; heights, confined spaces, high speeds, darkness or infectious diseases. Other anxieties are tolerated and thought to happen as part of life, such as looking foolish in front of others, disapproval from friends and family, or fear of the unknown. Some anxieties are thought to be 'all right' for certain ages, or to be gender-specific, for instance, a small child crying. A noise, a smell, certain lighting conditions can also bring flashbacks to past events that trigger anxiety – perhaps reviving memories of a critical incident in the past.

However, for some children with BESD excessive anxiety amounts to a significant mental-health problem. When we recognise anxiety in a child, we are likely to be responding to externalised signs as the actual anxiety can remain hidden within a child, in whom it is likely that the stress hormone cortisol is flowing throughout the body, interfering with the production of calming neurotransmitters such as serotonin and the endorphins.

Because of acute and chronic anxiety a child might resist going to school, show excessive mood swings, at times refuse to talk, have difficulty in forming or maintaining relationships, or have difficulties in concentrating in class (being inattentive and easily distracted). The child might display physical (somatic) symptoms such as headaches, nausea, palpitations, breathlessness, feeling dizzy. She/he could develop obsessions or phobias, have disturbed sleep patterns, could self-harm or develop eating disorders (Cowie *et al.* 2004; Stallard 2009).

A 'panic attack' is an extreme form of anxiety, involving intense terror lasting from several minutes to several hours (see Chapter 8).

DEPRESSION

On occasion, we can all feel down, and that feeling may be reinforced by the particular balance of neurotransmitters and other hormones flowing around our brain and bodies at that time. Sadness and tears are a normal part of life and not necessarily a sign of mental disorder. Here we are considering more serious states, i.e.:

- depressed mood
- 'depressive syndrome'
- 'depressive disorder' that is a psychiatric illness.

Depressed mood

This is:

A state of profound unhappiness and sense of dejection (dysphoria) that is more than normal sadness. The person cannot see any bright spots to his or her life, and there is a loss of emotional involvement with either other people or activities. It is associated with negative styles of thinking. (Elliott and Place 1998, p.176)

The presence of some such feelings can be a *normal reaction* to a *distressing event*, but the feelings should be *in proportion* to the importance of the event, and the overall intensity won't be too great. A depressed mood is also the way in which negative thoughts can become attributed to all aspects of life: when thinking about the past a person may have feelings of guilt and shame and be frightened of repeating past mistakes; contemplating the present, the person is convinced she/he is a failure and feels helpless; anticipating the future there is an expectancy that the worst will happen, accompanied by a feeling of hopelessness.

Depressive syndrome

This is indicated by a cluster of syndromes, including depressed mood, tearfulness, irritability, loss of appetite, sleep disturbance, poor concentration and loss of energy.

Depressive disorder

This is present when a psychiatric diagnosis of depression has been made, i.e. by a psychiatrist using the American Psychiatric Association's *Diagnostic Statistical Manual* (DSM-IV, APA 2000). Such a diagnosis is based on typical symptoms but they must be present for a specific (usually a long) time and clearly impair the person's functioning. Persistence and degree of impairment distinguish the *disorder* from the *syndrome* (Elliott and Place 1998; Verduyn, Rogers and Wood 2009).

Children with BESD in your setting are most likely to be in a 'depressed mood'. This may be accompanied by difficult, disobedient or aggressive behaviour or by withdrawn and quiet behaviour – sometimes with a mixture of both. Less frequently, pupils will have with a depressive syndrome or depressive disorder, which might take the form of extreme anxiety, self-harm, attempted or completed suicide.

Major depressive illness is found in 1.8 per cent to 2 per cent of children and equally for both sexes before puberty; 5–10 per cent will have a major depressive illness during their teenage years; 22 per cent of girls and 13 per cent of boys show symptoms of depression in Year 8 (12–13 year olds) (Cowie *et al.* 2004; Elliott and Place 1998). The gender difference probably occurs because girls internalise their anger to a greater extent than boys.

The presence of depression in children and in adults, can be explained by

- genetic inheritance and brain chemistry (problems with particular neurotransmitters, for instance the monoamines)

- traumatic historical events (for instance bereavement)

- separation and divorce

- risk factors in the general home or neighbourhood environment.

Common symptoms of depression are sadness and misery; poor concentration; lethargy; social withdrawal; loss of interest in things; a negative view of the self, self-deprecation; a negative view of the world and the future; feelings of hopelessness and futility; high levels of impulsivity; guilt; feelings of persecution; eating too much or too little (poor appetite); sleep disorders; irritability; impaired social relationships; underachievement at school.

Severe depressive syndromes and disorders are clearly the responsibility of general practitioners working with specialist CAMHS, who can help through family and individual therapy/counselling (including cognitive behaviour therapy); and/or medication.

SELF-HARM AND SUICIDE

Talbot (2002) noted that there were 140,000 referrals for self-harm in England and Wales a year and many thousands of these are children. In many cases self-harm accompanies a transient period of distress in a child's life. For others, it is an important indicator of lasting mental-health problems and risk of suicide. It should be noted that even repeated self-wounding rarely results in suicide – but in about 1 per cent of cases it does.

Self-harm:

- is rare in children under 12; peaks in mid-adolescence
- occurs in 10 per cent of teenagers aged 15 or 16
- is a condition in which girls outnumber boys 4:1
- usually takes the form of cutting – in 64.6 per cent of cases
- manifests in its second most common type as overdosing – in 30.7 per cent of cases
- occurs in young people who are more likely to employ poor coping strategies, such as blaming themselves or drinking alcohol.

Self-harmers may use more than one method in a particular episode but they are most likely to cut themselves (in 72% of cases); they may also burn their skin (35% of cases); hit or punch parts of their body (30%); interfere with healing wounds (22%); scratch (22%); pull hair (10%); and break bones (8%). In 74 per cent of cases they will harm arms, often wrists (74%); legs 44 per cent; abdomen 25 per cent; head 23 per cent; chest 18 per cent; and genitalia 8 per cent. Broken glass, needles, open scissors, razor blades, sharp blades, knives or cigarettes are the most common tools used. Cutting rarely leads to hospital referral. The latter is more common for overdoses (Cowie *et al.* 2004).

Risk factors associated with self-harm are:

- high levels of depression
- established drug and alcohol issues (regular life-style or addictions)
- increasingly drinking alcohol/getting drunk (new behaviour pattern)
- increasing consumption of cigarettes
- having fewer 'confidants' than other teenagers
- social issues (bullying; being in trouble with the police; having concerns about sexual orientation; recent awareness of self-harm by peers, i.e. 'copy-cat behaviour').

We clearly need to be watchful, looking out for the behaviour of small groups and peer-group pressures, particularly as 41 per cent of 'self-harmers' seek help from friends before acting. Children who say they are going to commit suicide must be taken very seriously. Over 80 per cent of teenagers who commit suicide first try to communicate their desperation to others. Suicide is associated with depressive illnesses, eating disorders, psychotic disorders such as schizophrenia, and alcohol and drug abuse.

Groups at increased risk include young south Asian women in conflict with their family. Young males can also be at risk: twelve young men take their lives every week in the UK and attempted suicides by young men have nearly tripled since the 1980s. Two-thirds of suicidal young men feel that they have no one to turn to for help. A 'lads' culture requiring young men to appear tough prevents many from seeking help. Young men living apart from their families as a result of family difficulties are especially vulnerable (Cowie *et al.* 2004).

EATING DISORDERS AND OBESITY

Serious eating disorders are a relatively common type of mental-health problem (affecting 1 in 100 adolescents), which can become life threatening or fatal.

Obsession with body image is closely associated with eating disorders and is of, perhaps, increasing importance: many girls will be influenced by waif-like or perfect female role-models. A study found that 40 per cent of teenage girls diet significantly and 7 per cent to extremes. This compares with 10 per cent of boys – 1 per cent to extremes (Elliott and Place 1998). About a third of both anorexic and bulimic patients say they have been sexually abused.

Once a child has anorexia or bulimia, they must receive specialist medical help, usually involving CAMHS. Practitioners in schools can play an important part in:

- trying to prevent or reduce the occurrence of these conditions
- watching out for tell-tale signs that may have escaped the child's family
- keeping a watchful eye over children who have been through specialist treatment.

Anorexia nervosa affects 0.7 per cent of the population, persists for years and can be fatal. It has three main features:

- determined food avoidance
- weight loss or failure to gain weight as a child matures, plus behaviours designed to bring about weight loss (e.g. vomiting, use of laxatives or excessive exercise)
- pre-occupation with weight and shape.

Commonly, anorexia starts (usually in adolescence) when a young person has been called 'fat' (that is, has been teased about their weight), after a period of dieting (88% of young people with an eating disorder have a history of dieting); after a pact with a friend; or after a virus.

Girls will deny being hungry, will hide their lack of eating, e.g. putting their school packed lunch in a bin. Sitting at table can be stressful and the girl will cut food into tiny pieces, avoiding swallowing it. The young person can be obsessed with exercise. Initial weight loss will at first be praised by her peers. However, girls with anorexia become less sociable and often stop meeting friends. They can be irritable and gloomy, appearing depressed. If anorexia appears before the age of 14 it might relate to the girl's fears about growing up and losing the child's body shape. This can link with girls choosing to dress in a childish manner (Cowie *et al*. 2004; Elliott and Place 1998).

Other risk factors associated with the development of anorexia are:

- family problems
- early feeding problems
- obsessive compulsive traits
- death of a close relative in childhood
- interpersonal problems
- low self-esteem at the age of 11–12 years
- unrealistic expectations as girls struggle to be high achievers (for example, watch out for excessive pressure on girls to do well at GCSEs)
- a family history of eating disorders
- severe stresses in the previous 18 months
- a change of school and other life stresses in combination.

If anorexia is suspected then a referral to the young person's doctor and/or to CAMHS should be brought about. Family therapy and individual psychotherapy can help. The first intervention is to stop further weight loss, usually using a programme based on behaviourist principles (rewarding desired behaviours, etc.). Powers under relevant Mental Health Acts may have to be invoked if the young person refuses treatment or hospitalisation in a specialist unit if this becomes necessary.

Increasing weight has to be a gradual process and the experience can be very frightening to the young person. The amounts of food expected to be eaten have to be built up gradually. The process requires patience, tact and the use of sedatives to allay the person's panic. Counselling will not focus on the disorder – rather it will try to show the sufferer that there is an enjoyable life beyond anorexia.

Outcomes remain very variable and child patients often develop their disorders again as adults. However, over half the girls are expected to recover a reasonable weight and for their periods to re-start. The prognosis for boys is poorer. In the long-term under half will maintain normal eating habits and a fifth will develop chronic illnesses directly caused by the anorexia. Five per cent of sufferers will die from a condition caused by it. The earlier the illness starts, the poorer tends to be the outcome.

Bulimia nervosa has only been recognised as a separate condition in the past thirty or forty years. Bulimia nervosa is characterised by an overwhelming fear of getting fat and an obsession about weight and shape. This leads to a powerful urge to eat that does not go away (seen in recurrent binges and feelings of loss of control), followed by behaviour that compensates or purges (e.g. making yourself sick, using laxatives, fasting or taking exercise). The risk factors are parental and personal histories of obesity and depression; critical comments by family on shape, weight or eating; negative self-evaluation; impulsive personality; or parental alcoholism.

Bulimia can be associated with self-harm (usually cutting), alcohol and drug abuse and sexual promiscuity. Over half of the women with bulimia are reported to have recovered and to be living normally ten years after the illness. Others will not recover fully and could have other mental-health problems.

Finally, *obesity* (not necessarily an eating disorder) is an increasing problem and is associated with low self-esteem and mental-health difficulties. Being overweight tends to link with being bullied or carrying out bullying. Peers and staff can have negative attitudes to overweight children, exacerbating their feelings of low self-esteem. Interventions that try to raise self-esteem include circle time and using 'Circles of Friends'. These approaches do not get to the heart of the matter but can lessen the social consequences and improve the quality of the obese child's life.

If you want to look at this area in more detail, we recommend you read Gowers and Green (2009), who mix research on eating disorders with advice on using cognitive behaviour therapy (CBT).

REVIEW:THE ICEBERG OF BEHAVIOUR

In this chapter we have looked at the development of the brain, attachment and needs theory, parenting styles, self-concept and IWMs, stages of development, risk and resilience, separation and loss and a range of mental-health difficulties. We have indicated that the cause of children and young people's BESDs and wider mental-health problems may lie deep within them, reflecting interacting biopsychosocial factors that can pass unnoticed – certainly by an unsympathetic society and much of the media. At other times the difficulties may be clearly 'externalised' and 'acted out'. A helpful way of concluding this chapter is to give a visual representation of the common metaphor, the 'iceberg of behaviour' (see Figure 3.4).

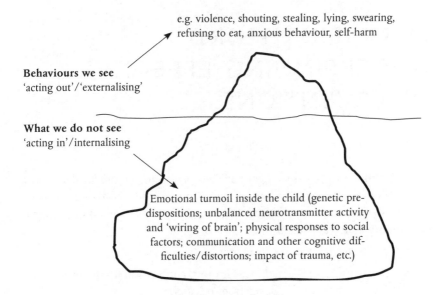

e.g. violence, shouting, stealing, lying, swearing, refusing to eat, anxious behaviour, self-harm

Behaviours we see
'acting out'/'externalising'

What we do not see
'acting in'/internalising

Emotional turmoil inside the child (genetic predispositions; unbalanced neurotransmitter activity and 'wiring of brain'; physical responses to social factors; communication and other cognitive difficulties/distortions; impact of trauma, etc.)

Figure 3.4: The iceberg of behaviour

Clearly, practitioners in educational settings cannot counteract all the risk factors facing children with BESD or undo much of the damage already present. However, where staff have understanding, commitment and knowledge of effective interventions (to be described in later chapters) this can have a positive compensatory effect.

NOTE

1   Mary Ainsworth, having worked with John Bowlby, carried out her seminal 'Strange Situation' study, observing how babies reacted when separated briefly and then reunited with their mothers. Based upon the responses observed, Ainsworth *et al.* (1978) descibed three major styles of attachment; secure attachment, abivalent-insecure attachment, and avoidant-insecure attachment, and avoidant-insecure attachemnt. Later, other researchers added a fourth attachment style called 'disorganised-insecure' attachment.

CHAPTER 4

FURTHER THEORY UNDERPINNING EFFECTIVE INTERVENTIONS

When Colin Smith (1988) suggested 'There's nothing so practical as a good theory' he was, of course, talking of research and evidence-based 'theory' – not untested personal convictions. We, too, believe that some knowledge of such theory is useful since it:

- promotes reflection on practice

- re-assures professionals – as it often confirms that what we do is in fact in line with messages from research

- lessens unwarranted personal guilt-feelings when things go wrong, as theory can show us it is not personal or our fault

- sometimes opens our eyes to new ways of working.

In a climate of increasing individualism (Layard and Dunn 2009) and possibly 'toxic childhoods' (Palmer 2007) this approach is particularly important as we seek to address complex problems.

In Chapter 3, we looked at the biology of child development, mentioned the ecosystemic approach and described human needs (Abraham Maslow's Theory of Motivation, an essential part of the humanistic perspective). We cannot consider these further other than to note that some humanistic and ecosystemic beliefs influence perspectives that are covered in the pages below. Humanistic writers such as Maslow, like modern positive psychologists, wanted science to move away from a possible pre-occupation with pathology and fixing of deficits to identifying and building on people's strengths. In this chapter we focus on key ideas from the psychodynamic, behaviourist, cognitive behaviourist (extended into 'mindfulness') and finally 'positive psychology' perspectives. For readers who wish to delve deeper in this area we recommend Ayers, Clarke and Murray (2000) and Porter (2000).

THE PSYCHODYNAMIC APPROACH

The psychodynamic perspective goes back over a century to the pioneer writings of Sigmund Freud, but has been refined by many writers since. Psychotherapists and psychiatrists undertake extended training in this approach, which often involves delving deep into painful memories from long ago in the young person's past when very young. Intervention focuses on a person's view of him or her self and feelings about other people, particularly family. Mental health professionals will sometimes conduct regular sessions with a client spread over many months. Obviously such in-depth exploration should be left to those fully qualified, given the stressful forces that such work can unleash in the child.

However, understanding some key ideas associated with the psychodynamic approach can be helpful to educational practitioners, for instance, appreciating how behaviour is often driven by unconscious impulses or knowing that terms we sometimes use, such as 'denial' or 'transference' are 'psychological defence mechanisms' identified in psychodynamic theory.

According to this perspective, many behaviour difficulties originate in a person's maladaptive responses to the constantly interacting forces, both conscious and unconscious, within a person's psyche. Crucial to a child's healthy development is the development of his or her ego, the mechanism by which he/she makes sense of his/her world, a person's 'psychological gatekeeper'. Whether the ego grows healthily will have been determined by the experiences very early in life. In Chapter 3, we looked at *attachment* and *bonding*, ideas which were part of the psychodynamic tradition. Children who do not form firm attachments at an early stage are unlikely to have a healthy ego or 'ego boundaries' and will not develop the secure emotional base on which many aspects of good child development are built. Of interest is the psychodynamic approach's notion of the *superego* (roughly equating to a person's conscience). This helps to keep in check the instinctual and sometimes powerful sexual or aggressive urges of, what Freud called, the *id*. The latter is a more primitive, less restrained part of the personality, which is governed by both ego and superego.

For some children with BESD it can be important to discuss their past experiences (in particular their early childhood) and how these experiences affect their feelings and behaviour now. The understanding gained can free the children to feel more in control; more at ease with themselves and able to make better choices about what happens to them in the future.

The externalised challenging behaviour of the children that we encounter may be an '*acting out*' of inner, deep seated trauma or unresolved unconscious conflicts. However, the view of some workers in the 1950s that 'acting out' (including extremes being allowed to happen e.g. smashing furniture, windows etc.) was a necessary part of therapy for children then called 'maladjusted' lost credence as the years went by.

The psychodynamic approach is associated with *psychological defence mechanisms*. When working with children with BESD we are likely to encounter these when the child feels his or her self-worth (ego) is under threat because of the difficulty of the task, fear of being shown up in front of others or perhaps because unconscious contact has been made with aspects of their inner selves which create anxiety (Ayers *et al.* 2000). Defence mechanisms include those descibed in Table 4.1:

Table 4:1: Defence mechanisms

Defence	Definition	Example in school or care situation
Denial	Children or adults denying or forgetting painful events or feelings	Children experiencing difficulty with a task will defend their self-esteem by denying the difficulty and avoiding the task, e.g. saying: 'This is too easy for me. This is for babies...'
Rationalisation	Explaining behaviour after the event to hide the real reason for your action from yourself and from others.	Children who do not give in homework might say they had forgotten to take it home rather than admit it was too hard and they could not do it.
Regression	Process whereby the child tries to avoid anxiety by partial or total return to an earlier stage of development.	In the care situation or classroom a child cries or acts like a young child to avoid tackling a task she/he feels is too difficult.
Transference	Process by which person projects unconscious feelings or intentions onto another person.	A child who repeatedly 'acts out' with the teacher by 'putting' into the adult feelings the child is experiencing, e.g. anxiety, aggression, anger.

Other defence mechanisms include 'projection', 'splitting' and 'idealisation' (see Ayers *et al.* 2000; Delaney 2008; Greenhalgh 1994).

THE BEHAVIOURIST APPROACH

Many approaches that are used to motivate or control children can be linked to the 'behaviourist' theoretical perspective, for example, rewarding desired behaviours ('positive reinforcement') and giving sanctions for ('punishing') undesirable behaviours. Aspects of behaviourism have proved useful at individual, class and whole-school levels, as the star charts, the 'smiley' stickers, and the points and token systems used in educational and care settings all suggest. These can help to provide encouragement, reinforce the predictability of some behaviour and provide the security some children with BESD need. However, as we explore later, behaviourist approaches have limitations and can fail to teach the behaviours that we often expect them to.

Behaviourist theory dates back to before the 1920s to early researchers wanting to bring a more scientific understanding of animal and human behaviour – and, importantly, how to change it. Their experiments included Pavlov discovering that dogs salivated when a bell rang (because they associated the bell sound with being rewarded with food). Behaviourist experiments progressed through the doubtful ethics of giving aversion therapy (e.g. electric shocks) to humans, to arrive at a set of useful principles which now run through much work with children.

Some of the key behaviourist principles are as follows:

- Behaviour – good or bad – is 're-inforced' by the response it gets.

- There is value in careful observation and recording of behaviours to provide a scientific base for further action.

- Rewarding desired behaviour can be a powerful way of changing behaviour through both tangible (e.g. sweets, points, tokens) and intangible means (e.g. encouragement, signs of approval and praise).

- Punishment can suppress unwanted behaviour – but rarely helps the person to lasting change and can have undesirable side-effects.

- Ignoring behaviour is often better than punishing it.

- Humans copy the behaviour of people they respect, trust and like.

Although behaviour policies in schools are underpinned by some of these ideas we would urge caution about settings relying too heavily on sanctions and rewards. We would stress the importance of also cultivating, sometimes teaching, pro-social skills behaviours such as how, in a calm and polite manner, to make your views known.

The behaviourist perspective stresses that it is important to *observe, record* and *analyse* [ORA] actual behaviours before setting clear targets for children. ORA establishes a reliable 'baseline' on which interventions can be based rather than people relying on hunches, instincts, vague feelings or what an influential colleague in the staffroom keeps saying about a child. Consideration should be given to the way behaviour is taught and modelled throughout the school and class before any targets for practice and improvement are set. Teaching behaviour should be regarded in the same way as teaching a particular aspect of a subject – for instance, fractions – with the same approach adopted to mistake making and possible barriers to learning.

As with other subjects any targets set should be 'SMART':

'SMART' Targets

S   pecific

M   easurable

A   chievable

R   elevant

T   ime-limited.

Other key aspects of behaviourist theory include:

- **The ABC of behaviour (Antecedents – Behaviour – Consequences):** When examining how children behave, it is helpful to both them and us to look at the factors that precede a particular behaviour ('antecedents') and what the behaviour leads to ('consequences'). ABC analyses should be made factually and accurately: practitioners should not infer or generalise from a particular event.

- **'Modelling':** The modelling of desirable behaviour by staff, for example, through punctuality, use of polite, quietly spoken language, empathy or values and beliefs is also very important. Children often absorb and copy the behaviours of respected adults or peers.

- **'Time-out':** The act of removal of the child from the place and the people who generally provided the positive reinforcement for the child (sometimes by providing social contact and interaction with the child; sometimes by *encouraging* his or her unwanted behaviour) can stop the child behaving in the undesired way.

An important aspect of the behaviourist perspective is the rewarding of desired behaviour. Reward systems can range from points or merit certificates through to small sums of money or vouchers for shops, the choice sometimes being made in negotiation with the pupil. BESD and 'short stay' schools usually offer a mixture of extrinsic rewards and verbal reinforcement (adult approval and praise) sometimes given at weekly celebration assemblies.

School policies should stress the dictum 'Catch them being good', i.e. instead of staff issuing frequent reprimands for infractions of minor rules, noticing and commenting on the things that children do well (e.g. being polite or showing kindness to others or following a school rule) (Madsen *et al.* 1968, cited in Cole *et al.* 1998). They also need to take into consideration 'How many chances?' and 'How much take up time?' should be allowed for children to follow instructions (Rogers 2009).

Principles governing the use of rewards include the following:

- **Rewards have to be earned.** Pupils with BESD will not respect rewards perceived as being unearned nor respect staff for giving them too freely. Rewards can become appeasement – or, as Dweck (2006; 2009) found, counterproductive, encouraging a fixed rather than a growth mindset.

- **Rewards must relate to clear, agreed targets.** Targets should be specific, limited in scope to maintain a child's focus, realistic, negotiated and agreed as worthwhile by the child with BESD. Global injunctions on a child's Behaviour Plan or Report Card 'to behave' or 'be good' are of very limited use.

- **Rewards must be given at appropriate time intervals.** Large rewards offered half-termly or weekly may not work as well as small rewards offered daily or half-daily or after attainment of targets for a particularly problematic lesson with a particular teacher.

- **Praise should be delivered appropriately.** Praise can take many forms and some pupils may be embarrassed by public praise – for instance, lavish words in front of their peers (Hanko 1994; Rogers 1994) but will respond to nonverbal communication (e.g. a thumbs up or nod of the head). Praise might best be offered in private. Consideration should also be given to the reason for which the praise is being given (achievement or effort?) and whether it is likely to promote the desired 'growth' mindset (Bronson and Merryman 2009; Dweck 2006; 2009).

- **Rewards should come from a 'significant other'**, i.e. a person respected by the child. Rewards or sanctions given by staff perceived by the child as being hostile or indifferent are likely to be ineffective.

- **Rewards of an emotional rather than a tangible nature** are likely to have a more enduring effect. Producing the desired effects by bribing with physical gifts is not a sensible way of proceeding.

Behaviourist approaches clearly have their limitations.

- They can have little impact on children who have undergone deep trauma or loss and who either cannot, or do not, choose to 'play by the usual rules' – and might even get re-inforcement and greater attention through flouting them, although this may be at considerable loss and discomfort to themselves.

- Second, there is the challenge of getting the child to 'generalise' – that is, to replicate on a regular basis – newly acquired behaviours when the perhaps unnatural and contrived system of extrinsic rewards (e.g. weaning children off sweets, treats) are removed. A reward might be good at containing unwanted behaviours but can it be made to help a child to become self-managing?

- Third, there is a danger that behaviourist approaches will be applied as cold, mechanistic systems (e.g. the unforgiving 'three strikes and you are out', or points systems/tokens approaches). Behaviourist interventions have to be delivered in a framework of *warm, positive relationships* between staff and children. They must 'have a heart', touching and engaging the emotions of the children, who have to know that they are valued, and preferably liked, by the member of staff.

THE COGNITIVE-BEHAVIOURAL APPROACH

This approach developed partly because of therapists' dissatisfaction with earlier behaviourist approaches (Stallard 2009). In contrast to the sometimes cool and calculating behaviourist perspective, a cognitive behaviour therapy (CBT) (or for non-specialists, a 'cognitive behavioural approach') is very much concerned with examining heart, emotions and feelings.

Cognitive behaviourists maintain that it is not so much the actual situations or events that make us depressed (or angry or over-anxious or obsessive) – rather, it is *we* who induce these feelings within ourselves through our deeply engrained thought patterns. As Rogers wrote:

> The fundamental maxim behind cognitive-behavioural theories is that thinking, emotion and behaviour are inextricably involved with each other. Self-defeating behaviour is related to self-defeating thinking, which in turn is related to feeling 'down'. (Rogers 1994, p.46)

The constant interaction of thoughts, feelings and behaviour is demonstrated in the 'cognitive circle':

A situation or event occurs, which gives rise to:

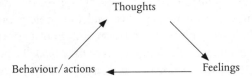

Children who are anxious or depressed often interpret what is happening to them as an unfair or an unjustified attack on them, or believe they can have little or no control over what happens to them ('learned helplessness'). There is a clear overlap here with our description of 'Internal Working Models' (IWMs) earlier. Such children *think*:

- the good things that happen to them are due to external factors
- the bad things that happen to them are their fault, due to their failings that they *feel* they cannot change
- their *thinking* and *feelings* then govern their *behaviour*.

They can set themselves unreasonably high expectations, then blame or punish themselves when they cannot achieve these aims. For example, if a child with BESD has a general belief that he is 'useless' in class, every low mark or comment by a teacher helps to confirm for the young person that this is a true summary of the situation.

It is a difficult challenge to change such thinking and feelings (even to motivate the child to *want* to change – see McNamara 2009). It helps if you can find out what the child is thinking and saying to themselves through their 'self-talk'. What sort of internal dialogue happens when they are confronted with something that triggers or maintains a negative mood (of depression/anxiety/anger etc)? Fox (2001, p.24) gave a list of common thoughts that can cause problems. This list included:

- 'I'm no good'
- 'Everyone is against me'
- 'I should be better than others'
- 'Adults should trust me'
- 'I must never show I'm weak'
- 'No one likes me'.

Many children with BESD are trapped in thought patterns that make them feel worse about themselves and the world around them. They expect scary things to happen and not to be able to cope. They frequently look out for threats and judge themselves harshly. These thoughts lead to anxious feelings in the body (racing heart, shortness of breath, dizziness, perspiring, feeling sick or needing the toilet). This results in anxious behaviour, which is seen in avoiding scary places or situations and poor performance of tasks. When faced with a new or challenging event they *think* 'I can't do this' or 'It will go wrong'. They then *feel* scared and anxious. If they *behave* by avoiding the challenge they start to think 'I'll be all right now... I'm safe' and they feel relieved (Stallard 2009).

Cognitive behaviour therapy is a 'talking' treatment, meaning that at its heart is an ongoing conversation between the helper and the helped. The intervention seeks to identify how negative thoughts affect the child and then look at ways of tackling or changing those thoughts, thereby helping the child feel better. Unlike the psychodynamic approach, it focuses on 'here and now' difficulties rather than focusing on the causes of distress or symptoms in the past.

Stallard (2009) stresses that the approach must involve a collaborative partnership between clinician, child and parents – an approach that is very different to the 'expert/professional' relationship that many children and families may have experienced and still expect. It is established early in the process that the child is the expert on his or her own experiences and interests, with the parents providing an alternative perspective and information about what may or may not help.

CBT has been found to be helpful in relieving anxiety, depression, panic, agoraphobia and other phobias, bulimia, OCD, post traumatic stress disorder and schizophrenia. CBT with the child can usefully be accompanied by family therapy, which seeks to increase the chances of a more positive emotional atmosphere at home. If you want to explore this area in more depth we recommend that you read Stallard (2009), Verduyn *et al.* (2009) and Gowers and Green (2009). 'Solution-focused brief therapy' is a specific branch of CBT and is described in Chapter 8.

MINDFULNESS

'Mindfulness-Based Cognitive Therapy' is an off-shoot of CBT, and takes the psychology and neuroscience behind CBT and then melds it with the wisdom of Eastern meditation and yoga. Williams, Teasdale, Segal and Kabat-Zinn (2007), who are cognitive scientists, first had to overcome their scepticism that meditation could be a way of breaking the cycle of recurrent depression, but, along with Crane (2009) and other researchers, eventually came to be firm and persuasive advocates of this approach.

Referring to the role of neurotransmitters and other hormones without actually naming them, Williams *et al.* (2007) note how anxiety and depression, often resulting from over-busy pressurised lifestyles, give us aches and pains as well dysregulating our eating habits, sleep and energy levels. Negative thoughts or images in the mind link to a sensation in the form of a contraction, tightening or bracing in the body somewhere. The thought may be accompanied by a frown, a stomach churning, a pallor in the skin, or a tension in the lower back. They see these as part of freeze, fight or flight responses linking to the limbic system in the brain. As noted in the section above on CBT, the state of our bodies interacts with the state of our minds. They go on:

> It's not just that patterns of negative thinking can affect our moods and our bodies. Feedback loops in the other direction, from the body to the mind, also play a critical role in the persistent return and deepening of unhappiness and dissatisfaction... Our bodies function as highly sensitive emotion detectors. They are giving us moment-to-moment readouts of our emotional state. (Williams *et al.* 2007, p.26)

A problem for many children and adults is that they find it difficult to look at these 'moment-to-moment' readouts. They are too busy having depressing cognitions, perhaps falling victim to damaging 'rumination' (that is, going over and over negative thoughts from the past or worrying about the future, sometimes in the vain hope of *thinking out* answers). Williams *et al.* point out that rumination is 'a heroic attempt to solve a problem that it is just not capable of solving' (p.45). Rumination actually makes our ability to solve problems worse.

Children and adults may also be striving to achieve goals, driven on by stressful 'coulda, shoulda, woulda, oughta' thoughts. Either way, they do not respond to the messages from their body and do not seek to harness their natural defence systems, by 'tapping into the inner calm and happiness that is present in all of us' (Williams *et al.* 2007, p.82 – see Chapter 3 on calming neurotransmitters). In Western cultures, we have not, as a rule, been taught to be attentive to our physical selves as a way of relaxing or self-healing. We have often been told to 'keep a stiff upper lip' or 'just get over it!'. We have to be helped to be aware, to be mindful of what our bodies are telling us.

We can help young people (and perhaps ourselves?) to give more attention to becoming 'mindful' of the here and now, of 'being' in the present, including the promotion of greater appreciation of some small pleasures that all of us find at moments in a day (e.g. eating an apple slowly using all of our senses). Through working at being mindful of our breathing (described by Williams *et al.* 2007, p.76, as the 'gateway to awareness'), relaxing and stretching our muscles, scanning our body for areas of stress; through using all our senses – our eyes to notice pleasant sights (e.g. a clear blue sky) or ears (e.g. to focus on calming music or birdsong) or sense of smell (e.g. to savour pleasant aromas) – we can unleash our body's natural calming systems. By being mindful, our attention is diverted from damaging rumination over past events and feelings – also, possibly, from stressful obsession with the future ('to do' lists and rigid timescales). Through mindfulness, we can recover our ability to think effectively. Williams *et al.* (2007) use the analogy of a jar of muddy water. Shake it and it is cloudy. Put it down and the mud settles to the bottom leaving clear liquid above. The problems are still there (the mud) but they are no longer clouding our thinking and judgement: seeing things more clearly, we are more content.

Williams *et al.* (2007) and Crane (2009) offer an approach that helps people sidestep the cascade of mental events that draws so many children (and adults) down into depression and despair, through reading their 'physical barometer' and activating natural resources within themselves. However, the particular course they champion requires many weeks of guided work and it is far from easy for the child or adult with mental-health difficulties to make routine the essentially simple daily practices advocated. However, even a little 'mindfulness' can help and we will return to some of its suggestions for both children and stressed practitioners in Chapter 8.

POSITIVE PSYCHOLOGY

During the 1990s psychological theory saw a shift in emphasis from a concentration on what might have gone wrong in the development of a child to a new stress on understanding and building positive aspects of human life, earlier seen in the humanistic psychology of the mid-twentieth century, when Maslow had used the term 'positive psychology'. This movement is particularly associated with the eminent American psychologist, Martin Seligman and his many publications (e.g. Seligman 1993; Seligman *et al.* 2005), whose overarching concern is to promote what he calls 'optimal human functioning'. It is associated with a concern for promoting 'emotional intelligence' (e.g. Goleman 1996).

An excellent summary of positive psychology's focus on promoting emotional well-being, happiness and resilience can be found in Boniwell (2006). However, she, along with Baylis (2009), warn against a simplistic acceptance of all that is claimed by positive psychology (not by Seligman), given the links between some positive-psychology publications and commercial interests and the sometimes sub-optimal research methods used, using easily accessed but not necessarily representative cohorts for questionnaire surveys that suggest *correlations* rather than causation. As Boniwell (2006, p.107) says 'Positive psychology aims to improve too many things, often without knowing exactly what the connections between them are.' However, similar caveats can be attached to much research claimed to underpin other theoretical perspectives and Boniwell is right to stress the achievement of positive psychology in generating much sound science (involving empirical as well as qualitative research), which supports approaches that sit comfortably beside much of what practitioners in educational settings try to achieve with children with BESD.

Positive psychology suggests that we *can* have a good impact on children's 'subjective well-being' (SWB) in areas such as improving their optimism (promoting 'positive realism'), social connections and friendships, their motivation, their coping strategies, their view of their own health, their actual physical well-being – in short, in areas associated with the *Every Child Matters* agenda and the social, emotional aspects of learning (SEAL) programmes in schools. Boniwell (2006) cites work that suggests we can assist in the promotion of positive emotions that:

- **broaden children's attention and thinking** – facilitating children's enjoyment and interest, which helps them to become more creative, see more opportunities, be more open for relationships, play more, and be more flexible and open-minded

- **helps to displace or undo negative emotions** – it is difficult to experience both negative and positive emotions at the same time

- **enhance resilience** – enjoyment, feelings of happiness, contentment, satisfaction, warm friendships, and affection all help our ability to cope with, and sometimes to solve, problems

- **broaden children's psychological repertoire** – through building children's cognitive and social skills

- **trigger an upward psychological spiral** – reversing the downward spiral caused by an excess of negative emotions.

There are clearly similarities here with aspects of CBT and mindfulness – indeed, Boniwell (2006) advocates muscle relaxation, yoga and meditation to increase positive emotions. She wants us to find positive meaning and experience in our daily routine activities (echoes of mindfulness) and to reframe them in positive terms. We need to dispute the pessimistic explanations that can dominate our self-talk (echoes of CBT and, indeed, of the ecosystemic approach). She advocates 'active mood management', which can be promoted through exercise, relaxation and music. A warning: be aware that positive emotions are not the *temporary* pleasant sensations generated by eating chocolate or ice cream!

Negative emotions are a part of living and are still needed since they can bring about positive effects. Boniwell notes that coping with negative emotions, e.g. associated with suffering and loss, can build up qualities such as endurance, modesty, care and empathy. Trauma or crisis can lead to major and beneficial personality change. She suggests as a rule of thumb for good emotional health, that there should be a ratio of 3:1 between feeling positive and negative emotions.

Positive psychology is also concerned with inducing 'flow', a major component of happiness and well-being (Csikszentmihalyi 1990). In psychological terms, this is the equivalent of what athletes call 'being in the zone' or, as others say, in 'a heightened state of consciousness'. It means identifying and promoting how a child's attention is totally captured by an activity so that 'time flies' and their interest in other activities disappears. This psychological state is reached when we are challenged and absorbed by an activity that is just within our capabilities, often stretching us to our limits – but not beyond. For practitioners with children with BESD this means finding activities that really capture a child's interest, then gradually increasing the difficulty of that activity as the child's skills grow. Taking a wider view, it means encouraging people to reallocate time away from often apathetic and passive activities such as watching TV to 'flow inducing' activities. There are, of course, some bad examples of 'flow' – for example, obsession and possible addiction to gambling or extreme sports.

REVIEW

Our experience indicates that practitioners who study and reflect upon key elements of psychodynamic, behaviourist, cognitive and mindfulness theory, and positive psychology, gain an improved understanding of the iceberg of behaviour mentioned in Chapter 3. They increase their capacity to seize even the fleeting moments that occur in the school day or evening care hours to observe, listen and talk to children, to gain more insight into their strengths as well as the emotional turmoil inside the child and to instigate helpful interventions. In practice, what they do is eclectic, using approaches that are underpinned by aspects from all the different perspectives described above and in earlier chapters.

We end with a caveat – we must not indulge in amateur psychiatry. Deep application of some theoretical approaches has to be left to trained psychologists and CAMHS professionals, including qualified psychotherapists and counsellors.

PART 2

HELPFUL
INTERVENTIONS

CHAPTER **5**

WHOLE-SCHOOL INFLUENCES

Pervading attitudes, policy and practice at the whole-school level filter down to class groups and to individual pupils and are therefore important for the child with BESD. Research on leadership, ethos and behaviour influencing guidance on teaching, learning and behaviour designed for the whole-school population (e.g. DfES 2006a; 2007a) overlaps considerably with advice produced by studies of effective provision for pupils with BESD (e.g. Ofsted 2003 and 2005). Both sets of findings and advice should therefore be heeded.

The over-arching whole-school issue is the creation and maintenance of an inclusive ethos for pupils with BESD, as discussed first below.

INCLUSIVE VALUES AND ETHOS

Schools successful at helping children with BESD have an understanding and inclusive ethos (Daniels *et al.* 1999; Ofsted 2003). After extensive research, Ofsted (2005) identifies factors in this:

> A school's ethos provides the context within which children feel secure, know they are valued as individuals, are safe from emotional and physical harm and are able to discuss their interests and voice their fears in a supportive atmosphere. The development of a school's ethos falls to the senior management team but its growth and maintenance depend on the involvement and co-operation of the whole staff. Inspection and research continually reaffirm the importance of consistency in the way staff themselves behave and act in and around the school. This particularly helps boys to behave better and achieve more. (Ofsted 2005, paragraph 39, p.10)

Ofsted's findings overlap with, but are expanded by, other work on ethos (e.g. Daniels *et al.* 1999; Fullan 2003). These include factors listed here but considered in more detail in separate sections below:

- style and effectiveness of leadership
- 'critical mass' of staff committed to inclusive values
- clear whole-school learning and behaviour policies 'owned' and consistently applied
- caring, sharing and learning communities
- skilled teaching, responsive to BESD and other SENs
- staff understand, respect and listen to pupils with BESD, encouraging their participation
- SEAL and promoting health and well-being
- an outward-looking attitude, with staff open to working with other agencies and to engaging with parents, families and carers.

LEADERSHIP

An inclusive whole-school ethos is unlikely to be realised without strong, skilled, energetic and 'emotionally intelligent' leadership that generates direction, coherence, cohesiveness and high expectations of, and for, all (Ofsted 2005). Leadership is far more than just efficient management: leaders must demonstrate passion and enthusiasm. The extensive literature identifies the following leadership characteristics:

- creating energy
- valuing people
- building capacity for learning
- meeting and minimising crises
- articulating and developing the vision
- securing the environment
- reflecting and charting improvement.

Fullan's work (2003; 2005; 2009) enlarges on the above: successful leadership involves a 'moral imperative' to create coherent, values-driven communities, and to pursue improvement through developing skills and leadership qualities in staff. School leaders should have a clear vision of goals and understand the change process. They should avoid wishful thinking and blame; know when to be fearless and when to be cautious; embrace diversity; focus on fundamentals; not over-plan or micro-manage. Heads should believe and encourage 'distributed leadership', keen to build trust and teamwork through delegating responsibilities to colleagues, thereby building their capacity to lead others (see also Bush and Glover 2003). They should empower members of staff through 'knowledge creation' (enhancing understanding and skills through regular professional development – also advocated by DfES 2006b); be clear about what they are *not* trying to achieve; and work to improve the quality of relationships. At the heart of the process are relationships (Fullan 2003). Fullan (2005) also stresses how important it is for leadership to be outward-looking, keen to engage with other schools and services in their district.

Part 2 of the Steer Report (DfES 2006b) adds further practical advice, saying senior staff should be seen out and about around the school buildings monitoring staff and pupil understanding and application of school policies. This document also notes that governors should play 'a pivotal part' in 'identifying and developing values and expectations that are shared by pupils, parents and staff' (DfES 2006b, p.5).

The factors outlined above are very much in keeping with the types of successful leadership suggested by government and independent research into provision for BESD (Cole *et al.* 1998; Cooper *et al.* 1994; Daniels *et al.* 1999; Ofsted 2005).

A CRITICAL MASS OF STAFF COMMITTED TO INCLUSIVE VALUES

In most schools there are likely to be a range of attitudes to pupils with BESD, with some staff feeling that it is beyond their responsibilities to provide for challenging and disruptive pupils. This is far from being just a mainstream school problem – practitioners in special or 'short-stay' schools may give up too quickly, thinking a particular young person is better placed elsewhere. However, in schools that provide well for pupils with BESD, there is clearly a *critical mass* of influential members of staff (including most of the senior leadership) who are concerned about the needs of pupils with BESD and who are very reluctant to resort to exclusion of such children, even when they test the school to the limits. In such schools a tipping point has been passed ensuring that the attitudes of this critical mass predominate (Gladwell 2000).

The importance of this critical mass lies in the influence these teachers have on the creation and ownership of the school's behaviour policy and also in the strength of the positive relationships some of these staff have formed, partly because of their values, with particularly challenging pupils.

Such staff understand the emotional underpinnings of pupil behaviour and the sometimes fractured lives outside school of many pupils with BESD. They have an empathy for the pupils and their family's difficulties. The critical mass remains optimistic, avoiding debilitating fatalism about the future of these children, instead sustaining a belief that their school could help pupils with BESD to improve their behaviour and achievement. They also tend to avoid the use of the term BESD, preferring to see each child as an individual without a label (Daniels *et al.* 1999; 2003).

WHOLE-SCHOOL LEARNING AND BEHAVIOUR POLICIES

Learning and behaviour policies are considered together because they are both crucial to effective provision and influence each other. Both Ofsted (2005) and the current government guidance on *School Discipline and Behaviour Policies* (DfES 2007a) recognise this. DfES (2007a) endorses the Steer Report's (DfES 2005a; 2006b) firm view that raising standards in teaching and learning are an important way of improving behaviour.

There is substantial evidence that clear and positive whole-school policies consistently applied and regularly reviewed by staff and pupils are an essential part of good practice for all settings attended by children with BESD. The content of such policies should reflect the values and beliefs (that is, the ethos) espoused by the critical mass of inclusive staff. The policies should give a framework that facilitates the daily practice of individual teachers and support workers, facilitating helpful relationships between staff, between pupils, and between staff and pupils.

The policies should take the form of succinct written documents, complete with pro formas, flow-charts for referrals and clear accounts of routine procedures. They must include descriptions of the links that should exist between the different elements of the school structure, e.g. between subject departments and special needs/support for learning.

In relation to teaching and learning (largely beyond our scope here), the policies should:

- stress the need to have high expectations of academic progress
- outline a variety of ways of fostering an appropriate climate in class including motivating pupils including the appropriate use of praise
- offer advice on responding to barriers to learning.

In relation to 'behaviour', DCSF (2007a) repeats the Steer Report's recommendations for topics to be considered and covered in school's behaviour policy. These are:

- a consistent approach to behaviour management, teaching and learning
- school leadership
- classroom management, learning and teaching
- rewards and sanctions
- behaviour strategies and the teaching of good behaviour
- staff development and support
- pupil-support systems
- liaison with parents and other agencies
- managing pupil transition; and
- organisation and facilities (paragraph 3.1.9).

Regular audits of behaviour are also recommended (DfES 2007a) to identify strengths and weaknesses, with tools provided by the National Strategies for this purpose advertised along with CPD materials to address weaknesses (e.g. the 'Improving Behaviour for Learning' DVD designed for secondary schools; DfES 2004b)

To add a little detail to the Steer list, the school's behaviour policy should be prefaced by the school's mission statement and general aims, followed by data on the school community and a statement of the rights and responsibilities of governors, staff, pupils and parents/carers. This would be followed by an overview of expectations of learning and behaviour, with emphasis on the prevention of unacceptable behaviour rather than responses to it. The policy could appropriately include:

- approaches to encouraging good behaviour/clear boundary setting and specifying how positive behaviour is modelled, taught and reinforced
- classroom strategies to promote a learning climate with minimal conflict, including routines for starting and ending lessons
- school-wide routines for transitions, including from lesson to lesson
- corridor and playground expectations and staff responsibilities
- links to other school policies (e.g. SENs/operating the Code of Practice)

- details on 'positive behaviour' rewards, certificate, 'celebration' systems

- systems for reporting and recording worrying or unacceptable behaviour

- advice on working with parents and carers.

DCSF (2009c) also makes the link between good and outstanding behaviour in the 'vast majority' of schools and the part played by the promotion of SEAL. They might also have added paying attention to the holistic concerns of the *Every Child Matters* five key outcomes (see Chapter 3). The school's policies for the promotion of social, emotional and physical health should also be referred to and linked into policies for learning and behaviour.

Lack of consistent application of policies across staff groups (e.g. between one department and another in a secondary school) leaves pupils with BESD confused and (as with all ambiguous situations that they face) can lead to feelings of threat and subsequent fight, flight or, indeed, 'flock' (antisocial group) activity. However – and this is a difficult dilemma in relation to some children with BESD – there is a need for some 'clinical elasticity' (Redl 1966) and 'rubber boundaries' (Amos cited in Cole *et al*. 1998) in applying expectations to pupils with individual needs and different capacities for following routines. Skilled practitioners are those who can engineer a degree of flexibility in certain circumstances and manage to persuade the other children that what was done in relation to a particular child was 'fair'.

Giving a thorough induction to newly appointed staff in policies is, of course, crucial – particularly given the high turnover of staff in many of the settings attended by children with BESD.

Adherence to policies should be an integral part of the ongoing monitoring work by school leaders. Where there is resistance to regular usage of such policies staff development should follow. Policies should be subject to frequent discussion amongst staff and with pupils, and review where necessary and possible revision. Behaviour policy reviews should happen regularly and be open and consultative if reflection and self-evaluation amongst staff is to be promoted and the stakeholders are to feel 'ownership' of the process. Imposed policies tend to be subverted, circumvented or ignored.

CARING, SHARING, LEARNING SETTINGS

Cole, Visser and Daniels (2001), Ofsted (2003) and Daniels *et al*. (2003) researching good practice in mainstream schools in relation to BESD and permanently excluded young people found staff showing a particularly high degree of *caring* for children, even for those who challenged staff the most. The child with BESD was still seen as a valued part of the school community and, significantly, the staff were reluctant to attach any label to him or her, still referring and thinking of Ryan or Stephen (see Chapter 1) as an individual with particular strengths and needs. Their *mis*behaviour was confronted but it was the 'act' that was condemned and not the 'actor'.

This research also found *sharing practice* between staff that helped to make real the factors outlined in the sections above. Teamwork was the norm and a collegiate approach (frequently talking to and listening to each other) demonstrated.

There was also a willingness on the part of staff to *learn* through being receptive to the ideas and advice of their colleagues. With ongoing encouragement from school leaders, they learnt through reflection and self-audits that highlighted areas for improvement. Their leaders shared the view of Ofsted on the need for continuing professional development:

> Regular training, focused on classroom practice, combined with in-depth appreciation of child and adolescent development, is central to understanding and managing behaviour. (Ofsted 2005, p.10)

Assessment was valued and Dennison and Kirk's (1990) 'do–review–learn–apply' cycle was clearly in evidence (Cole *et al.* 2001). Effective schools were schools who reflected on past experience to help guide what they did in future. They had a problem-sharing and solution-focused approach that encouraged open discussion of classroom or playground-management issues. In one case-study in a secondary school the SENCo talked of 'tea-time therapy' when senior staff would discuss professional concerns with less-experienced teachers over a cup of tea in the staffroom at the end of the school day (Daniels *et al.* 1999). This was seen as a valuable mode of staff development akin to the teacher-support team approaches advocated in Creese, Daniels and Norwich (1997) or the 'coaching' and 'mentoring' approaches used in the present (see DfES 2005b).

DELIVERING SKILLED TEACHING RESPONSIVE TO BESD

In schools where pupils with BESD do relatively well, there persists a deep concern amongst leadership and other staff for these pupils' *educational* as well as their many and complex social and emotional needs (Ofsted 1999; 2003; 2005). As we have seen, children with BESD almost always have significant barriers to learning. However, leadership and staff try to ensure that these obstacles do not lead to feelings of pessimism amongst practitioners, either in planning or delivering the support needed.

Children with BESD retain a right to a challenging education that can open doors to a better childhood and adulthood – and some do exercise these rights. Ofsted (2005) and DCSF (2008a) stress that many schools manage to deliver skilled, responsive and differentiated teaching across the different subject areas, which results in effective learning for some pupils with BESD, and that school leaders have a duty to promote the delivery of this. Ofsted (2005) and Daniels *et al.* (1999) found schools that had staff with a range of effective styles and classroom-management techniques reaching out to some very challenging young people. In secondary schools, pupils with BESD are entitled to be helped towards a range of national accreditation. To help, there should be flexible timetabling, now emerging through the 14–19 curriculum developments that play to the individual strengths and sometimes side-step the weaknesses or difficulties of the individual child with BESD (the personalised learning of DfES 2006a). The calls from leadership in the secondary schools, in the aftermath of the 1988 Education Reform Act, for a freeing-up of the national curriculum has been heeded by government with a new stress on vocational training and the re-emergence of a skills-based curriculum in the Qualification and Curriculum Authority's Learning to Learn initiative.

School leaders should ensure that effective systems are in place and operate throughout their schools for assessing and responding to the additional learning needs of many children with BESD. Many of the latter have reading, writing and other communication difficulties. Their complex needs require close working between all staff. It is now mandatory for the SENCo to be a qualified teacher and it is recommended that she/he be part of the senior leadership team. It is clearly a duty of the SENCo to work closely with the subject teachers responsible for the child with BESD. However, as the SENCo's role seems to be under constant scrutiny as part of an ongoing review of SEN provision, the actual quality and extent of such supportive practice remains variable. There appear to be too many schools where SENCos, some departmental heads and managers responsible for 'behaviour' each act separately, to the detriment of the ethos and effectiveness of the school and where BESD is confused with 'disaffection' (Daniels *et al.* 1999; 2003).

The SENCo will be active in the school's 'provision mapping', a term that has recently arrived through the National Strategies and denotes a part of the strategic planning across a school year for children with SENs. It should be an easily understood overview – a summary chart – of the resources available to support children with additional needs. It must include support for children with BESD – Ofsted (2006) found that the could in fact be the last to have their SENs recognised or provi National Strategies see 'provision mapping' as a key means of the quality of teaching, promoting inclusion and bringing the appropriate additional support to children with SENs. Provision mapping should be a whole-school issue involving all stakeholders, including subject teachers who should have the chance to make the case to the SENCo and other senior staff for extra resources in support of the child with BESD ahead of the finalisation of the map.

If a child with BESD is deemed to have a disability, then school leadership should also ensure that 'reasonable adjustments' are made in line with the DDA Act 2001.

RESPECTING AND LISTENING TO PUPILS WITH BESD AND ENCOURAGING PARTICIPATION

A common theme of young people excluded from school who talked to Daniels *et al.* (2003) was the contrast these teenagers noticed between some of the staff at the schools that had excluded them and the teachers and support workers they met at their new schools (sometimes other mainstream schools, sometimes 'short stay' or special schools). Similar evidence was found in Cole *et al.*'s (1998) national study of BESD schools. Children used to being dismissed and rejected with their views going unheard by school professionals now spoke approvingly of the respect and attention given to them in their new settings. At last they sensed they could express views that would be heard, and this novel experience helped them to feel valued and as belonging to their school or unit.

Since that research, the ECM Agenda (DfES 2003b) and recent National Strategy approaches to learning typified in *Assessment for Learning* (DCSF 2008c) have made schools look in some depth at the part children and young people play in influencing their schools and settings, as well as in reviewing their own progress and contributing to planning their future learning. The many and various systems of peer review, peer mentoring and peer support are beginning to impact on school practice (e.g. Cowie, Hutson, Oztug and Myers 2008; Cowie and Jennifer 2008) and Sellman (2009), probably to the benefit of pupils with BESD.

Active listening to the pupil voice is now a well-established part of primary practice for children and school councils and pupil-representation groups are increasing in number. This is a re-emergence of practice seen many decades ago in some pioneer schools for 'maladjusted' children (see

Bridgeland 1971; Cole 1989). It is particularly pleasing to note the increase in pupil advocacy in statutory assessment and the way that some authorities have responded to this need by creating more child-centred SEN reviews.

Unfortunately, initiatives such as these can be viewed with suspicion and fear by some staff. Where schools have adopted student assessors, and where pupils are routinely involved in the assessment and appointment of staff, tensions can sometimes still exist. Despite this predictable resistance, the current stress on enabling pupils to express their views and to contribute to how their schools are run is to be welcomed. Whole-school policy and practice that contributes to student voice and participation and that reaches pupils with BESD fits the type of collaborative approach advocated in Cooper, Smith and Upton's (1994) seminal book.

SEAL AND PROMOTING HEALTH AND WELL-BEING

SEAL is a comprehensive approach in English schools to promoting the social and emotional skills that underpin effective learning, positive behaviour and well-being. The programme has five competency areas, which the programme seeks to develop in children – self-awareness, managing feelings, motivation, empathy and social skills. It is designed as a whole-school approach and it is clearly a duty of school leaders to view it and promote it as such (DCSF 2007a). The programme appears to be useful in adjusting and improving ethos in many schools and is likely to have benefited many children with BESD (although firm research data are still lacking). Suggestions on how to make SEAL permeate school life rather than being confined to PSHE lessons will be made in later chapters.

In terms of promoting wider well-being, the government's healthy schools advice is useful reading for school leaders and all staff. DfES/DoH (2007a and b) points out that schools have a duty to promote the general well-being of pupils under the Education and Inspections Act of 2006. It also makes frequent reference to the valuable potential contribution of SEAL. Near its start, it lists the eleven key principles developed from the National Healthy Schools Programme Whole School Approach that should guide what schools do. These principles correspond closely to the sub-headings of this chapter. In the context of addressing the needs of vulnerable children, it asks schools to consider: 'Do we have a team of people in the school who are able to identify children and young people experiencing, or at risk of experiencing, behavioural, emotional and social difficulties? Do they have adequate time to dedicate to this role? (p.17). It sees BESD as a whole-school issue, along with anti-bullying, promoting physical health and many other topics that tie in to the five outcomes and 25 aims of the *Every Child Matters* framework.

Three years ahead of this advice, Cowie *et al.* (2004) proposed that every school should have school guidelines on identifying and addressing mental-health problems. To be effective, all staff (having gained familiarity with the content and trained in how to use them) should contribute to their implementation and annual review. The school might have a Mental Health Co-ordinator (a role suggested by the Mental Health Foundation 1999) who could oversee mental-health guidelines and act as liaison between staff and outside agencies. We return to mental-health issues in Chapter 8.

'OUTWARD-LOOKING SCHOOLS'

The phrase 'outward-looking schools' is increasingly being used to describe settings that set great store by working in partnerships with other schools and support services (as advised by Fullan 2005). Effective practice with children with BESD clearly requires this (Cole *et al.* 2001; Ofsted 2005) and indicates that such work should be driven from a senior level. In the holistic children's services and *Every Child Matters* age, schools must seek out and use the skilled assistance that is available from beyond the school in support of children with BESD. There are obvious needs to be met, e.g. in terms of multi-agency assessments and interventions. We look at this topic in more detail in Chapter 9.

An 'outward-looking school' should also have the willingness and capacity (i.e. time and staffing) to work closely with parents, families and carers, given that many of the problems of children with BESD will relate to the child's experiences at home. How to do this is considered in Chapter 10.

REVIEW

In this chapter we have made the predictable but crucial point that leadership, policy and practice at whole-school level all have an important impact on the classroom and individual experience of the child with BESD. Key factors contributing to a necessary inclusive ethos have been sketched. These include: styles of leadership; a critical mass of staff with inclusive values; appropriate whole-school learning and behaviour policies; caring, sharing and learning settings; leaders' concern for skilled teaching responsive to BESD; respecting, listening and encouraging the participation of pupils with BESD; a stress on SEAL; and being an 'outward-looking school'.

CHAPTER 6

HELPFUL GROUP INTERVENTIONS IN CLASS AND AROUND SCHOOL

Children and young people with BESD are a diverse and imprecise grouping, consisting of pupils each with their own individual aptitudes and needs. This said, there are effective general classroom and group approaches to teaching, learning and developing well-being that commonly help to reduce these pupils' behavioural difficulties, encourage their social skills and provide them with emotional support. In this chapter we consider these general practices in and around the classroom. In fact these approaches are likely to be helpful to nearly all pupils but they are of particular importance to pupils with BESD.

We consider:

- the part played by practitioners in lessening or increasing BESD
- teaching strategies, including the National Strategies' '*Quality First Teaching*' and '*Assessment for Learning*' (DCSF 2008c)
- the positive impact of established and rehearsed routines
- curriculum entitlement and flexible curriculum delivery that plays to pupil strengths
- building emotional well-being in the classroom
- specific forms of group intervention ('circle of friends' and 'nurture groups')
- checking and adapting the behavioural environment (physical features including classroom layout)
- checking and adjusting staff's personal and, sometimes, emotional contribution to the behavioural environment.

DO WE SOMETIMES MAKE BESD WORSE?

Despite deep-seated 'bio', 'psycho' and 'social' factors, much BESD is a response to immediate environmental factors including the relational style and teaching skills of school practitioners. While a child's inner difficulties clearly create serious obstacles to teaching and learning and often link to disruption (see the 'Iceberg of behaviour' in Chapter 3), it is clear that staff can both lessen or, unintentionally, exacerbate the children's behaviour difficulties. This can be seen when shadowing pupils with BESD, who can be observed creating extreme difficulties in one class and then going across the corridor to another lesson and responding within acceptable bounds, sometimes very well – without in the meantime taking any medication or becoming involved in a playground fracas or unsettling communication from home. Classrooms in BESD schools that bring together groups of pupils who have been highly disruptive in mainstream settings can be quiet, purposeful environments with little outward sign of disturbed behaviour (Cole *et al.* 1998; Laslett 1977; some Ofsted school inspection reports). Similarly, in mainstream settings, some children with BESD behave well for some teachers but are severely disruptive for others (Daniels *et al.* 1999; Ofsted 2003). Disruptive behaviour is often 'situation-specific', relating in part to how practitioners in school settings operate, whether they are identified as 'deviance-provocative' and 'deviance-insulative' practitioners, to use Jordan's (1974) terminology (cited in Smith and Laslett 1993).

Enhancing staff skills is an aspect of school life to which more time and resources should be devoted, as pupils with BESD tend to be the first to respond with disruptive behaviour to inappropriate or unskilled teaching or support. These children, lacking a growth mindset and often basic knowledge and skills, become easily frustrated, have limited attention spans, give up on tasks and are frightened of new work. Probably linking to imbalances in the biochemistry of their bodies, they also have low anger thresholds. These factors will readily come into play when teaching or support is 'just satisfactory', particularly if the approaches used exacerbate the children's low self-esteem and 'show them up' in front of their peers.

Practitioners are assisted by regularly checking the 'behavioural environment' (Daniels and Williams 2000) discussed further below, as well as their own emotional state, preparedness and approaches used. It is with good reason that the first assignment set on specialist BESD training course is often 'Staff create BESD: discuss'. We should not feel unfairly provoked when asked to reflect on this proposition.

SKILLED CLASS TEACHING AND CURRICULUM DELIVERY REDUCES BESD

Ofsted (2005) provides a succinct overview of what is required (see Table 6.1). Schools that cope well with 'difficult' children are characterised by having many talented staff who are able to form positive relationships with challenging young people. They know their pupils as individuals, remembering their names, and having awareness of their personalities, interests and friends. Staff do not need to be masters of psychoanalysis or psychology but they *should be* well organised, consistent, humorous, calm, enthusiastic, skilful in delivering their specialist subjects, capable of setting clear boundaries, flexible, understanding of 'behaviour' causation and empathetic (Cole *et al.* 1998). A girl in Year 10 in a mainstream comprehensive with a statement for BESD, described good staff as:

> Teachers who understand you and take an interest in you. After you have finished your work they ask you how you are. They socialise. You get to like them. (Daniels *et al.* 1999, p.83)

Table 6.1: Ofsted (2005) on effective teaching and learning

Effective teaching and learning
Extracts from Ofsted (2005) 'Managing Challenging Behaviour'
• A positive classroom ethos with good relationships and strong teamwork between adults encourages good behaviour. Late starts to lessons, disorganised classrooms, low expectations and unsuitable tasks allow inappropriate behaviour to flourish.
• Learning is best when staff know pupils well and plan lessons which take account of the different abilities, interests and learning styles.
• Pupils often react badly when staff show a lack of respect for or interest in them.
• The most effective teaching for learners with the most difficult behaviour is little different to that which is most successful for all groups of learners.

A Year 10 boy who used to have a statement for BESD enlarged on this: 'They [the good teachers] are polite and treat you with respect'. He added that it was when others shouted at him or did not show respect that he responded in kind (Daniels *et al.* 1999, p.84). Moving beyond this research into BESD, a survey by Hay McBer (2000) found Year 8 pupils describing a good teacher as: kind, generous, listens to you, encourages you, has faith in you, keeps confidences, likes teaching children, likes teaching their subject, takes time to explain things, helps you when you're stuck, tells you how you are doing, allows you to have your say, doesn't give up on you, cares for your opinion, makes you feel clever, stands up for you, makes allowances, tells the truth and is forgiving. Successful teachers, without seeking it, can come to be seen as friends and helpers by children with BESD particularly where form tutors *embrace* rather than resist their pastoral role as mentors and supporters of pupils at risk (Munn, Lloyd and Cullen 2000).

There is substantial evidence, gathered over decades, showing that when these practitioner traits are in place and teachers are masters of classroom craft, then behaviour difficulties at a class level will tend to decrease (e.g. Kounin 1977; Reinart and Huang 1987; Smith and Laslett 1993, or Cole *et al.* 1998; Ofsted 2005).

Beyond personal traits, but partly interlinked, are the key features of teaching described in the National Strategies' *Quality First Teaching* (QFT), Wave 1 (universal) class teaching (DCSF 2007c).[1] Relating in particular to good literacy and good mathematics instruction, good teaching displays the following characteristics:

- It is lively and engaging.
- It is a carefully planned blend of approaches that direct children's learning.
- Children are challenged to think.
- The teacher provides good support but requires independence in the pupils as and when appropriate.
- There is an appropriate balance between adult-led and child-initiated activity.
- Pitch and pace of lessons are sensitive to the rate at which the children learn, thus helping to sustain concentration and motivation.
- Expectations are kept high.
- (In literacy) the strong interdependence between speaking, listening, reading and writing should underpin planning and provision for learning.
- The maths or literacy skills and knowledge that children are expected to learn are clearly defined.
- The teacher has clearly mapped out how to lead the children to the intended learning.
- Children know they can discuss and seek help as and when they need to.

- They like challenge and enjoy opportunities to practise and apply their learning.

- Over time, they can identify their attainment and progress (and should be encouraged to do so).

- They can support one another in group work and are happy to share their ideas and to explain their reasoning and methods.

- Children needing extra support are identified early and receive early intervention to maintain their progress.

- (In maths) the teacher recognises that mathematics is a combination of concepts, facts, properties, rules, patterns and processes.

- 'Leading children's learning' requires a broad repertoire of teaching and organisational skills (directive and less directive techniques; appropriate use of questions).

- (In maths) teaching is sequenced to incorporate practical, visual and ICT resources that children can use to test and confirm their learning; children have access to these resources and understand how to use them.

- (In maths) models and images are demonstrated and displayed to support methods, promote thinking and develop strategies.

- (In maths) the teacher balances the need for precision with the flexibility to use alternative methods.

- (In maths) there is a balanced approach allowing for mental and written work in order to ensure both are developed, practised and applied.

- Teachers have good subject knowledge and an understanding of progression in the curriculum.

- Teachers recognise that some teaching approaches are better suited to promote particular learning outcomes.

These key features are linked to English and maths teaching in primary schools but also apply to secondary schools and to other subjects.

There are further highly relevant aspects of QFT. Clear objectives and well-planned, structured lessons have been covered above but attention also needs to be given to the following:

- **Building on prior learning:** QFT builds on pupils' prior learning. This is crucial for pupils with BESD. If there is a significant gap between their knowledge and skills and what the teacher thinks they can do, with inappropriate lesson planning resulting, then disruptive behaviour is likely to ensue and 'within child' anxieties increased. Attention has to be paid to their common lack of reading, writing, communication and maths skills (Ofsted 1999; 2003; 2005).

- *Assessment for Learning* **(AFL):** (the National Strategies' favoured term). Regular, accurate assessments must be made of where these children are at, which approaches work best for them, what targets are realistic and how progress towards them should be monitored.

- **Pupil participation:** In keeping with *Assessment for Learning* principles, pupils with BESD should be active participants in AfL. They, as much as the teacher, should be party to the objectives set, how they best learn and how their progress will be measured. Clarity, organisation and structure in these factors are crucial. Beyond AfL there should be: regular pupil involvement and engagement with their learning; high levels of interaction for all pupils; an expectation that pupils will accept responsibility for their own learning and work independently – while providing sufficient support to children with BESD in pursuit of these aims.

- **Personalised learning approaches/differentiation:** QFT requires focused lesson design with sharp objectives – yet flexibility must be built in so as to enable the teacher to try different routes to the desired end, finding the approach that best engages the individual child with BESD. Where the curriculum allows, a *personalised* approach (matching teaching to the pupil with BESD's interests and their preferred learning style, and building on his or her strengths) will also help. *Diffferentiating* topics by task or expectation and accepting different levels of success is also appropriate for teachers to use with pupils with BESD, particularly where they have learning difficulties other than 'behaviour' – but differentiation should not be an excuse for low expectations.

Further QFT characteristics, also very important to working with BESD, include:

- appropriate use of teacher questioning, modelling and explaining
- an emphasis on learning through dialogue, with regular opportunities for pupils to talk both individually and in groups (many pupils with BESD find writing tasks very difficult – and need to practise oral communication skills)
- regular and appropriate use of encouragement and praise to engage and motivate pupils.

The current government guidance on BESD reiterates much of the above. In relation to curriculum and BESD it says (DCSF 2008a, paras.109–127):

- What is taught should be 'balanced and broadly based'.
- Use the National Curriculum flexibly.
- Curriculum should be carefully sequenced to build on previous. learning/experience ['small steps' learning].
- Does not have to be taught in individual subjects (a themes and topic approach may be a more appropriate way to deliver the national curriculum).
- Use highly interactive lessons.
- Use groupwork to promote speaking and listening.
- Use work-focused learning for 14–16 year olds (e.g. through the new Diplomas).
- Give opportunities to students to show responsibility/leadership.
- Find time to work at conflict resolution/building/keeping friendships.
- Provide support through identified adult ('keyworker'/mentor idea).
- Emphasise personal life-skills and essential life-skills.

Further useful advice in relation to curriculum delivery has been offered in many books on classroom management and repeats well-supported views (e.g. Galvin 1999 and Ofsted 2005). This advice includes the following:

- Restrict the number of curriculum activities happening at one time.
- Have a balance of activities – whole group, small group, pairs, individual, teacher talk, seat work, practical work.
- Make sure pupils have appropriate time to complete an activity.
- Questioning is highly effective if:
  - a balance of techniques are used: open/closed/speculative/factual
  - structured to match pupils' ability levels so that all are involved
  - staff allow learners time to respond.
- Mix oral instructions with visual clues.
- Set realistic timescales for each task.
- Give appropriate and speedy feedback to pupils about their work – orally and marking with written comments.

- Address the class quietly with confidence.

- Use humour appropriately to make the pupils feel at ease and motivated.

- Have a sense of grouping within the whole-class group, showing variety and flexibility in how groups are set up; making sure you are clear on what basis pupils are grouped; having group sizes and structures appropriate for the task.

- Have all necessary materials ready ahead of the lesson wherever possible.

Galvin (1999) offers further good advice, drawing together the wisdom of many (e.g. Smith and Laslett 1993) and anticipating materials now to be found on the Behaviour For Learning (2009) website. He stresses the importance of knowing what is happening in your classroom and demonstrating on a regular basis that you have 'situational awareness' by commenting on what is happening in the room. He could also have used the term 'withitness' (Kounin 1977 – comparable to 'having eyes in the back of your head'). Teachers should make sure that most pupils are where they can be seen by the teacher for most of the time. Galvin talks of making the classroom your territory by:

- moving around all areas of the classroom

- moving physically closer (but not too close or in a way that could be seen as threatening) to potential difficulty

- having awareness of pupils who might be having problems with the task

- sometimes standing or sitting behind the class rather than at the front.

The Behaviour For Learning website (Behaviour For Learning 2009) offers wise advice to new teachers (also of relevance for 'older hands' and for support staff) about projecting confidence through body posture and expression (appearing confident, e.g. entering the room purposely; standing straight with feet slightly apart; shoulders back and arms unfolded; using gestures to make points but avoiding over-dramatic ones; when sitting down, keeping a straight back to avoid looking defensive). Daniels et al. (1999) saw teachers who were skilled in the use of eye-contact for engaging interest or in using 'the look' to express disapproval. They gave instructions in an authoritative manner.

It could be helpful to reflect and perhaps work on the tone of voice you use – as well as the choice of words. Rogers (2000) offers good advice on not being 'snappy', rude, sarcastic or short-tempered, and on being decisive, assertive and caring in what you say. It can help to make a connection on an emotional and caring level by taking opportunities to say a child's name and exchange a few friendly words as children enter the class or in the corridor outside, e.g. 'Good morning, Ashley'.

Successful communication is, of course, a blend of the spoken, the written and the unspoken (nonverbal communication). Much of what we communicate is through body language, and only a minority through tone of voice or actual words, the proportion varying from one situation to another.

Under pressure, it is easy to fall back into a negative mode, drawing attention to shortcomings rather than encouraging desired behaviours. It helps to be guided by the old adage (particularly when a child like Ryan is 'acting out'): 'four positives to one negative'. Avoid if possible 'Don't do...' language. 'Walk slowly' is better than 'Don't run!', or 'Share the crayons, thanks...' is better than 'Don't fight over the crayons'. Where possible give a child a choice: 'Sit down in your seat or you'll choose to sit in the quiet corner.' Draw the disruptive child's (Ashley shouting out again?) attention to the way another child is doing something right: 'Jane, I really like the way you are sitting quietly with your hand up.'

Ofsted (2005) notes that practitioners who are effective in reducing unacceptable behaviour are quick to intervene and to divert pupils' attention. They apply a variety of strategies to engage and hold pupils' interest and so minimise the impact of negative behaviour. When behaviour is more difficult they adopt a consistent and non-confrontational approach and they always show respect for pupils.

In terms of approaches to avoid, Ofsted (2005) noted the common tendency of teachers to give too many oral instructions with the result that pupils became confused – and this precipitated disruptive behaviour. Another failing found in many settings was the unhelpful assessment of pupil work such as giving only limited or unhelpful oral and written comments. The *Managing Challenging Behaviour* report also found in a small proportion of the schools some staff showing a lack of respect by shouting at pupils, making fun of them, making personal remarks or using sarcasm. Pupils, particularly those with BESD, will react badly to such comments and also to staff who come too close, grab, hold or touch them even in mild restraint (the issue of physical restraint – sometimes necessary – is considered in more detail later).

It is over twenty years since the Elton Report (DES 1989) but this was grounded in extensive research and offers timeless good advice. It urged teachers to be:

- flexible in order to take advantage of unexpected events rather than being thrown off balance by them. Examples would include the appearance of the window cleaner or a wasp in the middle of a lesson
- continually observing or 'scanning' the behaviour of the class
- sparing and consistent in use of reprimands. This means
  - being firm rather than aggressive
  - targeting the right pupil
  - criticising the behaviour and not the person
  - using private rather than public reprimands whenever possible
  - being fair and consistent
  - avoiding sarcasms and idle threats
- sparing and consistent in use of punishments. This includes
  - avoiding whole-group punishment which pupils see as unfair
  - avoiding sanctions that humiliate pupils as this breeds resentment.

The Behaviour For Learning (2009) website gives guidance on having clear procedures for the different stages of lessons and a sense of timing. There is guidance on meeting and greeting, the settling-down phase, giving the lesson a clear structure (a beginning, middle and an end, fitted into the given time slot). Extra care needs taking over transitions within lessons – make these smoothly and efficiently. Advice is given on clearly marking the boundaries between activities. Galvin (1999) had earlier advocated using 'switch' signals to change activities, giving advance warning of what is about to happen. Transitions between lessons also have to be handled carefully (these can, of course, be particularly difficult times for the child with BESD).

THE POSITIVE IMPACT OF ESTABLISHED AND REHEARSED ROUTINES

The lifestyles of pupils who develop complex BESD can be chaotic, characterised by a lack of consistent direction or patterns to home life, including irregular eating and going to bed very late, with the latter resulting in a shortage of sleep that probably affects their hormonal balance, mood and ability to concentrate in class. Their BESD may also have been exacerbated by the unpredictability of the actions and expectations of the adults around them. School-life should, and can, be a very helpful counterweight. Children with BESD benefit and respond with improved behaviour and learning when they know where they are, the staff who they are with and what is going to happen next. They can react very badly to altered personnel, e.g. supply teachers or adjusted timetables, coping poorly with the different or the unexpected. Structure and routine provide emotional support to them (Cole *et al.* 1998; DCSF 2010; Redl 1966), fostering a sense of belonging and helping them to make and sustain personal relationships. Classroom and corridor or playground routines that are well known to pupils with BESD can make a significant contribution to reducing their disruptive behaviour – and also to 'acting in' disturbance.

It helps if children with BESD know what is expected during the entire school day (from before breakfast club starts to the end of the extended day). Each subject/class teacher should have a re-assuring routine for meeting and greeting children before they enter the classroom. There should be clear routines for:

- getting to seats
- getting out materials
- accessing equipment
- getting work marked
- asking questions
- taking turns
- getting the attention of the class
- changing activities
- making up uncompleted work
- having back-up activities for pupils who finish first
- giving out administrative information
- going to the toilet
- clearing up
- leaving the room to go to the next lesson
- going out into the playground or lunch areas
- catching buses or going home on foot at the end of the school day
- after-school 'extended curriculum' activities.

Seating plans, especially in secondary and special schools, help pupils with the most challenging behaviour to settle quickly (Ofsted 2005).

Children with BESD will also be helped if school staff pay close attention to the issues raised in Table 6.2, which focuses on routines outside the classroom.

Table 6.2: Do pupils understand school rules and routines?

Answer the following questions – in general terms and then in relation to children with BESD with whom you work:

		In general			To your children with BESD		
		Yes	Some-what	No	Yes	Some-what	No
1	All staff know and apply the behaviour policy for out of class?						
2	Corridors, playgrounds and other social areas are well supervised?						
3	Problem areas of the school site are identified, and difficulties addressed?						
4	Routines for movement around the school site are clear?						
5	Rules for short break times are understood by pupils?						
6	Rules for short break times are being applied by all staff?						
7	Rules and systems for lunchtime understood by pupils?						
8	Rules and systems for lunchtime systems understood by all staff?						
9	Break times rewards/sanctions system clear to/applied by all?						
10	Effective systems in place to resolve pupil conflicts?						
11	Range of activities/equipment available for break times?						

If there have to be changes to a child with BESD's routines – whether short-term (e.g. because a teacher is away or an altered timetable during SATs or because of a school trip) or long-term (e.g. a change of class or timetable) – staff should outline what is to change and rehearse the altered procedures with the child. Taking the time and trouble to do this is likely to forestall and avoid disruption, and reduce anxiety and upset as well as showing children that they matter and are included in plans.

There should also be clarity about what sanctions might be applied if rules are broken, both in class or elsewhere on the school site.

BUILDING WELL-BEING IN THE CLASSROOM (SEAL)

DCSF (2009c) notes that social, emotional and behavioural skills (SEBs) underlie almost every aspect of school, home and community life, including effective learning and getting on with other people. Working at developing SEBs, it says, is:

> fundamental to school improvement... Where children have good skills in these areas, and are educated within an environment supportive to emotional health and well-being, they will be motivated and equipped to: be effective and successful learners; make and sustain friendships; deal with and resolve conflict effectively and fairly; solve problems with others or by themselves; manage strong feelings such as frustration, anger and anxiety; be able to promote calm and optimistic states that further the achievement of goals; recover from setbacks and persist in the face of difficulties; work and play co-operatively; compete fairly and win and lose with dignity and respect for competitors; recognise and stand up for their rights and the rights of others; understand and value the differences and commonalities between people, respecting the right of others to have beliefs and values different from their own. (p.2)

The guidance (current in 2010) for the National Strategies 'Social and Emotional Aspects of Learning' (SEAL) programmes in secondary schools makes similar claims. The programmes build on earlier work that showed the importance of 'whole-school' approaches, where all staff actively work at developing the children's 'emotional literacy'. The effective use of SEAL in all classrooms could be particularly helpful with pupils with BESD. Although it is taught in discrete topics it should also permeate much teaching across the curriculum. Crucially it should also be part of the modelling of behaviour and relationships by staff members. It is clear that as excellent as these SEAL teaching materials are, they will have little sustainable impact if they cannot be exemplified in the relationships observed within the school, the policy formation and in whole-school practices – for example, using the teaching materials on empathy while making insufficient response to pupils' individual needs. Schools where SEAL is seen merely as part of curriculum to be taught for an hour, say, on a Monday or Tuesday morning (thus disregarding the intentions of the SEAL framework) are likely to reap little benefit.

DCSF (2007d, p.49) says 'There is clear evidence...that "universal" approaches that target everyone are better at preventing and managing issues than approaches which target only those experiencing problems'. A good backdrop of universal provision is 'the best platform from which to provide more intensive help'. It points out that it is less stigmatising for pupils with SEN to receive most of the help they need from the same people who are providing it for everyone. It claims research shows that the processes that help those with difficulties help *all* children:

> it is just that those with particular needs require more of them. These processes include: intervening early; teaching skills; promoting self-esteem; giving personal support; building warm relationships; setting clear rules and boundaries; involving people in their learning; encouraging autonomy; involving parents/carers; creating positive climates and taking a long-term, developmental approach.(DCSF 2007d, p.49)

The government's SEAL approach to promoting SEBs is represented in Figure 6.1, which shows provision in terms of three waves – universal provision (Wave 1), targeted group work (Wave 2) and individual support (Wave 3).

So-called 'focus groups', DCSF (2007d, p.51) says, are designed to provide a safe and supportive environment where specific skills can be developed and practised at a level matched to that of the individuals involved. Realistically the guidance recognises that some pupils with BESD may find it hard to acquire social and emotional skills within a group context and may require Wave 3 work. The Government rightly believes that SEAL Wave 2 work 'has a valuable contribution to play for all pupils who attend learning support units (LSUs) and pupil referral units (PRUs)' (DCSF 2007d, p.51).

DCSF (2009d) outlines key hopes of the SEAL primary-schools programme, which are relevant to both working with groups of children with BESD and to individual work. The materials are designed to promote:

- **Self-awareness:** to help children to have better and more realistic understanding of themselves, helping them to 'know how they learn, how they relate to others, what they are thinking and what they are feeling' to assist in organising themselves and planning their learning
- **Management of feelings:** through promoting a range of strategies to recognise and accept their feelings. It is hoped 'They can use this to regulate their learning and behaviour, for example, managing anxiety or anger, or demonstrating resilience in the face of difficulty'

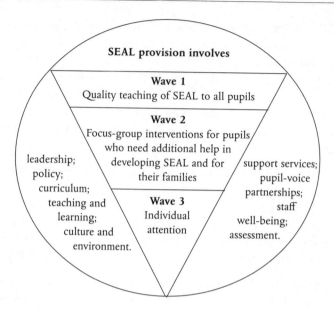

Figure 6.1: DCSF's universal approach to promoting social and emotional skills
Source: DCSF 2007d

- **Motivation:** thereby enabling learners to take 'an active and enthusiastic part in learning. Intrinsically motivated learners recognise and derive pleasure from learning. Motivation enables learners to set themselves goals and work towards them, to focus and concentrate on learning, to persist when learning is difficult and to develop independence, resourcefulness and personal organisation'

- **Empathy:** i.e. 'understanding others, anticipating and predicting their likely thoughts, feelings and perceptions...seeing things from another's point of view and modifying one's own response'

- **Social skills** that enable children to 'relate to others, take an active part in a group, communicate with different audiences, negotiate, resolve differences and support the learning of others'.

The SEAL programme offers a structured, whole-curriculum framework and resources; a 'spiral curriculum' that revisits each theme (and the skills associated with that theme), offering new ideas yearly, so that a child entering the school aged four or five years and leaving at the end of Year 6 (aged 11) will have experienced each theme, at an appropriate level, each year. Children should be able to demonstrate progress in SEBs as they progress through the school. The programme:

- makes suggestions for work on each assembly or group-time theme in each year group

- provides materials to teach children how to use thinking skills and feelings together

- suggests 'a potential whole-school or setting focus' for noticing and celebrating positive behaviours, e.g. one week 'catching children being kind' or another 'catching children resolving an argument well'. Any member of staff (not just the classteacher) can nominate a child for a reward.

The SEAL programme resources suggest several ways through which teachers can help children:

- develop a vocabulary of feelings

- express feelings

- use calming-down strategies

- link thinking and feeling

- counteract 'emotional hijack'

- understand feelings of 'threat', 'fight' and 'flight'

- manage anxiety, anger and fear

- respond to loss and changed life circumstances.

Conflict resolution is one key area of learning. This is an on-going theme in the resources, embodied in the 'peaceful problem-solving' and 'problem-solving processes'. There are also activities to encourage children to become *assertive*, under the 'Good to be me' theme. *Motivation* is tackled through the 'Going for Goals!' theme, drawing, perhaps controversially, on the claims of 'multiple intelligences'. DCSF (2009d) believes this helps children consider the question: 'How am I clever?' rather than the more usual 'How clever am I?', and provides an opportunity for children to consider their particular strengths in learning by seeing, doing or talking and listening.

Three ways to *calm down* are suggested in the materials: distraction, exercise and relaxation, and approaches to help children relax include visualisation and physical relaxation.

SEAL resources also draw on *solution-focused thinking*, encouraging children to look at times when they have been successful; identify goals, 'miracles', dreams or preferred futures; set targets to help them to reach their goals or preferred future; use scaling to identify and support the process.

DCSF (2007d) provides interesting and challenging suggestions for how 'SEAL', interpreted very broadly, can be fostered through class teaching in all standard areas of the National Curriculum, for example:

- **arts subjects**, e.g. experiencing and expressing emotions through seeing, listening and taking part; co-operation and communication with others; building self-confidence; using drama to teach assertiveness, negotiation or other skills directly

- **English language**, e.g. developing an emotional vocabulary and expressing feelings; developing positive self-concept apparently through talking and writing about themselves (though no research is given to underpin this assertion)

- **English literature**, e.g. encouraging empathy, broadening and deepening emotional experience

- **Geography**, e.g. seeing the world from another's point of view

- **History**, e.g. developing tolerance, understanding and empathy through exploration of past experiences

- **ICT**, e.g. creating good presentations suited to the needs of others; making sense of information

- **modern foreign languages**, e.g. developing listening skills and expressing and discussing feelings and opinions.

Opportunities for SEAL in maths, as well as some of the suggestions for other subjects, do seem somewhat tenuous, with evidence for making the links not provided in this document at least. However, we support the general point of trying to infuse all subjects with the development of SEAL and believe this could lead to a change of culture in many classrooms, producing a climate that is more inclusive for children with BESD.

There are also other approaches to promoting aspects of SEBs through structured programmes, some of which were used in English schools before the advent of SEAL (e.g. Cole, Visser and Daniels 2000), while in Scotland the Australian 'Bounce Back' resilience-building programme (McGrath and Noble 2010) is meeting with a positive response. With a new UK government in power since May 2010, the future of SEAL might become uncertain, leading to alternatives being used more widely.

SPECIFIC GROUP APPROACHES

There is an extensive literature on the value of circle time, a practice that is now commonplace in many schools (e.g. Mosley 2004) and that can be useful in promoting social and emotional skills in children in BESD (or, if handled badly, in precipitating difficult behaviour). Here we look at two more specialist group approaches, 'circle of friends' and 'nurture groups'.

Circle of friends

Farrell (2006a) advises that setting up a circle of friends can be an effective way of offering support to withdrawn, isolated, teased or otherwise vulnerable children with BESD (in this present instance, those suffering from obesity). The teacher starting a circle of friends is usually supported by someone (perhaps from outside the school or perhaps working in a support role in the school) who has experience of using this approach.

This person, the facilitator, will hold a preliminary discussion with a larger group of the peers of the 'victim' – the 'focus child'. (The focus child will usually not be present at this but will have been approached before this happens.) The facilitator finds out from the peer group the situations involving the focus child in which things go well and situations where they go badly. The peer group then consider their feelings when they have felt left out, teased or lacked friends. The facilitator asks for ideas to improve the situation – these might be suggestions such as sitting next to the focus child in a lesson or talking to him or her in the playground.

The facilitator then asks for volunteers to form a circle of friends. Later, staff decide which volunteers will be chosen, selecting perhaps six children. The 'circle' then meets with the focus child and tells him or her all the positive things that were said and discusses how the focus child would like to be included in what they do. The circle meets perhaps weekly to discuss how things are going. This kind of support can last for a term or sometimes longer (Farrell 2006a). A variety of this approach is the 'Circle of Support', as described by Mosley (2008).

Nurture groups

Nurture groups provide an extended and compensatory nurturing experience in schools to children, who usually have BESD, and whose early life experience has given them a poor start in life. These are often children with insecure and damaged attachments who have been subject to various risk factors. The children go to a carefully planned nurture room (operating under a variety of names) in their primary schools for a time-limited period, prior to full re-inclusion into their normal mainstream class. There has also been some experimentation with nurture groups in secondary schools.

Bennathan and Boxall (2000) state that since their first introduction more than thirty years ago, this approach has proved an effective model of early intervention. Nurture groups that carefully follow their advice can:

- help these children feel valued and partners in education
- build up confidence and self-esteem
- teach children how to make good relationships with adults and with each other
- improve attendance and attainment
- provide support to parents.

Nurture groups help promote the five key outcomes of *Every Child Matters*, can help long-term inclusion, contribute to better mental health in the future and, it is claimed, assist in breaking the link between a poor start in life and later youth offending.

Nurture groups should take the form of a small supportive class of up to 12 children, usually in a mainstream primary school. This should provide a secure, predictable environment in which the different developmental needs of each pupil are catered for (emotional, social and, at times, physical – e.g. through sharing food). It should be staffed by two adults, usually a teacher and a learning support assistant, and pupils attend regularly for a substantial part of each week. There will be a focus on emotional and social development as well as academic progress. Pupils must remain on their mainstream class roll, with an expectation that they will return to their class in two to four terms (Nurture Group Network 2010).

A nurture group can be an integral part of an individual school or a resource for a cluster of schools. School leaders must ensure that children attending the nurture group remain members of a mainstream class where they register daily and attend selected activities. There must be a pattern of attendance whereby children spend part of each day in the nurture group or attend for regular sessions during the week. The two adults staffing the group must work together modelling good adult relationships in a structured and predictable environment, thereby encouraging children to begin to trust adults and to learn.

The Nurture Group Network goes on, a nurture group must:

- Offer support for children's positive emotional and social growth and cognitive development at whatever level of need the children show by responding to them in a developmentally appropriate way.

- Supply a setting and relationships for children in which missing or insufficiently internalised essential early learning experiences are provided.

- Ensure that relevant national curriculum guidelines are followed for all children.

- Be taken full account of in school policies, participate fully, and be fully considered in the development and review of policies.

- Offer short or medium term placements, usually for between two and four terms, depending on the child's specific needs.

- Ensure placement in the group is determined on the basis of systematic assessment in which appropriate diagnostic and evaluative instruments have been used, with the aim always being to return the child to full-time mainstream provision.

- Place an emphasis on communication and language development through intensive interaction with an adult and with other children.

- Provide opportunities for social learning through co-operation and play with others in a group with an appropriate mix of children.

- Monitor and evaluate their effectiveness in promoting the positive social, emotional and educational development of each child. Recognise the importance of quality play experiences in the development of children's learning. (*What is a Nurture Group?*, Nurture Group Network 2010)

An assessment tool designed for use with nurture groups is the Boxall Profile (Boxall and Bennathan 1998), discussed later.

Cooper and Tiknaz (2007) give an account of the research that supports the nurture-group approach but see a need for more independent studies. One such study was Reynolds, MacKay and Kearney (2009), psychologists who gave a favourable account of nurture groups in Glasgow. This research needs to be seen alongside a report by HMIE (2009) on the wider operation of nurture groups in Scotland, which echoed Cooper and Tiknaz's concern that some schools were not fully following the precepts laid down for a 'classic nurture group' in Bennathan and Boxall (2000), thereby leading to mixed results. However, we are persuaded by our own experience and contacts with colleagues that nurture groups *do* have a valuable part to play and have made a large contribution to the alleviation of BESD – as well as making school cultures more inclusive.

CHECKING THE BEHAVIOURAL ENVIRONMENT: PHYSICAL DESIGN AND LAYOUT

'We shape our buildings – and they shape us', Winston Churchill is supposed to have said (Maier 1981, p.40). Ofsted believes that physical factors have:

> a significant impact on the behaviour of pupils…a welcoming and stimulating environment tends to foster good behaviour. In many schools senior staff…ensure that the cleanliness and brightness of accommodation are maintained. A high priority is placed on the condition of the buildings and much thought is given to how they are used. When damage occurs it is quickly repaired. High-quality displays celebrating pupils' achievement are evident in communal areas and classrooms. (2005, para.84)

This advice echoed earlier research: 'The buildings themselves can have a psychological significance' wrote Wilson and Evans (1980, p.190). Behaviour seems to respond to, and can be shaped by, the physical environment (Cole *et al.* 1998). Colour, light, form, space and acoustics can be used positively to induce mood change and pro-social actions. Even sound, in the guise of 'mood music' or Mozart flowing through a classroom's airwaves, can soothe 'uptight' pupils and staff.

Conversely, the physical environment can precipitate the undesirable. Where there is a lack of personal 'territory' this can exacerbate feelings of low self-worth: a child's ecosystem has lost its centre. Violence increases in confined spaces: if large groups of any humans, particularly pupils with BESD, are compressed into cramped spaces, whether classrooms, corridors, or dinner-queues, there tend to be problems for staff. Physical lay-out – nooks and crannies of large sites that are difficult to supervise – can increase opportunities for bullying. Dingy classroom décor and dilapidated plant encourage a lack of respect for property, leading to further damage. Echoing corridors and bare-boarded rooms can precipitate a crescendo of shouting and argument (one worries about the modern trend in new school design away from carpets and adequate sound-proofing).

An attractive, comfortable and comforting physical environment is a sign of a caring school that recognises the importance of allowing for pupils' physiological and affective needs. It can allow response to Maier's (1981, p.37) observation that 'Bodily comfort speaketh the loudest', when it comes to meeting vulnerable children's needs. It should also allow for privacy in the 'fish bowl of group living'(p.43) in a care home or in, our major concern here, educational environments.

In short, how staff, within the constraints of existing architecture, design and resources, mould the physical environment, can assist or obstruct pupils' emotional well-being and receptiveness to teaching and learning. Thinking of *your* classroom, could you improve it to reduce the BESD of the children with the greatest needs?

Might you re-arrange furniture to allow you:

- to see what is going on better?

- to move around easily so you dominate the 'action zone', the key area of the traditional classroom that tapers away from the teacher's desk?

- to place a child like Ryan away from distractions, yet still within the 'action zone'?

- more space for children to access resources?

Could you and colleagues create a quiet, comfortable zone, with a rug, where those who are upset might recover or the anxious child can find respite from the normal bustle – or a small group could work, or an occasional one-to-one chat take place? Are there practical ways of dampening down noise and vibrations from voices or from scraping furniture (carpets and soft furnishings can be useful here)?

Might behaviour be worse because of a lack of ventilation or too much heat or cold? Is the lighting as good as it could be (avoiding glare or dark corners)? Are materials and equipment properly prepared, neatly laid out and clearly labelled?

Other considerations for classroom layout and environment include:

- Use the wall space for attractive displays.

- Try to avoid bottlenecks and high traffic areas.

- Try to keep academic work areas away from sinks and doors.

- Change the classroom layout to suit different tasks.

- Ensure space for personal belongings – coats, lunchboxes, bags.

All these physical aspects of classroom teaching and learning (as well as providing opportunity to offer small-group or individual support) are important. Similar attention paid to the corridor or playground could also be helpful.

YOUR PART IN LESSENING BESD

·School practitioners benefit from regular review of their own practice, sometimes drawing on the help of friendly colleagues who might be their mentors or coaches or fellow members of a 'teacher support team' (Creese *et al.* 1997; DfES 2005b). This self- and assisted-review can help in identifying your, sometimes, unintended part in exacerbating the behaviour of some pupils. School leaders should be pro-active in creating school climates in which such review is the norm.

There are times when, unintentionally, *we* light the blue touch paper to a child's 'acting out'. What we do, what we say and the nonverbal messages we convey to our pupils are in part produced by our own emotional state. In the same way as for the child, our amygdala and hypothalamus give us intense feelings of anger, frustration and distress. Where possible – although sometimes it cannot be – it helps to be aware of, evaluate and counteract our negative feelings before reacting to the child's behaviour.

As our emotional thermometers rise, using 'self-talk' can make a difference. Children with BESD can pick up quickly on:

- our mood (tell yourself – 'I mustn't let my anger show', consciously try to keep calm and controlled)

- our attitude ('Be more patient with Cameron – he always finds this activity challenging')

- our facial expressions ('Cheryl could see me thinking "Oh no, not her again!"')

- anger or irritation shown in our use of our voice (remind yourself 'Raising my voice will make things worse!').

If possible, resist the putdowns that are on the tip of your tongue ('You're acting like a Y4!') or sarcasm ('Ryan, that was really helpful – not!'). Pay attention to other 'give-aways', e.g. how you are standing: your proximity to a child might be an intrusive and provocative act given his or her mood at that moment (although at other times it could be a useful approach to nipping trouble in the bud).

In the aftermath of a difficult situation, perhaps later on in the staffroom with a colleague, you can anticipate what Stephen might do the next time – and rehearse how you will react, increasing the chances of your emotions being in check when he challenges you again. We know that if our calmness, empathy, consideration and respect for pupils slip, then life in the classroom becomes more difficult and leads to a shortfall in the standards we should model. If we are to develop the five core areas of SEAL (self-awareness, managing feelings, motivation, empathy and social skills) in our pupils, we need to set an example.

REVIEW

In this chapter we have considered general factors that affect children with BESD. These include the skills, moods and attitudes of practitioners, which can either diminish or exacerbate the feelings, emotions and behaviour of all pupils, but particularly those who are troubled and tend to be troublesome. We stressed the supportive power of well-established daily routines. We described key elements in skilled teaching, looked at the promotion of SEBs in class and thought about using the physical environment to good effect. We have also stressed that many behaviour difficulties in children are situation-specific, responding to the factors described above, which make up the overall 'behavioural environment' in class, school buildings and playground.

NOTE

1   The DCSF National Strategies (NS) promote a 'Waves of Intervention Model' to assist the inclusion of children with SENs. It is visualised as a triangle. At this triangle's wide end is Wave 1 which encompasses what should be on offer for all children: high-quality everyday personalised teaching for every child ('Quality First teaching' or 'QFT'). In the middle of the triangle is Wave 2. This descibes targeted small-group additional intervention for pupils. At the triangle's sharp end is Wave 3. This is about intervention for children for whom QFT and Wave 2 catch-up programmes are not enough. Wave 3 is likely to involve more intensive programmes, involving more individual support or specialist expertise.

CHAPTER 7

THE INDIVIDUAL CHILD FROM AN EDUCATIONAL PERSPECTIVE

> Children and young people who are troubled and suffering emotional distress not only trouble others with whom they come into contact, but find it difficult to be available for learning, and often give the impression of being stuck, somehow frozen, in their difficulties. (Greenhalgh 1994, p.1)

How do we help children with BESD to become unstuck so that they can be more receptive to teaching and learning? There are no easy answers but in this and the following chapter we outline factors that clearly help.

It is neither possible, nor desirable, to be dominated by a policy of *waiting* until children with BESD are in a regular settled frame of mind before we have some normal educational expectations of them. That time might never arrive: we have to start sometime – preferably *now*. There is perhaps more scope to allow for 'readiness' and 'mood' in small special-school environments or 'units'. In mainstream settings, increasingly complex timetables at secondary level and the demands made on primary practitioners can constrain flexibility. Also, 'waiting till ready' can create the very real danger, as HMI and Ofsted have long noted (Cole 1989; Ofsted 1999), that where an overly 'therapeutic' approach largely displaces an educational one, it can lead to unnecessarily low educational expectations and poor and narrow teaching, which can further increase the children's disadvantage.

'Waiting till ready' further denies practitioners a range of approaches that can have quick impact: skilled teaching can be engaging, motivating and divert troubled children from disruption and damaging rumination, taking the child from negative to positive frames of mind. The evidence from HMI (Ofsted 1999; 2003; 2005) is fairly compelling: some mainstream schools, and many special schools and PRUs have succeeded in being both highly caring and supportive environments addressing underlying social and emotional difficulties while, at the same time, making challenging educational demands on children with BESD. The task for educational practitioners, in Greenhalgh's (1994, p.1) words, is to strengthen the children's 'inner resources so that they may become more self-aware, autonomous and open to learning'.

In this chapter we look at educational factors that can help individual children such as Cameron and Stephen (see Chapter 1). These include:

- the teaching intervention cycle

- assessment and planning

- responding to special (or 'additional') needs

- individual support through personalised learning

- staff language and communication

- rewarding behaviour in a way that encourages a 'growth' mindset

- managing difficult behaviour in and beyond the classroom (applying sanctions, pre-arranged sanctuaries for 'cooling off', access to speedy backup)

- helpful use of support staff

- handling transitions.

It helps to keep the names of individuals in mind when discussing these topics, remembering research findings that the best practitioners (e.g. Daniels *et al.* 1999) are reluctant to use labels or to think in terms of '*the* BESD child'. Each child in their care is unique: Cheryl is so different from Ashley or Ryan. Planning and intervention for each one has to identify and reflect individual strengths and needs.

THE TEACHING AND LEARNING INTERVENTION CYCLE

A careful and strategic approach is needed towards teaching and learning. To achieve desired change, detailed assessment should occur regularly and then progress should be made round the teaching/intervention and learning cycle throughout a child's educational career (see Figure 7.1).

Reflective, well planned and engaging practice, based on the bedrock of a strengthening positive relationship between staff and the child (see Chapter 8) is the key. Progress round each cycle will rarely be smooth. There will be times when it is necessary to make tactical retreats or respond to the unexpected (both helpful and unhelpful) as mental-health or social issues

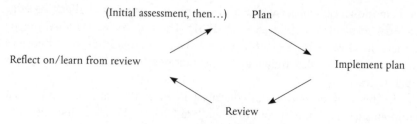

Figure 7.1: The teaching intervention cycle

dominate. There could be times when a new master plan or shorter-term contingency plan is necessary well ahead of statutory assessments or the work setting's usual schedule for reviewing children, such are the dramatic life-events in some children's lives; or key-staff may go off on unexpected long-term absences, or sometimes a child reacts with extreme and negative responses to the best-laid plans.

The strategy represented in Figure 7.1 should be used to identify and address needs in a holistic manner that takes into account the interacting bio-psycho-social nature of BESD (Cooper 2005 - see p.47). Approaches to teaching should allow for 'biological' factors sometimes apparent in SENs such as SLCN, ADHD, ASD, sensory impairments or learning difficulties as for emotional/psychological and social influences.

ASSESSMENT AND PLANNING

We can, and should, measure, monitor and reflect on progress in classroom areas such as language, reading and mathematics skills and attainment. However, we do need to show caution towards calls from government for 'evidence-based' practice beyond these areas. Is it really possible to get sufficiently inside a child's mind to make an accurate assessment of his or her generalised feelings or overall sense of well-being or mental health difficulties over time? Can we completely guard against the impact of our own mood or recent experiences of a child's challenging behaviour to be completely objective as we fill in an assessment schedule on a child? We would opt for a mixed approach, believing that assessment and then planning for intervention with the child with BESD has to remain in part creative art as well as attempted science through the use of, where possible, standardised assessment tools.

We note the caution of Dr Thomas Achenbach (1991) who devised the Child Behavior Checklists (CBCL), detailed instruments widely employed in over fifty countries for decades. After years standardising these, he noted that there was 'no well-validated criterion for categorically distinguishing between children who should be considered "normal" and those who might be seen as "abnormal"' and that, with respect to mental-health syndromes, 'children are continually changing' (Achenbach 1991, p.45). He warned that:

> All assessment procedures are subject to errors of measurement and other limitations. No single score precisely indicates a child's status. Instead, a child's score on a syndrome scale should be considered an approximation of the child's status as seen by a particular informant at the time the informant completes the CBCL.

Achenbach's frankness mirrors the doubts of others expressed in the BESD and mental-health literature (see Cole and Visser 2005). The latters' literature review for Ofsted (2005) also contained the following warning from a Canadian psychiatrist – note from a *senior medical professional* – who said:

> Efforts to create categories within what is a heterogeneous and wide-ranging collection of behaviour patterns are commendable attempts to bring order out of chaos; yet they are essentially both arbitrary and artificial and have serious limitations, particularly as guides to treatment and prognosis. In reality the behaviour disorders of childhood and adolescence are a very mixed bag of social–behavioural–emotional disorders, which usually have multiple causes. A comprehensive formulation of each case is more important than the assigning of a diagnostic label. (Barker 1996, p.13)

It is wise to be sceptical about some diagnoses and allocations of children to categories of a medical nature particularly if a full assessment has not been made by a fully qualified psychiatrist. Was the assessment made carefully and properly, i.e. with a child extensively observed at different times while interacting with different people in contrasting settings (home, different classes, out and about with peers in playground or downtown) by a skilled medical practitioner (in which case we *should* respect the judgement), or was reliance based on parental or other professionals' reports or loose assertions (see Colley 2010; Cooper 2001; Visser and Jehan 2009)?

We are also wary of the regular recording of the minute details of a child's outward behaviour each day or week. With the best intentions, practitioners can mislead themselves in their observations and record keeping, wanting a child to progress for his or her own sake, but also in part to prove that they, the staff, are doing a good job, and in part to produce 'evidence-based practice' to impress schools' inspectors. Sadly, what one person sees as 'naughty but normal' can be seen by another professional as a deep sign of disturbance or even malicious intent and such a judgement can ignore the practitioner's own role in producing the child's behaviour. Different teachers can place ticks in starkly different points on assessment scales, when purportedly measuring and assessing the same child in similar situations and similar mood. Occasionally, even, a setting may not want a child to progress on an assessment instrument, fearing that that could lead to the loss of resources from their local authority at the next review meeting. Furthermore, a deep concentration on assessment can lead us to focus on fault and remedy and to adopt a very mechanistic medical approach to problems that actually require more complex responses. A careful and deliberate look at what works for a child in a given environment might better identify solutions than completing a general assessment tool.

There is a further problem: many standardised tests with high levels of validity and reliability (e.g. Achenbach 1991) are not available for use other than by licensed professionals, usually educational psychologists or trained mental-health professionals. Also, some worthwhile measures are long and time-consuming if used properly and at the prescribed intervals.

We therefore view some 'behaviourist' texts (including some recent American books on 'Functional Behavior Analysis') with disappointment – surprised that working with children with BESD (which is so much about engaging with feelings and emotions and mental health) can be discussed in what can seem such a cold, clinical and tidy way. The apparent resistance of busy professionals in America and in this country to devoting much working time to filling in assessment forms is to be expected, given that the data resulting could be of limited value in firmly demonstrating a child's difficulties or progress.

These caveats stated, we accept that observation, recording and planning can undoubtedly be aided by completing appropriate schedules and assessment forms – we just think it can be dangerous to rely on them *too* much.

In addition to deploying the usual methods for measuring progress in classroom subjects (an important function necessary to guard against low classroom expectations for the child with BESD), does your school have access to materials used by your local behaviour-support service or behaviour partnership?

The long-established Boxall Profile (Boxall and Bennathan 1998, being revised in 2010) is not restricted to use by specialists. Although it takes time to become familiar with its format and intentions the effort *is* worthwhile. The profile is a good, if expensive, aid to assessing and helping individual children and a way of developing staff's observational skills and understanding. The assessor rates the child on 34 items including uncontrolled emotional outbursts, sensitivity to disapproval, disruption, wandering attention, and listlessness. Scores are then grouped to give an indication of how well or how poorly a child performs in important areas relating to BESD.

The 'Strengths and Difficulties Questionnaire' (Goodman 1997) is a quick, easy-to-use and free assessment tool available (with supporting materials) from the SDQ website (see 'Recommended Resources' at the end of this book). This aid lists features of 'BESD', sub-dividing 25 items into 5 groups: emotional symptoms, conduct problems, hyperactivity, peer problems and 'prosocial' (sociability). This has been subject to wide standardisation and has proved useful in many situations.

A recent series that provides a range of materials for the assessment of mental health and well-being is Frederickson, Dunsmuir and Baxter (2009) – in particular, McCrory and Cameron's (2009) list of measures for resilience and Booker and Faupel's (2009) selection of tools for assessing social behaviour. If your setting can afford this quite expensive resource, it will provide you with a selection of potentially useful materials to guide your work and to assist in referrals on to other professionals. Faupel's (2004) 'Emotional Literacy Assessment and Intervention' tool is also useful for identifying strengths and weaknesses and suggesting strategies for intervention. This tool includes items to be completed by the teacher, the pupil, and parent or carer, which means that it considers issues from various different perspectives and actively involves the child and so can be a useful aid in later 'counselling'.

In relation to measuring and monitoring classroom behaviour, materials available from your behaviour support or educational psychology service are likely to provide a means of observing and recording the usual aspects of a child's behaviour (much of it not particularly 'BESD'). If these are not available – or have not been standardised – then you could construct your own pro-forma with a three- or five-point scale to cover each of the following:

- **Response to classroom rules and expectations:** Punctuality; how enters/leaves class; in or out of seat behaviour; having right materials; respecting own and others property; talking out of turn; interrupting others; hindering other children; disrupting others; responses to changes in routine.

- **Attitudes and performance in class work:** Starting, completing or refusing to work; contribution to group or class discussions; amount of errors/standard of presentation of work; impulsivity; distractibility and attention difficulties; confidence to try new tasks; frustration levels; motivation; avoidance tactics; signs of additional special needs (see section above).

- **Response to staff:** Argumentative; rudeness or possible physical abuse of staff; manipulative or provocative behaviour (where? when? and why? taking into account corridors, break-times and playground); response to sanctions; attitude to discussing difficulties with staff.

- **Relationships with peers:** Trustful or distrustful; co-operative or unco-operative; argumentative/verbal abuse of peers; understanding or intolerant; tendency to fight/physical abuse of peers; stirs up conflict between peers; gives in to bad peer pressures; attention-seeking through poor behaviour; manipulates peers; accepted or rejected; sociable or tends to keep own company; lying, spitting or other particular anti-social behaviour; inappropriate sexualised behaviour.

- **Emotional and social development:** A simple instrument would cover your assessment of the child's confidence, inter-personal skills; self-esteem (feelings of self-worth or view of him/herself); ability to express feelings; anxiety and tearfulness; response to criticism; response to different types of encouragement or praise.

When using the data produced by checklists, it is important not to focus too much on the negatives. More progress can be made by reflecting and building on areas of comparative strength. As the National Strategies' *Assessment for Learning* stresses, assessment should be positive and 'formative'. It should involve the child in the process (as a key part of 'personalised learning' – see paragraph 82 of DCSF 2008a), promoting reflection in him or her as well as in staff, and achieving agreement on opportunities to develop strengths and key needs; setting appropriate targets as well as suggesting modes of intervention most likely to address identified issues.

IDENTIFYING AND RESPONDING TO SPECIAL (OR 'ADDITIONAL') EDUCATIONAL NEEDS

Assessment should explore any cognitive learning difficulties that a child with BESD may have. As the BESD Guidance (DCSF 2008a) requires, this must happen if schools are to carry out their duty to follow the SEN Code of Practice's 'graduated approach' (DfEE 2001a). Thorough assessment should happen before a child is allocated to the stages of 'School Action', 'School Action Plus' or (compulsory for special-school placement) a 'statement of special educational needs' is made. Assessment should also precede annual reviews of 'statements'.

Literacy difficulties

It is essential to recognise and to address the well-established overlap between behaviour difficulties and difficulties in reading and writing or specific learning difficulties ('dyslexia'). One major study (Ofsted 1999) noted that in relation to pupils with BESD in special schools, their 'prior learning in literacy and numeracy was often a history of repeated failure and a constant source of frustration' (para. 42, p.12). This report went on: 'Successful learning in these essential skills was often reflected in improved behaviour indicating how damaging to pupils' self-esteem their lack of progress in learning to read and write had been.' Research in mainstream schools indicated the same happening there (e.g. Daniels *et al.* 1999; Ofsted 2003; 2005). Challenging behaviour in class was linked to pupils with BESD finding learning difficult because they lacked basic literacy skills. The link with speech, language and communication difficulties (SLCN) is less well explored (and therefore merits quite detailed consideration below). The work of Cross (2004) highlights many of these concerns and is well worth studying. Behaviour difficulties are made worse by attentional difficulties and sometimes by unrecognised hearing or visual problems.

It can be helpful – and *essential* in special schools where children with moderate learning difficulties (MLD) are openly mixed with children of 'average intelligence' with BESD – for subject teachers and special teaching assistants (TAs) to have some knowledge and experience of the elements of teaching reading, as most teachers working with children with BESD will find they need to provide assistance in this area. It is likely that some staff in your school, certainly the SENCo, will be well versed in this respect and able to provide guidance. If you are working with children with moderate learning difficulties the advice offered by Farrell (2006b) could be useful. Information about dyslexia is also available on the internet or in Farrell (2006c).

Speech, language and communication needs

SLCN hinder the communication and learning of about 7 per cent of all children (Tommerdahl 2009), with boys affected more than girls. The term 'SLCN' can be applied to any type of communication difficulty linked to speech or language. However, the term is more often used in relation to the situation where the speech and/or language difficulty exists in isolation from any known medical cause such as hearing difficulties, psychological reasons or any health problems.

SLCN frequently interact with BESD. Symptoms are detectable from babyhood but often missed. Children with SLCN are likely to be late talkers; have difficulties with close social relationships and accessing the curriculum and be more prone to psychiatric disorders. SLCN could cause BESD due to difficulty in communicating with others but early psychiatric difficulties could lead to poor behaviour, by limiting the interaction between parent and child – thereby limiting the child's experience of language.

It is helpful to make the distinction between 'language' and 'speech'. *Language* refers to a system of rules about language sounds, word meanings and grammatical word combinations that people use to communicate. *Speech*, on the other hand, is what we use to *express* language. Speech difficulties are generally easier to recognise than certain types of language difficulties as they are more evident.

Children with BESD commonly experience difficulties with:

- speech – clarity and fluency of speech

- expressive language – vocabulary and combining words to make sentences and longer sequences of language

- receptive language – understanding words, sentences, narratives

- functional and social use of language – using language and understanding verbal and nonverbal rules of communication.

As DCSF (2008d) points out, speech and language difficulties often lead to low self-esteem, particularly in children of junior or secondary school age. Predictably, such pupils may have difficulties with literacy, particularly in;

- decoding and segmenting words for reading and spelling, comprehension of reading

- understanding vocabulary to access the curriculum, such as concept language for mathematics

- higher-order language skills, such as predicting an outcome in science; developing learning through conversations with peers.

They can also lack skills in social interaction – for instance, not possessing a good understanding of reciprocity or awareness of the motives, thoughts and feelings of others. They can be withdrawn, fearful of company, or present with acting-out behaviour.

Links between SLCN and BESD often increase as the child grows older, unless targeted assistance is provided.

Ideally, every child with BESD would be assessed formally by a qualified speech and language therapist. However, the resources are often not available for this, and most teachers and SENCos are unlikely to hold specialist qualifications in SLCNs. It is therefore useful for teachers and assistants working with children with BESD to be familiar with language structure in order to inform their practice and to alert them to when they should press for expert advice on helpful interventions.

Language can be broken down into *language production* and *language comprehension*. The most useful classroom tool in evaluating language production is observation. Tommerdahl (2009) recommends that a pupil's language be observed in various settings and with a range of conversational partners. She suggests a sample of 10–30 minutes in total (depending upon how much the child speaks) to allow the teacher or colleagues to develop preliminary ideas of the child's strengths and weaknesses, particularly when used in conjunction with other language assessments.

There is not space here to look in detail at language comprehension. This happens within the child and is far more difficult to assess. Tommerdahl (2009) says that teachers need to be creative in devising activities that test comprehension at various levels, and makes various practical suggestions for assessing the linguistic components described above. How successful these means of exploring language comprehension are will depend on the pupil's co-operation, the time available and, perhaps, environmental factors. The information gathered by a teacher (sometimes a skilled TA or the SENCo) must be put to effective use. If you did the observation and/or transcription then you should discuss the findings with the SENCo and other teachers who share responsibility for the pupil. The data should also be used to inform visiting speech and language teachers, therapists or educational psychologists, as a prelude to their giving practical advice on how to tackle the child's difficulties.

Having established the child's SLCN, you and colleagues must, of course, move on to thinking through how these impact on the child's learning across the different areas of the curriculum and the possible effects on his or her internalised and externalised behaviour. It is best to involve the child in these discussions and in planning ways to address the difficulties. It is advisable to look at how the pupil can be supported in an indirect manner, using his or her strengths to compensate for speech and language difficulties. It can be helpful to write down questions about a lesson, speak to the teacher in private after a classroom session, or work in small groups. A pupil's physical position in the classroom might also be relevant, possibly getting them to sit in a seat from where they can always see the teacher's face in order to help them monitor language sounds through lip-reading or through teacher expression.

Staff can also help pupils with SLCN by paying close attention to the language they use themselves. It is worth checking that you:

- signpost important points
- write down key words
- explain new or complicated vocabulary.

As part of your professional development plan, you might record yourself giving lessons, and then evaluate the language you used, looking for elements that might cause difficulty to these students. The aim should be to avoid unfamiliar idioms or phrases that are ambiguous.

ADHD

As important as focusing on SLCN is the need to take into account the attentional and/or hyperactivity difficulties of many children with BESD – which commonly earn them the label 'ADHD'. When working with such children it is to be hoped that a multi-modal approach be used, trying hard to apply educational, psychological and social approaches, as advised by Cooper (2001) and other commentators. There should not be *over-reliance* on medication, given the clear social and sometimes situational factors that can exacerbate or lessen ADHD. However, drugs *do* continue to have a place (NICE 2008), particularly as the evidence for psychosocial approaches working effectively and consistently is varied (Colley 2010). Indeed, some children might be impossible to manage without carefully administered psychostimulants such as methylphenidate (e.g. 'Ritalin'). Advice referred to in DCSF (DfEE 2001b) remains pertinent for children said to have ADHD (although the recommended approaches seem relevant to many other children with BESD who don't have the ADHD label).

Strategies that teachers could implement are:

- seating the child nearer to the teacher and away from distractions (e.g. the window)
- setting short, achievable targets and give immediate rewards when the child completes the task
- use checklists for each subject, outlining the tasks to be completed, and individual homework assignment charts
- use large type, and provide only one or two examples per page. Avoid illustrations that are not directly relevant to the task
- encourage the pupil to verbalise what needs to be done – first to the teacher, and then silently to themselves

- use teacher attention and praise to reward positive behaviour; and give the pupil special responsibilities so that other children can see them in a positive light
- keep classroom rules clear and simple.

For readers wanting further, highly readable, guidance on working with children with ADHD Martin Kutscher's (2008) *Living Without Brakes* is recommended (although it is written with American schools and society in mind).

Autistic spectrum difficulties

Screening should also have taken place for other possible difficulties. It is quite common, for example, for children towards the milder end of the autistic spectrum (perhaps having aspects of Asperger's Syndrome) to be seen as having BESD. Good advice is given in Jones (2002), Farrell (2006d) and the National Strategies Inclusion Development Programme (IDP) (DCSF 2009d) in relation to autistic spectrum difficulties (ASD). The latter contains a useful self-evaluation checklist and then connects to introductory information. It stresses the contrasting and individual difficulties that children with ASD have with:

- social interaction with peers and adults
- being aware of, and understanding, their emotions and those of others
- language and communication (specific difficulties in the understanding of use of speech and nonverbal communications such as gesture or facial expression)
- changes to routines or the familiar
- predicting what will happen next
- over- or under-sensitivity to sight, sound, taste, smells and touch.

In short the IDP offers a good basic course that is well worth following as part of your school's professional development programme.

Sensory difficulties

Moving on to sensory SENs, it is far from unknown for a child with BESD to have hearing or visual impairments that could have escaped detection and continue to pose obstacles to learning. In relation to both, the difficulties, once diagnosed, could be simple and remediable. Examples might be clearing wax from the ear or getting the child to the optician where the necessary lens or glasses can be provided (although persuading a child to wear spectacles in class can sometimes pose a serious challenge). The difficulties could, of course, be more serious, and diagnosis may establish impairments that the child has to learn to live with and for which staff need to make appropriate adjustments, working wherever possible with the child and family. A detailed look at teaching children with sensory – and physical – impairments is offered in Farrell (2006e).

Teamwork and the SENCo

Identifying and addressing SENs requires close working between different staff members in mainstream settings – in particular, between teachers, learning support and inclusion staff. It helps if the SENCo is an influential and expert member of staff, who is a part of the school leadership team. Teachers with concerns about a child with BESD's possible additional learning needs must have easy access to the SENCo. The latter should also be a valuable source of advice on practical approaches and methods to use. The SENCo should also have been given real influence over how the school deploys its extra resources, including use of teaching or special-needs support workers, parents, peer-tutoring, cross-age tutoring and mentors, that is, over what should, and actually does, go into the school's provision map (see Chapter 6).

INDIVIDUAL SUPPORT THROUGH PERSONALISED LEARNING

The BESD guidance (DCSF 2008a, paragraph 82) reminds us that personalised learning involves:

- effective assessment for learning (which we have already covered)
- teaching and learning that builds on the learner's experiences (and, by implication, strengths)
- a curriculum delivered flexibly ('an enriched curriculum with a guaranteed core')
- effective use of support staff and new technologies
- using extended services beyond the school (which is covered in a later chapter).

It will help to reduce the individual learner's BESD if the curriculum can be related to areas of life that are familiar and relevant to the child and in which the pupil already has some knowledge, progressing carefully just beyond the child's 'comfort zone' in small steps, into his or her 'zone of proximal development' (ZPD) (Daniels 2001).[1] Perhaps the teacher or support worker can tap into the child's existing knowledge and interest in his local community and town, or his or her liking for television programmes, a particular football team, or dance.

The manner in which teaching and learning occurs is also an issue. If pupils with BESD are asked to do tasks at which they have often failed or that they have found very difficult (perhaps because of reading or writing weaknesses), they are, of course, likely to display disruptive behaviour, their negative cognitive cycles having been activated and the stress hormone cortisol starting to flow through their bodies (see Chapter 3). Or, with their self-esteem under attack, they will perhaps retreat into themselves, feeling helpless, fearful of experiencing once again, inadequacy and humiliation in front of their peers. If, on the other hand, the learning task is planned to build on the pupils' relative strengths, then there is a greater chance of a positive response.

Research into learning styles has seemingly run into a complicated blind alley with over fifty styles being claimed (Coffield *et al.* 2004), but the simplicity of Kolb's (1984) model remains persuasive. He identified four styles of learning: 'abstract conceptualisation', 'reflective observation', 'concrete experience' and 'active experimentation'. Cole *et al.* (1998) and Daniels *et al.* (1999) found that most children with BESD were reported as preferring the last two modes.

Developing young people's writing skills is clearly important. However, there can be some sympathy for a Year 10 girl, who complained to Daniels *et al.* (1999) about her mainstream school experience: 'All we do is write, write, write.' 'Get them writing' is an old piece of advice given to new teachers embarking on their careers in secondary schools, but teachers spoke persuasively of the dangers of an over-use of this approach. Too many writing tasks can underscore the weaknesses of learners with BESD. 'Getting them writing' also leaves less time for oral approaches such as group discussion, even though the latter is often enjoyed more by pupils (Duffield 1998) and can build on their skills with the spoken word.

Teaching can be helped by adapting the curriculum so that it involves many pupils' 'natural propensities' for the practical or sometimes creative and artistic, and the verbal rather the abstract or the written. Maybe even PE and sport can be used as vehicles for getting across aspects of other different subject areas. The BESD Guidance advises that the National Curriculum is used flexibly and that subjects do not have to be taught as discrete entities. For Key Stage 4 pupils, the advice to increase relevance to young people by stressing 'work-focused learning' is well founded.

If you are a primary school teacher or teaching assistant spending each day with a particular child it should be easier to identify the best types of approach. In secondary school, where contact is less, the challenge is greater but remains crucial. As the National Strategies and DCSF guidance stress, involving pupils in their work planning and assessment will help.

Flexible timetabling is also important. Full inclusion with their regular class for all of every lesson could be unwise in the short to medium term and some withdrawal for small group or individual work could be beneficial.

STAFF LANGUAGE AND COMMUNICATION

Bill Rogers' advice on building and maintaining relationships through your choice of calm and respectful language (spoken or unspoken) is particularly useful (Rogers 2000; see also Delaney 2008). Nonverbal language has been recognised as important for many decades (see Redl and Wineman 1952). Rogers recommends using previously agreed, privately understood signals between adult and the individual child with BESD (a simple example would be a 'thumbs up' or a disapproving look accompanied by lifting a finger). The aim is to use a non-obtrusive sign of disapproval – or encouragement. Rogers talks of the importance of 'directional' language – focusing on the desired behaviour rather than on the one we do not want, for example: 'I want you to wash your brush before putting it away' rather than 'Don't leave your brush like that!' or avoiding the unnecessarily negative 'I'm sick and tired of you talking!' by substituting 'Keep the noise down, Ryan, thanks!'. Rogers goes into detail that cannot be included here on the value of 'reminding language', which is often so appropriate for children with BESD, who can be genuinely forgetful of what has been asked or explained. Such memory lapses could also be explained by these children's minds being filled with unhappy thoughts or irrational anger or anxiety as a result of their biochemical balance being upset. A simple example would be the teacher saying 'slow down in the corridor' or using a previously agreed sign of two downward facing fingers, indicating 'walk!' to the child with BESD who sometimes runs.

Rogers (2000) urges teachers not to rush instructions and to use pauses to good effect: 'Stephen (pause), facing this way and listening, thanks.' He advises staff to allow 'take-up time', i.e. allowing the instruction or request 'to sink in' and for the child to do as requested – but not instantly. He goes into the advantages of 'tactical ignoring' (see also Redl and Wineman 1952), describing this as 'the teacher's conscious decision to ignore certain behaviour and keep the focus on the flow of the lesson, or on acknowledging and reinforcing positive behaviour' (p.111). He notes the difficulties of applying this but sees it as useful for pupils' 'whining, calling out, sulking and pouting, the "tsk, tsks" when you ask a student to pack up and the sighs' (p.111). See also Delaney (2008) on the effective use of silence as an aid to communication.

In contrasting situations, for example, where safety may be a factor, Rogers offers the old advice of saving the big voice for the big occasion. It may sometimes be necessary to raise your voice, to give the 'Stop!' command loudly in order to ensure the child's or group's attention is gained and they are ready to listen, but then, as soon as possible, drop the volume as you give an unambiguous command to move away or put something down or whatever other action is needed. As most experienced practitioners will advise less-aware newer colleagues, over-use of requests in a loud voice rapidly undermine a teacher's or teaching assistant's authority and will damage relationships with the child with BESD.

Staff can also be helped by mentors or other colleagues to reflect on and adapt the language they commonly use: cutting down the critical comments; replacing long and unnecessary phrases with crisp, assertive but positive alternatives; stripping out 'the don't's' and replacing them with 'dos'; using a volume and a tone of voice that does not inflame a situation; or, perhaps, avoiding the use of the spoken word altogether in some situations. Making positive language an inbuilt habit can be particularly useful in terms of building a better working relationship with an individual pupil with BESD and persuading him or her to behave in the ways you want them to.

Delaney (2008) suggests that it can be best to show the pupils that we are human by admitting to mistakes and by then attempting to find solutions by working together, thereby modelling to children social skills and how to repair relationships.

The advice in this above section applies to working with any child, but, if followed, can make a significant difference to how a volatile or perhaps seriously depressed child with BESD (whose body's biochemical balances may be unusual) responds to you. Using embedded positive language can make the difference between preventing and provoking very serious behavioural outbursts, and lifting or exacerbating a child's depressed mood.

REWARDING BEHAVIOUR TO ENCOURAGE A 'GROWTH' MINDSET

As described in Chapter 4, behaviourist-learning approaches, particularly seen in incentive and reward systems, have been found useful in reinforcing routines and good order. They have also helped to develop pro-social be-haviours in the individual child with BESD – and continue to do so in some circumstances. After observation and tallying of behaviours on frequency charts, specific target-setting can be discussed with the child, linked to clear-ly defined reinforcement. Systems can range from points or merit certificates to shop vouchers – the choice being made in negotiation with the pupil.

However, this type of approach does have its limitations and must not become bribery or appeasement characterised by 'empty praise' and easy reward-winning. Carol Dweck's (2006, 2009) work, recently popularised by the journalists (and parents) Bronson and Merryman (2009) in a chapter called 'The inverse power of praise', refers to recent studies showing the damage to which over-praising and rewarding can lead. An example is given in Meyer, Reisenzein and Dickhauser (2004) which indicates that by the age of twelve, pupils can believe that earning praise from a teacher is actu-ally a sign that they lack ability and that the teacher thinks they need extra encouragement. They have noticed that children who are falling behind receive lavish praise. Teenagers sometimes in fact believed it was teacher's criticism that showed a positive belief in the young person's ability.

Learners can believe that practitioners lavishly using praise are really saying that the pupils have reached the limits of their ability. Conversely, if staff use careful, constructive criticism the child thinks the teacher believes he or she can progress further and learn more. The over-praised child can become risk-averse, less persistent at difficult tasks and less independent learners – as well as more competitive and critical of others as they seek to preserve their self-image.

There is clearly a dilemma here for practitioners working with children with BESD. Rewards, praise and a culture of encouraging troubled and trou-blesome children remain very important. Children have to be encouraged to believe that it is worth making an effort, trying and trying again, sticking at tasks that are within their reach (i.e. in their ZPD). So, the manner in which, and the reasons for which, reinforcement is given are clearly key. Practitioners (and parents) have to be sincere in the praise they give, and have to relate it to specific and real achievement, which the child knows required effort with the child genuinely having tried hard. Lavish reward should not be attached to, say, gaining full marks on an easy test that the child knows required little effort on his or her behalf. Encouragement and reward should be given for concentrating on a task, making effort, sitting down with a teacher to examine where she/he went wrong and how she/he might do better when attempting the task afresh. This type of reward is more likely to induce the desired 'growth mindset', better equipping the pupil for improved future cognitive and social functioning. Bronson and Merryman (2009) conclude from a wide study of recent evidence that: 'A child deprived of the opportunity to discuss mistakes can't learn from them' (p.22). Brushing aside failure and just focusing on the positive is often not doing the child any favours.

The skilled practitioner will bear all the above considerations in mind and will know which reward is most motivating and appropriate for Ashley, Cheryl or Ryan – and also *how* it should be given. Repeated and quite lavish rewards may not be as effective as a simple smile of approval from a significant other. You will also be aware of *where* rewards and praise are best given – in full gaze of the pupil's peers at a celebration assembly or in front of the class, giving a deserved public boost that will be appreciated by the child (or will this, instead, diminish the young person's 'street cred'?). A reward might only be appreciated if given unobtrusively away from an audience, and delivered with the minimum of fuss.

BEHAVIOUR IN AND AROUND THE CLASSROOM

This section should be considered alongside the content of Chapter 8, which goes into more detail about helping children to regulate their emotions (including the management of anger).

Applying sanctions

Many pupils with BESD can and do accept sanctions or consequences perceived by them as fair – unless the young person has become very alienated from the school community and has very poor relationships with most staff. Government guidance on discipline and behaviour policies (DfES 2007a) outlines a range of common sanctions and the manner in which they should be given (section 3.6). It is important that sanction systems do not dominate approaches and that they avoid being mechanistic and punitive (thereby failing to achieve the necessary balance between overall fairness and allowing for individual capacity and difference). There are some children who always seem to be being punished – and to, sometimes, harmful effect. If suppression of unwanted behaviour is not working, more subtle, holistic approaches, described elsewhere in this book, are indicated. Rigidity in the application of sanctions can lead to the danger of simplistic interpretations of, for example, Assertive Discipline[2] (Canter 1990).

The application of sanction systems to the individual child must be accompanied by regular monitoring by school leaders or staff who are 'significant others' to the child. The style of this monitoring does not need to be punitive. For example, a headteacher was observed in a secondary school sitting next to a child at school dinner to chat to him informally at the same time as checking teacher entries on the pupil's lesson report card: the message was that it was the pupil's bad behaviour and not the child that had been criticised (Daniels *et al.* 1999).

Pre-arranged 'sanctuaries' for cooling off

The physical environment should be used as an aid to managing an individual child's extreme behaviour. It is helpful for there to be a comfortable *physical and private space* (a room or an area) to which a child can be directed or self-refer, to be used as a haven or sanctuary when the child is at risk of, or is actually, displaying a damaging behavioural outburst. If possible, this sanctuary will be close to, but separate from, their classrooms. A risk assessment should have been made of the likely scenarios following a particular child's challenging behaviour, e.g. following a violent outburst, and of the degree of supervision required actually provided. It can become part of a child's individual behaviour plan (understood by subject teachers and support staff) for this pupil to go to this designated space from class, or as an escape from the playground situation, when:

- they are losing control through anger
- they feel the need for 'time out' from provocative peers
- they are feeling overwhelmed by anxiety
- they need to talk with the specialist staff
- a subject teacher decides that the child's behaviour has become too disruptive.

Pupils can return from this sanctuary to rejoin their usual groups when they are ready, often when the biochemistry of their bodies has re-adjusted and their emotions are once again effectively self-regulated.

Beyond the classroom

Helping the child with BESD through the school day outside the classroom can be a challenge, requiring planning and regular review, as well as team work between teaching and support/care staff responsible for breaks and lunchtimes. Experiences outside class can clearly contribute to or detract from the child's 'availability for learning' (Greenhalgh 1994, p.1). For healthy social development, children need a mixture of structured and unstructured time, of being organised by adults with the growing child's interests at heart and of being allowed freedom to grow emotionally and socially through play and social interaction in school corridors, in school halls, dining area, on the playground or playing fields.

Planning of the child's day should cover arrangements for transport to school by taxi or bus (Laslett 1977) and, where relevant, breakfast club. At these times and throughout the day, how can the child be helped to avoid, or to cope with, possible teasing and scuffles in the playground or toilets or corridors? If senior staff, teachers and lunchtime supervisors as well as an allocated support assistant can work together according to a plan to keep a close eye on the child from the moment he arrives at school – perhaps asking peer mentors or 'buddies' to watch over him – the chances of settled behaviour in the classroom increases. Hopefully over time, this supervision will become unobtrusive and from a distance, allowing for greater freedom for the child and 'normal' interaction with his or her peers. Sometimes it is boredom that induces difficult behaviour, so the more the school offers by way of structured or semi-structured activities at break and lunchtime the better. Could the child with BESD be given individual activities to do (say on a computer) or gradually involved in semi-supervised group activities? If there is danger of an outburst, be clear which member of staff – or perhaps peer mentor – is to guide the child to the 'quiet zone' on the playground or into a calming corner of the classroom.

In terms of corridor behaviours it could be useful to rehearse procedures for walking along corridors from one lesson to the next. To help you anticipate and respond to 'trouble', it could be worth observing and recording days of the week, timings of problems when a particular child gets very upset or causes problems. Monday mornings, after a difficult weekend at home, is a common time to expect trouble.

In residential special schools and care homes, the sharing of food is held up by some writers (e.g. Dockar-Drysdale 1968) as presenting opportunities for the delivery of high-quality care and social interaction. It can be an important part of addressing basic needs and can be about far more than merely filling hungry stomachs. Cole *et al.* (1998) observed a few 'family-style' meals, which could be viewed as therapeutic experiences. More recent research via visits to boarding schools has shown such practice continuing in some very caring settings. There can be talk and controlled humour, turn-taking and the gentle coaxing of manners where staff and children sit at a table together. However, in an era of TV dinners and fast-food, the importance attached to the sharing of food in traditional style may seem less important. Certainly some 'good practice' schools have opted for cafeteria-style feeding, with staggered starting and finishing times. This approach can lessen the management problems of having a large number of volatile pupils close together, resulting in serious behavioural challenges, but, nonetheless, one feels that sometimes opportunities are being lost for cementing relationships between individual child and member of staff when they are no longer able to spend time at a meal table together.

Time outside the classroom can be a wasted opportunity when residential schools merely provide basic supervision, dinner, bed and breakfast. To borrow Miller and Gwynne's (1972, cited in Cole 1986) concept, staff 'warehouse' the pupils rather than adopt a 'horticultural' approach, which fosters personal growth through the provision in the care hours of good primary care mixed with a rich range of activities. The term '24-hour curriculum' is an exaggeration but it rightly stresses the need to consciously use breaktimes, evenings and (in seven-day boarding) weekends to aid the social and educational development of the pupils (while, of course, leaving sufficient time for relaxation and unstructured play).

Access to speedy back-up

When particularly challenging incidents occur in class, corridor or playground it is essential that fast assistance is on hand from experienced colleagues. Staff must not be isolated, without recourse to help for health and safety and, perhaps, safeguarding reasons but, also, so that other pupils do not experience excessive disruption. There will be times when even the very best of staff will need quick back-up. Cole et al. (1998) and Daniels et al. (1999) found such 'catcher systems' to be widely valued. Their role was to distance the pupil from the incident, give the child space to calm down and regain dignity and later to talk through what happened.

Of course, a correct balance has to be achieved. Front-line staff cannot relinquish their own responsibilities. They need to show their mettle by sorting out most challenges without assistance from colleagues. They have to retain control and work through challenges to their relationship with the child during the testing times. If they seek assistance too readily then pupils' respect for the adult will be diminished. It can become the norm for a child to manipulate a situation, to 'play up' in dramatic fashion merely to gain access to a senior member of staff, whose company the child enjoys or with whom she/he has a particularly good relationship. In weaker educational settings this can become a very time-consuming role, detracting from school leaders' other duties.

If a child becomes a regular source of very serious challenges then a Pastoral Support Plan might be appropriate (see Chapter 9).

HELPFUL USE OF SUPPORT STAFF

In recent years there has been a massive expansion in the use of teaching assistants and other support staff in class in order to help to reduce pressures on teachers. Blatchford *et al.* (2009) reported on this topic, although not with specific reference to children with BESD, so the benefits and disadvantages of this expanded support remain unclear for our purposes here. In terms of the general SEN population, teachers appreciate these arrangements and the supported children are thought to make social and behavioural gains but not necessarily academic progress. As Blatchford *et al.* (2009) point out:

> We have seen that teachers like this [support] because it then allows them to work with the rest of the class where the level of work is generally at a higher level. But it also means that the pupils in most need are often supported by staff with lower levels of subject knowledge, compared to teachers. (p. 134)

This is a drawback to which school leaders should give careful consideration in relation to the individual child with BESD. Is the child's educational potential being aided or hindered by the possible over-use of classroom support?

The quality of support provided is also likely to relate to the nature and extent of training that has been provided to the teaching assistant or other support worker, and possibly to issues such as career pathways – which are also matters for school leaders.

A third issue is the manner in which support is given to pupils with BESD. From the perspective of the child, what works best? Some children, often pupils with MLD as well as behaviour difficulties, are at ease having a support assistant physically beside them. Such pupils in secondary schools might have grown used to such an arrangement in their primary schools and have become heavily reliant on and even to expect and to enjoy the presence of support 'velcroed' to their side. In contrast, other pupils dislike being seen to be the recipients of such support, thinking this 'shows them up' in front of their peers. Schools need to consider how and when support should be offered, taking into account the feelings of the child. A support worker might bide her time and wait until the teacher is moving round a room offering support to other children so that it is not unusual or stigmatising for her to go over to help a child who is uneasy about her presence.

Useful support can also be offered by staff and volunteers not directly employed by the school. Pupils can value talking to the school nurse, visiting behaviour-support service teachers or youth workers. The ethnicity of helpers can also be a factor: Bengali children who received counselling from a Bengali educational welfare officer were appreciative, and black pupils often appreciate support from black adults (Daniels *et al.* 1999). The worth of adult mentors is increasingly being recognised, particularly where the mentor shares the same ethnic heritage (DfEE 1999).

HANDLING TRANSITIONS TO NEW CLASSES OR SCHOOLS

Transitions are difficult for all children and advice on handling them has particular importance for the child with BESD, who can be at his or her most troubled before and after a move to a new class or school – especially the move to secondary school. The contrast of being with a class teacher and perhaps a support worker they know in a small primary school and experiencing subject-based lessons taught by ten teachers in different rooms in a large secondary school often exacerbates BESD. Key Stage 4 pupils could also experience intense anxiety about moving on to Further Education college.

Staff who are trusted, liked and respected by children such as Ryan and Ashley need to prepare them for the transitions. It is helpful to talk through, and perhaps rehearse, scenarios, introducing them where possible to key people in the new setting. Some schools create 'Transition Groups' for vulnerable children to prepare them for new expectations and routines (see Grant and Duthie 2009). Visits should be made to the new school or college. Once the pupil has moved to the new setting, key staff should be helping the children with BESD adjust to the new setting, supporting them as necessary for months after the move.

REVIEW

We have looked in this chapter at ways of helping children such as Ashley or Ryan to become more open and 'available for learning' (Greenhalgh 1994), including strategic and tactical assessment and planning, responding to additional SENs, building in small steps on a child's strengths through personalised learning, rewarding progress but in a way that encourages a growth mindset, coping with behaviour difficulties in and around class, using support staff and paying close attention to major transitions. For the best outcomes, these factors should be considered in the context of the child's wider emotional well-being needs, to which we turn next.

NOTES

1   The ZPD is associated with the Russian L.S. Vygotsky and is discussed in detail in Daniels (2001). In layman's terms, ZPD is used to denote the new learning that is within the range of a child or adult at a given time, but only if the learner receives some support, for example, if the teacher provides the initial 'scaffolding' of the concept or task, in or on which the learner can build. The 'scaffolding' makes possible the learner's initial success but the student then moves on to grasp the concept or carry out the task unaided.

2   This approach originated in the USA. It is based on a firm set of rules, sanctions and rewards. It stresses that teachers have a right to teach and pupils have a right to learn. It can be applied across a whole school or individual classrooms. When misbehaviour first occurs, the teacher gives the child a warning (without punishment) but if the misbehaviour is repeated it leads to an increasing tariff of sanctions. Rewards may be stars, merit marks, playtime or prizes (see Montgomery 1999).

CHAPTER 8

WELL-BEING, MENTAL HEALTH AND THE INDIVIDUAL CHILD

There is considerable truth in the old adage 'It's good to talk!' Talking is at the heart of building well-being. We use spoken language to communicate, to comfort, to encourage, to have fun and to express feelings. It is central to creating and maintaining supportive relationships with children with BESD (and their parents and carers) and to tackling their troubled and troublesome behaviours and feelings – or filling their minds with happier thoughts.

However, the timing and type of talk needs to be appropriate and should also involve careful *listening*. Many children with BESD will have experienced years of being *talked at*. Also, the troubled young person might not want (or be able to find the words) to communicate with us through the spoken word. When directed at problem-solving, talking can precipitate negative patterns of thought and unhelpful rumination. Furthermore, McCarthy (2008) points out that children often succeed in saying more about their feelings and experiences by communicating *nonverbally*. Perhaps we, too, are stuck, not knowing what or how to communicate through speech – or we struggle to make sense of what a child is trying to say. It is often then better to build relationships, to help children feel better about themselves, through *doing*. We can encourage positive thinking and well-being through play, physical activity or art involving little talking.

In this chapter, after looking at factors in building and sustaining relationships, we consider the capacity of talking (including 'active listening') and doing approaches to building well-being and to repairing damage in individual young lives. We then move on to safeguarding and positive physical handling (including touch). There follows an extended section on handling negative emotions (intervening early to prevent crises; sensitive handling during and after an angry outburst). Discussion then moves to cognitive-behaviourist approaches to promoting more positive thinking (including mindfulness and 'solution-focused brief' approaches). Later in the chapter we consider responses to mental-health difficulties commonly present in the troubled individual child (responding to panic attacks, unhappiness associated with loss, parental separation or bereavement self-harm and eating disorders).

FACTORS IN CREATING A HELPFUL RELATIONSHIP WITH A CHILD WITH BESD

Skilled practitioners often say *the* key to success with children with BESD is to 'work through relationships'. But what does that mean and how can it be achieved in a busy lesson or, usually, a group situation outside class? The answer is that it is very difficult and takes time, determination and great commitment – particularly with children like Cheryl or Ryan or Ashley. Given their past experiences of life (being let-down, being ignored, being loved then pushed away, being maltreated), such children can be very suspicious of adult attempts to get closer – that is, to make helpful reciprocal relationships possible. They can react with further 'acting out' behaviour as a defence mechanism, continuing to test you, to see if you really care, see their good side and believe in them – to check you will stick with them in the long term. The term 'unconditional positive regard' is a powerful way of stressing that staff working successfully with children with BESD will go that degree further in terms of commitment and empathy, to form the crucial relationship from which helpful intervention proceeds. As one experienced practitioner said: 'It's about being there for the kids...you give of yourself and they see you give' (see Cole *et al.* 1998).

Gradually the child can be convinced that you are worthy of his or her trust and respect, as someone who gives them some of what they need and that you are a model whose behaviour is worth copying. You become a person they wish to please – and whose goodwill and care they do not wish to lose. Children with BESD sense your values and your feelings about them (Redl 1939 in Cole *et al.* 1998; Ofsted 2003) and, as the earlier discussion of neuroscience has suggested, children use their 'emotional brain' (particularly the limbic system) to a far greater extent than adults. As their prefrontal cortex is not fully developed they are able to read and respond to nonverbal clues more quickly, thus sensing your feelings towards them.

Building the necessary positive relationship will be helped if you:

- reach out to the child through sharing the child's life a little – beyond teaching your subject(s). Work at creating an *emotional* link with them through

- o making time to talk (e.g. in the corridor, after lessons), using regular small exchanges of friendly and encouraging words, showing you notice them and see them as worthy of your attention

- o listening to what they have to say and viewing this as important, wherever possible giving them your full attention

- o learning more about their life (e.g. about their family and home), so you develop the knowledge to show empathy and understanding when events beyond the classroom are particularly hard for them

- o storing what they tell you, gradually creating a memory bank to which you can refer in future conversations

- o remembering their achievements or examples of doing things right, how they were successful in confronting problems in a pro-social way – or how they avoided angry outbursts, so you can refer back to this later

- o remembering their birthdays

- establish what they like and take an interest in, e.g. football, types of music

- do as many activities as you can *with* them, sharing life experiences, e.g. go on school trips so they see you outside your usual classroom role, hopefully sharing an activity that is fun and captures the child's interest

- appreciate their strengths and seek to build on these

- encourage them frequently in a way that builds a growth mindset, finding the methods of praise to which the pupil is most receptive

- involve them in discussions about their work and problems

- trust them to do jobs (i.e. tasks they can complete partly to please you, partly to show they can be trusted to help)

- being firm but fair – at the same time knowing their individual traits where some flexibility is needed (a challenge!). There are times when structures/rules need to be a little flexible. (Cheryl might argue with some logic, 'We're all different! It's not fair if we're all treated the same'.)

- demonstrate you care by sticking up for them, acting as their advocate when they are blamed wrongly or their needs are ignored

- model behaviour that shows patience, respect, good humour and calmness for the child to copy

- engage the child through humour and gentle banter – of course, avoiding put-downs or sarcasm posing as humour
- when reprimanding the child, do it in a way that 'depersonalises' the issue. Soon after, seek to praise or encourage them, remind them you still value them
- split the bad things they do from the child itself – still see good in them. Show this through spoken words such as 'Ashley, doing that was *not* like you!'
- do not harbour grudges – forgive
- use first names and engaging 'I' language ('I want you to…' rather than a straight command), which, while being assertive and expecting compliance, builds rapport between you and the child.

TALKING AND LISTENING

We avoid the use of the terms 'counselling' and 'therapy'. In the hands of trained CAMHS professionals, person-centred and/or psychodynamic counselling and cognitive behaviour therapy do have an important role to play. However, those of us who are not fully qualified counsellors or therapists must not go beyond our levels of competence, although we can still use aspects of what these professionals do – such as using 'active listening'. This means genuinely absorbing what the children think and say, treating their views with respect and, where possible, responding to their ideas in and outside the classroom. It can be a challenge to work active listening routinely into pressured daily lives where usually staff are responsible for large groups of children (in this respect we can envy CAMHS professionals, who tend to work one-to-one or with small groups) but we do need to try to develop a high-level of skill in this area.

A good listener shows warmth and empathy, gives a child quality time, paying careful and undivided attention, and perhaps arranging for the interview or chat to take place in a private, quiet and comfortable place. A good listener:

- respects the child's feelings
- accepts as important that which the child sees as important
- does not offer unhelpful advice (e.g. 'You don't need to worry about that…'; 'When I was your age, I did not…')
- is non-judgemental
- helps the child to find words to express their feelings

- re-assures the child
- answers questions with honesty (rather than answer questions that should be, but have not been asked…)
- respects silence – does not rush to fill gaps in talk
- is aware of/takes account of cultural issues (e.g. degree of eye contact that a child is likely to be comfortable with)
- senses what the child does *not* say.

You can demonstrate your listening and hearing by 'reflecting back' ideas to show the child that you have understood what she/he has said. When doing this it is best to keep sentences almost as short as the child uses; to use some of the child's own words; to re-phrase questions that were not fully understood. The child could be asked to repeat what they have said they will do, to check that they have understood what they are agreeing to.

There are other aspects of active listening. Ask questions to establish meaning or to encourage the child to explore feelings. Use some *open* questions, i.e. those that allow some explanation in response rather than just a 'yes' or 'no' answer. (Instead of 'Do you like music/sport?' try 'What music/sport do you like?'.) Whilst a child is giving you an explanation, remember to keep conveying your interest, looking at them, nodding occasionally, and encouraging them to talk more.

It is dangerous to promise to keep a secret as promising this and then having to break such a commitment (e.g. if the child raises a child-protection issue) will affect the child's trust in you and other adults. If information has to be shared with someone else, give the child a choice in how this is done – it is always better if they can say something themselves, but accept that this may not always be possible. For example, if they are struggling with a topic in class, but their teacher is not aware of this, encourage them to tell their teacher, or offer to talk to the teacher yourself.

Sedgewick *et al.* (2005) warn that sometimes children will surprise you and may choose to talk to you about child-protection issues. If this happens, the organisation you work for will have child-protection procedures and these should be followed. Always explain to the child/young person what you are doing at each stage.

USING ART, CREATIVE ACTIVITIES AND PLAY

Art and craft, working with textiles, drama and music as well as wider creative expression (using imaginative computer programs or simple film-making techniques) should be an important component of the curriculum for children with BESD. Such approaches can have a powerful healing potential and have proved their popularity and worth in mainstream settings, special schools and PRUs for decades.

Art, creative activities and play can perform the Positive Psychology function of promoting well-being and self-esteem, because children with BESD enjoy them, believe they can get better at them and can often achieve considerable success in these areas. They offer opportunities for young people to become motivated, to get into Positive Psychological flow, thereby displacing at least temporarily sapping feelings of depression or stressful emotion. Art and creative work can play to children's strengths, which often lie in physical construction or figurative or 'modern' art work – rather than in formal 'reading and writing' classwork. These activities require experiential and experimental practical work – learning styles that tend to be favoured by children with BESD.

Also in the hands of skilled practitioners, art, creativity and play can be used therapeutically to explore feelings and to help young people come to terms with their problems. It is unlikely that many readers are qualified art or play therapists and we should be wary of amateur psychotherapy, but some activities can be used to open up opportunities. Talking with young children about worries is often helped if they are encouraged to draw or paint or work with clay. Sometimes depression is conveyed better in children's drawings than in their conversation (Barker 1995). Drama (informal, self-scripted or more traditional plays) can also be a powerful aid to addressing mental-health difficulties.

Therapeutic play can be aided by use of puppets or small toys. Children tend to reveal their preoccupations – both likes and dislikes – in play, and skilled observation can help understanding and the identification of ways of helping. It could be that the children indulge in a healing 'regression' to an earlier age – perhaps because they missed out on age-appropriate play when young. Structured and sometimes 'free play' can also foster social skills, which help the child with severe BESD to feel better about themselves.

SPORT AND EXERCISE

As indicated in Chapter 3, nowadays much more is being discovered about how physical activity – particularly exercise – can help boost the production of helpful brain-chemicals that have a positive effect on our moods (Department of Health 2004a.) Exercise:

- might be as effective for treating depression as psychotherapy

- helps to counteract phobias and panic attacks
- makes many people feel happier and more satisfied
- can promote social interaction/relationship building by getting people to go out and join groups.

It is therefore unsurprising that the Government is encouraging physical exercise as a way of assisting mental-health promotion, as well as dealing with the growing obesity epidemic.

Also of interest is research into national curriculum areas most enjoyed by children with BESD. This indicates that physical activity is one of the most popular parts of the curriculum (Cole *et al.* 1998), although for some – perhaps relating to body form or aptitude – it may be the most threatening, which can be a real challenge for teachers. Children with health and weight-related issues can find physical activities and timetabled PE difficult, particularly in today's society where they are constantly subjected to pictures of perfect body images that they cannot relate to. This group of children are often the target for bullying, particularly before and after physical activity, and staff should be sensitive to their needs and differentiate activities to encourage participation.

What opportunities are there for you and your colleagues to extend the range of physical, sometimes sporting, activity in the settings in which you work? What sports/physical activities are most motivating for the children you work with? It could be helpful to spend time thinking of ways around the obvious obstacles: lack of time, resources, staff skills – as well as health and safety issues.

THE APPROPRIATE USE OF PHYSICAL CONTACT

It is important to recognise children's need for affection and to acknowledge that they can sometimes benefit from an appropriate and agreed use of touch – the adult's arm round an upset child's shoulder, touching the lower arm as a sign of concern, holding a young pupil's hand; or responding to distress with a shoulder hug of reassurance. These are signs of liking and accepting a child. Indeed, it has been suggested that in the context of child-care: 'Touch is not only nice but necessary' (Keating, cited in Cole *et al.* 1998). Sunderland (2007) notes how appropriate touch can stimulate the brain to produce soothing chemicals – surely a factor that should be viewed as very important. Massage has been persuasively proposed as a way of easing stress and BESD (Bergren 2007). Appropriate physical contact is a natural and important part of creating warm, positive relationships, particularly for younger pupils – and staff in schools should feel freer to use it as part of their normal repertoire within the context of a described and agreed policy shared with stakeholders.

Recent guidance on what is termed 'Use of Force' (DCSF 2007b, paragraph 64) does allow that:

> There are occasions when physical contact with a pupil may be proper or necessary other than those covered in section 93 of the Education and Inspections Act of 1996. Some physical contact may be necessary to demonstrate exercises or techniques during PE lessons, sports coaching, or CDT, or if a member of staff has to give first aid. Young children and those with SEN may need staff to provide physical prompts or help. Touching may also be appropriate where a pupil is being congratulated or praised, or where the pupil is in distress and needs comforting. Teachers will use their own professional judgement when they feel a pupil needs this kind of support.

This seems a minimal and uncertain endorsement of what should be seen as a basic caring or instructional approach, worthy of open and confident support. There is passing reference to other guidance on the *Every Child Matters* site but paragraph 64 is all that is risked in DCSF (2007b). The very next paragraph 65 offers advice on the dangers of using touch (this advice, it is agreed, is sensible) because of cultural background or experience of abuse, 'There may be some pupils for whom touching is particularly unwelcome' and 'Physical contact with pupils becomes increasingly open to question as pupils reach and go through adolescence.' The guidance then goes on to warn staff to be aware that innocent physical contact can be misconstrued. They are clearly concerned about the links that can easily – and often wrongly – be made between physical touch and child abuse (indeed, these paragraphs appear under the sub-title: 'Dealing with complaints and allegations').

Hard evidence is lacking but we are left with the impression that too many staff are discouraged from using one of the most natural and effective ways of showing care and sustaining a healthy relationship. It is encouraging to observe that in some settings, appropriate touch is still used – and to very good effect. We can only hope that there will be a change in attitudes at national and local government level, so staff feel freer and better supported in this area.

'POSITIVE HANDLING' OR 'USE OF FORCE'

A guide to working with children with BESD would be incomplete without consideration of the fraught area of physical intervention. We are aware that highly experienced staff, trying to act in the interests of the child with BESD, or other children or of their colleagues, have made physical interventions and then found themselves the victims of distorted allegations made by pupils or parents (ATL 2009). No clear-cut advice can be given in a page or so, and practitioners therefore need to be alert to changes in government guidance on this area and also in guidance that might not sit easily alongside it on 'safeguarding' and children's and parents' rights to complain. Managerial staff must ensure that their own work setting has clear procedures and that staff are trained to a high level of preparedness and competence, and regularly refresh and update their skills. The aim should always be on avoiding 'use of force' through de-escalation or avoidance techniques (as approved courses that include physical interventions will stress) but some physical intervention will be inevitable.

The guidance in DCSF (2007b) was current in early 2010.[1] Rather than talk of 'restrictive physical intervention' (RPI) or 'physical restraint', this was entitled 'Use of Force'. This document states that the guidance is not a definitive statement of law as that is for courts to determine. However, the guidance is in addition to a common law right to use reasonable force in self-defence. The law governing 'Use of Force' is Section 93 of the Education and Inspections Act 2006, which says that school staff are able to use such force 'as is reasonable in the circumstances to prevent a pupil from doing, or continuing to do,' any of the following:

- committing any offence, or what would be an offence if child were older

- causing personal injury to or damage to property of any person

- prejudicing the maintenance of good order and discipline at the school or among any pupils receiving education at the school, whether during a teaching session or otherwise.

The guidance is for teachers or any person authorised by a head to supervise children at the school.

Then the 'fence-sitting' begins that leaves professionals working with challenging children with BESD in such an exposed and invidious position. The degree of support they receive from school leaders, governors, local authority or children's services or police (who ought to be consistently more realistic and understanding of school and care staff working with such challenging children) seems variable.

DCSF (2007b, paragraph 13) says there is no legal definition of when it is reasonable to use force. It depends on the circumstances of individual cases. The 'force' used should be the minimum needed to achieve the desired result. Those with disabilities can be restrained but should not be treated 'less favourably' than those without disabilities.

The section called 'Effective Practice for Schools' wisely advises the following:

- *(para. 18)* Schools should have an explicit policy on the use of reasonable force to control or restrain pupils: this should be communicated to parents and carers

- *(para.19)* no school should have a policy of 'no physical contact' as this denies statutory rights to teachers

- *(para. 23)* involve the SENCo in creating and reviewing 'Use of Force' policy.

The SENCo should be active in working with other staff, the child and parents to work out positive handling plans for individual pupils assessed as likely to need RPI. These 'positive handling plans' are to set out in written form techniques to be used in school records. These techniques should be compatible with a child's statement of SEN.

Paragraphs 34–38 advise on the actual 'use of force'. There then follows a section on staff training (paragraphs 39–42). Schools should set out their approach to relevant training for staff in the use of force:

- *(para. 39)* 'A school may decide that all staff who supervise pupils should have such training. However, individuals have statutory power to use force by virtue of their job. So a school policy cannot lawfully prevent teachers or other staff whose job involved having control or charge of pupils from using that power regardless of whether they have received training…'

- *(para. 40)* 'There will be particular training needs for staff working closely with pupils with SEN and/or disabilities. Risk assessments will help inform decision about staff training…'

- *(para. 42)* Training should include avoiding or defusing situations – particularly important for those working with SEN.

- Schools should identify and address training needs of staff. Reference is then made to DfES and DoH funding for BILD (the British Institute for Learning Disabilities), who assess, approve and supervise organisations providing training.

After each incident, recording and reporting are very important and paragraphs 43–55 offer advice on this, linking to a model recording form. Parents should be told of any incident. Staff are advised to attend to first aid needs and to consider if other agencies, e.g. CAMHS, should be involved. The guidance also talks of 'holding the pupil to account', e.g. punishing, giving opportunity for reparations, deciding whether exclusion might be the correct course of action. It is important to plan with the pupil so as to avoid a repetition. It is also important to support any emotional stress or loss of confidence in staff or pupil; to reflect, analyse and learn from an incident.

Finally, likely to send a frisson of unease through practitioners is the following from paragraph 59:

> 'Parents and pupils have a right to complain about actions taken by school staff. This might include the use of force. Schools need to make that clear.'

If a specific allegation of abuse is made against a member of staff then the school needs to follow the guidance set out in the current government advice on safeguarding children.

SAFEGUARDING ISSUES

Given the deeply troubled lives of many pupils with BESD, you may have serious worries about safeguarding/child-protection issues. You may have noticed features such as unusual mood, bruising, signs of physical neglect or possible after-effects of alcohol or substance abuse, likely to be associated with the child's life beyond school. It is important that such concerns are shared with colleagues and you know your school's procedures for reporting and referring on concerns.

You may also worry about events within school. Is the child falling into the 'wrong company', perhaps becoming a perpetrator or bystander to or victim of teasing or bullying? It is important to act early, even if your suspicions are weak. If you are not clear about the path to follow, talk to senior colleagues who *do* know – even if they decide that you are unnecessarily worried. This topic has been thoroughly covered in other publications, with Cowie and Jennifer (2008) offering a research-based account of effective approaches to reducing the impact of bullying at whole-school, class and individual level.

A HEALING APPROACH TO ANGER MANAGEMENT

There are few more stressful experiences for staff than the angry outbursts of children with BESD. The frequency of these, and the apparent triviality of the cause, might suggest learned behaviour or could perhaps be explained by the biochemical balances and circuitry of a child's brain – or a combination of both factors (see Chapter 3). A responsive and understanding approach is needed to volatile patterns of behaviour, intervening early in a preventive way wherever possible.

An outburst of anger can be viewed as the shape of a volcano, as shown in Figure 8.1.[2] From its summit, the volcano throws out rivers of magma as the child is out of control, hi-jacked by the alarm systems of the brain. She/ he is physically unable to respond logically to reason or logic. The explosion, if it cannot be avoided, is the time when a child's upper brain (his or her rational system in the cortex) has been pushed aside by the primitive instincts and emotions in the lower brain or limbic system. Progress from 'trigger(s)' (Stage 1) to 'calm regained' (Stage 6) can take an hour and a half or longer as the child's self-regulation system re-asserts itself and brings the brain chemicals back 'into synch'.

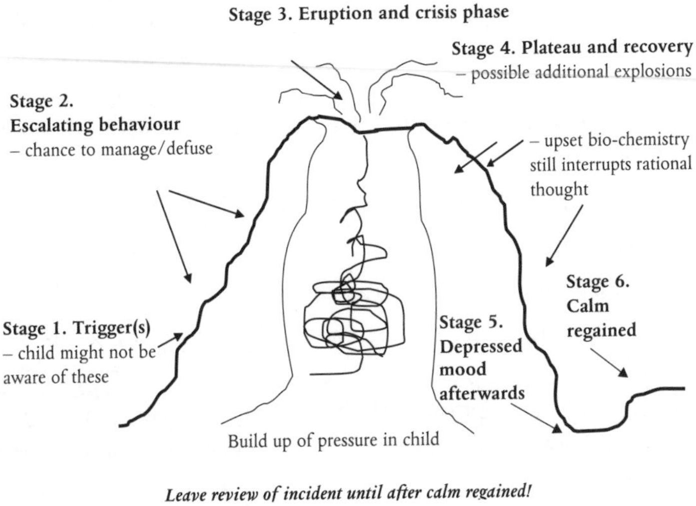

Stage 3. Eruption and crisis phase

Stage 4. Plateau and recovery
– possible additional explosions

Stage 2.
Escalating behaviour
– chance to manage/defuse

– upset bio-chemistry
still interrupts rational
thought

Stage 6.
Calm
regained

Stage 1. Trigger(s)
– child might not be
aware of these

Stage 5.
Depressed
mood
afterwards

Build up of pressure in child

Leave review of incident until after calm regained!

Figure 8.1: The 'Anger volcano'

There should be well-rehearsed strategies worked out ahead with an 'at risk' child. These can include preventative approaches as part of the pupil's educational and social individual programme (e.g. asking the child to keep a log over a period of weeks of what makes him/her angry, identifying triggers and supportive responses – see examples in Faupel *et al.* 1998). Triggers to outbursts might include the child interpreting events or situations as:

- a threat to feelings of belonging to the group
- safety or property being threatened
- being shown up in front of others
- frightening, anxiety-inducing events
- reminders of past failure or difficulty.

At Stage 1 (see Figure 8.1) you might see the beginnings of physical arousal in a child such as Ashley (see Chapter 1) as the brain demands more oxygen, and the heart has to work harder to gather energy stored in the muscles. You can first observe quickened shallow breathing, then blushing as the body temperature rises. There may be signs of sweating as the body tries to regulate its temperature. There may be indications of the child becoming agitated as blood flow leaves the digestive system to work elsewhere. The child may need to go to the toilet or be aware of 'butterflies' in his stomach or bowel. Sometimes this physiological response to fear (which causes the anger) can frighten the child further and it is important to work with the child to help identify the dangerous catalysts and the reactions they experience.

At the trigger(s) stage, the child can still be responsive to skilled intervention. Prompt action can allow the cortisol levels in his body to subside. He could be

- taught breathing exercises that calm his body down
- given a drink of water
- provided with comfort and security
- moved away from the source of his anger to a pre-arranged sanctuary.

We need to avoid exacerbating a child's feelings by questioning or starting a premature inquest. You could respond by offering the child some of the following:

- **active listening**
- **relocation** – moving the child away from the threatening place
- **'attention diverters':** do something different, e.g. chosen from a set of activities you know the child enjoys and that will take his or

her mind off the anger. This could involve humour, a powerful tool if used carefully

- **breathing techniques** – getting the child to breathe evenly and quite deeply or using approaches described later (see p178)
- other **relaxation techniques:** use relaxing music; or rehearsed 'self-talk'; visualise a favourite place – suggesting a physical technique, e.g.'Starting with the toes, consciously relax the muscles, working up through your legs, tummy, back, arms, shoulders, neck, face and scalp – until completely relaxed' (see Mindfulness, p.172)
- **'tension releasers'** – Long and Fogell (1999) and McCarthy (2008) note that physical activity can help children release their anger, e.g. modelling with clay, tearing paper for a beanbag, but they warn that excessive activity such as punching pillows or shouting out can leave children even angrier, sustaining the body's production of stress and arousal bio-chemicals.

In Stage 2 (see Figure 8.1) the *escalation phase*, there is still a chance, although this is fast reducing, to intervene before the explosion. The child's body is calling on its basic survival instincts deep in its 'reptilian brain' and is choosing 'fight' rather than 'flight' (see Chapter 3). There will be physical signs – tensions in the muscles, rapid breathing, red faces going *white*, speech might become quicker and louder. She/he will become obsessed with the perceived cause of the anger. As an automatic defence mechanism and bio-logical response, the stress hormone cortisol floods the child's prefrontal cortex thereby preventing thought and reason. At this stage the child will interpret neutral or calming behaviours (spoken or body position/stance, eye contact) as aggressive.

Staff should avoid comments likely to provoke, such as 'Pull yourself to-gether!' or 'Don't start!' or 'I thought you were more grown up than that!', as well as nonverbal signals that might be seen by the child as aggressive. Try speaking more quietly, avoiding direct eye-contact and sitting down rather standing near the pupil. Lown (2001) warns that once the child is well into the escalation stage only techniques familiar to and rehearsed by the child will have a chance of success. Staff should have worked out what the child is likely to do well ahead and to have planned suitable responses. If Stage 3 is reached and the volcano does erupt, are you familiar with your work-place's policy on handling the 'crisis phase'? Has this policy been thought through in relation to individual children such as Ashley?

The crisis and the plateau and recovery stages can last a long time and will, of course, be influenced by staff responses. We should pay attention to:

- **Posture:** keep hands visible, unfolded and palms visible; be at same level as child
- **Proximity:** Keep a reasonable space away – up to a metre
- **Eye-contact:** Allow the child to look away: do not stare or totally avoid eye-contact
- **Voice tone:** speak calmly but firmly making clear what is expected
- **Remove dangerous props**
- **'Fire drill':** other children should be told what to do (possibly leave the classroom. A named child goes to summon help from other adults) (Long and Fogell 1999; Lown 2001; Powell 2000).

Be wary of making physical interventions (see earlier section), although these might be unavoidable for health and safety reasons.

During Stage 4, the plateau and recovery phase (see Figure 8.1), there remains a danger of secondary or tertiary outbursts. This phase can last a long time and even longer if the child is subject to more 'triggers'. Their brain chemicals are still out of balance, hiding an often vulnerable and confused child. Tears do not mean recovery of a balanced rational state. During this phase, a child's guilt feelings could start to emerge. This period, requiring patience and a soothing approach as the pupil regains control, brings challenges for staff in mainstream schools particularly. There is a temptation – perhaps pressure – to send for senior staff members and to be seen publicly to disapprove of, or punish, such behaviours, even though the outburst was beyond a child's control. Where the roles and approaches of senior staff are not clear, or where there is an expectation that they will discipline the pupil in order to regain control (or make an example of the pupil to deter future outbursts) the situation can be made worse.

As the recovery phase progresses, and to ease the child's passage through the common experience of depressed mood, unhappiness and damaged self-worth at the end of the natural cycle (Stage 5), we can consider applying 'emotional first aid' (Redl and Wineman 1952). This can be more difficult to achieve in a large, mainstream school – but not impossible. What choices could such children be given about how and where to recover? In some settings, the child might be offered a drink, rest, warmth and perhaps appropriate physical contact and a soothing talk with a member of staff who is close to the child. They might appreciate time alone or a breath of fresh air or supervised walk that will stimulate calming bio-chemicals in the body. We should be flexible in the way we organise specialist BESD provision to allow emotional first aid to happen.

Any inquest into why the outburst happened should not start until much later when Stage 6, calm regained (see Figure 8.1), is finally reached – and then a direct discussion of the sequence of events may be unhelpful, merely exacerbating the child's negative thoughts about self and his or her surrounding world. It is advisable to avoid 'why?' questions that can re-ignite the anger. It might help to re-interpret the incident as one in which the child lacked the skills to get his or her needs met by calmer, more rational means. Discussion might involve looking for ways to help the child (and maybe others) to put things right and at how to handle situations better the next time. Rosoman (2008) offers a range of materials to use with a child to help manage his/her anger.

APPLYING COGNITIVE BEHAVIOURAL PRINCIPLES TO PRACTICE

We noted that children with BESD can have distorted thought processes ('cognitions'), which give them a skewed and, at times, unnecessarily pessimistic view of their own abilities or of the world around them. They attribute the good things that happen to them to external factors and the bad things to themselves and to their traits, which they think that they cannot alter. If we can help them to alter this thinking, we can assist them in changing mood, feelings and behaviour.

It can be useful to sit down with individual troubled children and together break down a perceived problem into its parts. A situation or event gives rise to:

- thoughts
- emotions
- physical feelings
- actions.

Each area can affect the others. How the child thinks about a problem can affect how the child feels physically and emotionally. Helping the child to analyse the situation like this can also alter what the child does about it.

There are contrasting ways of reacting to most situations, depending on how you think about them. Imagine yourself as a child with whom you work. You have had a bad morning in class (or evening in a residential special school) and feel depressed. As you walk down the corridor, someone you thought was your friend walks by and seems to ignore you. There is an unhelpful and a helpful way of interpreting what has happened (see Table 8.1).

Table 8.1: Unhelpful and helpful framing of events

	Unhelpful	Helpful
Thoughts	She/he 'blanked' me – she does not like me anymore	She/he looked worried – I wonder if something is wrong?
Emotional feelings	Low, sad and rejected	Concerned for the other person
Physical	Sinking feeling, low energy, nausea	None – feel comfortable
Action	Avoid the 'ex' friend when you meet in the playground	Speak to him/her to make sure all is well

The same situation has led to two contrasting results, depending on how the child thought about the situation. How the child thought affected what she/he *felt* and *did*. In the left-hand column of Table 8.1, the child jumps to a conclusion with little evidence – and this *matters*, because it has led to uncomfortable feelings and unhelpful behaviour that reinforce the child's bad feelings about him/herself. However, the child is helped to follow the actions in the right-hand column, there is a chance she/he will feel better about him/herself.

Fox (2001) gives good advice on how a child should be helped to build up a repertoire of 'best beliefs' to counter their old ingrained negative thought patterns. Rosomon (2008) offers photocopiable forms that could also be useful for you to use with children with distorted or overly pessimistic internal working models (IWMs) and depressed views of the world (see Chapter 3 re IWMs). Rosomon suggests the professional asks the child to fill in various forms – titled as follows:

- *Finding my positive qualities* ('What do I like about yourself? What do I do well – if not perfectly? What do other people compliment me on? What qualities do I value in others? Which do I share (even if only in some small way)? (p.229)
- *Good things about ME!*
- *What makes ME special!*
- *Nice things people say about ME!* (Rosomon 2008, pp.227–8)

These are just a few of the useful pages in this excellent resource book.

Elliott and Place (1998) suggest that cognitive behaviour approaches should be linked to reward-giving (although do remember 'mindset' considerations when giving rewards – see p.85). They suggest interspersing talking therapy (which could be practitioner and child in an informal 'counselling session') with routine sessions of physical activity or regularly playing favourite games 'to intrude upon the gloomy mood and, if well chosen, to give islands of positive feeling which can be gradually expanded and intensified' (p.184). In advocating the latter, they are reflecting the Positive Psychology described in Chapter 4. If focusing on an enjoyable activity helps the young person into a healing kind of psychological flow (see p.93) then that will be of further benefit and is likely to displace, at least for a time, negative thoughts and behaviour in the troubled young person. If you know children like Cheryl and Stephen and Cameron well, you are likely to be familiar with what captures their imagination, fires their motivation and induces Positive Psychological flow.

Squires (2002) is also recommended on ways in which you can help change children's thinking.

MINDFULNESS

In Chapter 4 we looked at mindfulness and its message that if we use all our senses to focus on the here and now state of our body and its immediate environment we can displace 'negative automatic thoughts' (NATs – see Wilding and Milne 2008) and escape from bouts of unhealthy rumination (that is, vainly churning over NATs again and again, thereby exhausting ourselves and increasing our depression). Being mindful, was seen by Williams *et al.* (2007) and Crane (2009) as a way of tapping into our natural ways of becoming calmer and content. Full training in mindfulness took months but we can adopt some useful ideas in educational settings.

The potential benefit in focusing on our breathing has already been noted earlier (p.168). The breath is seen by Williams *et al.* (2007) as a powerful way of diverting ourselves away from unhappy, stressful thoughts about past and future. Crane (2009) devotes a short chapter to 'The Three Minute Breathing Space' or '3MBS', saying (p.119) that this is essentially a 'mini-meditation' that could be incorporated into the working day to relieve stress or angry feelings. It has three steps:

- **Awareness** – Getting us to step out of auto-pilot, recognising our current experience. Having adopted an erect and dignified posture, either sitting or standing and possibly closing our eyes, we should ask 'What is my experience now?' Identify the *thoughts* in your mind; the *feelings* you have, facing any sense of emotional discomfort or unpleasant feelings, acknowledging their presence; the *body sensations*, picking up on tense muscles or frowning face or aches in the back.

- **Gathering** – Bring your attention to the sensations of each normal breath feeling the sensations of the air entering your nostrils, throat and windpipe, sensing the movement of the chest as the air comes in then falls away as you breathe out. You are advised to follow the breath all the way in and all the way out. By concentrating on your breathing you become embedded in the present moment, hopefully to the exclusion of negative thoughts on past worries or future stresses.

- **Expanding** – You are now advised to expand your awareness, becoming mindful of what is happening to your body beyond your breathing. Examine the sensations in the rest of your body, your posture, your facial expression, your shoulders, your legs. If you become aware of sensations of discomfort or tension, you should imagine yourself 'breathing into them on each in-breath and breathing out of them on each out-breath' (Williams *et al.* 2007, p.184), helping them to relax.

Repetition of the '3MBS' a few times a day is recommended by these eminent scientists (Williams is a clinical psychology professor at Oxford University).

Williams *et al.* (2007) also advocate the 'body scan', which might take the form of stressed children lying down and relaxing on an exercise mat. With eyes closed, they are asked to 'fall awake' by sensing their breathing and imagining the breath passing through the different parts of the body in turn – left leg, left foot, toes, right leg, right foot, toes, left arm, right arm, neck, back and so on. If they become aware of tension in any part then they are asked to 'breath into' where the stress is identified. Procedures such as these are claimed to help people relax even to the point where they get a calm, floating sensation in their bodies.

Williams *et al.* (2007) also suggest the 'Mindful Awareness of the Hands' exercise. They suggest you bring your attention to your hands then

> allow your awareness to fill your hands from inside to outside, from bones right out to the skin itself and fingernails. Open in awareness to any and all sensations in the fingertips, in the fingers, sensing the air between and around the fingers, feeling how it feels on the back of the hands. (p.101)

You are then asked to feel the sensation of touching the chair you are sitting on and thinking of the sensations experienced. 'Mindful walking' is also commended – not walking purposefully from A to B but without a destination, taking small steps while being aware of the small sensations of walking, the flexing of the muscles, the feeling of the foot against the ground. The aim is to be aware of your body as it is, not to achieve relaxation – although the latter can often be the outcome.

In the light of this research and the opinion of some colleagues working in the BESD field, it seems reasonable to extrapolate this kind of approach to highly strung children or depressed 'acting in' pupils, perhaps to be used alongside therapeutic massage (see p.162) or other ways of inducing a flow of calming neurotransmitters through our bodies. DCSF (2010) gives a video example of Tai Chi being used with children with BESD to similar relaxing effect.

SOLUTION-FOCUSED BRIEF APPROACHES

SFBA can take the lid off deep feelings in the child and family, which might then need more specialist support from CAMHS professionals. Nevertheless, educational practitioners without accredited qualifications can use aspects of this approach to good effect. A series of quality-time, one-to-one sessions between a skilled worker and a child can lead to beneficial change.

As the heading above states, this approach *focuses on solutions* and is *brief*, stretching over a few sessions (not over months or years, as can be the case with psychotherapy or person-centred counselling). It is therefore more affordable and, unsurprisingly, is widely used in a range of settings – clinical, social services and educational.

Like CBT (of which SFBA is a branch), this approach helps troubled children to alter their thought patterns by focusing on the positive and achievable. Like the behaviourist approach, it is concerned about the here and now and positive achievable targets for the near-future, rather than about exploring past and historical difficulties. It helps children to identify areas in themselves in which they are confident and proficient rather than highlighting their deficiencies.

The recommended process for using this in a school or child-care situation is that a referral is made to a key member of staff if there is cause for concern and a series of meetings are arranged. In the first session it is important to establish how the child perceives things and what she/he would like the situation to be. The American who pioneered SFBT, Steve de Shazer, would pose what he called the 'miracle question' in the course of this session. Also, involved would be 'scaling' (see below), whereby on a scale of 1 to 10 the child would rate him/herself in relation to the problem being discussed (see Figure 8.2).

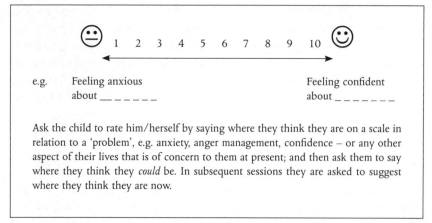

Figure 8.2: Solution-focused scaling

The techniques used in a typical SFBA interview are as follows:

- **General talk (not about problems):** Time is spent in general conversation rather than dashing into the issues causing concern. This helps to establish rapport and gives a sense of value to the child (she/he is not just 'a problem')

- **Goal setting:** These goals need to be clear, set by the client, and realistic. It is important to define indicators of success.

- **The 'Miracle Question':** This might be framed as – 'Imagine that after you have gone to bed tonight, while you are sleeping a miracle happens and the problem(s) that brought you here today are resolved. You do not know it has happened because you are asleep. When you wake up in the morning, how will you know the miracle has happened?'

- **Other person perspective:** It is important to encourage children to reflect on other people's perceptions of the problem and how they will see changes that are taking place. How will 'the other person' – perhaps the child's friends or parent – know that change for the better has happened?

- **Exception finding:** This involves exploring the times when the problem does *not* occur.

- **Scaling:** When the child has positioned himself initially on the scale, it can be followed by exploring:

  o 'What it is that tells you that you have moved on the scale?'

    o   'What would be a reasonable position on the scale to aim for next?'

    o   'How you will know you have got there?'

This is a particularly useful technique to develop in a school and/or care situation because progress can be shared regularly as child and key staff member meet around the school or care home.

- **Identifying personal resources:** The aim is to help the child (or parent) to identify their own personal resources to work towards solutions. It is important to make sure that any goal-setting is realistic and within them, but also that they have help to achieve the goals.

- **Coping:** This is exploring with the child how she/he copes with the problem, with the aim of identifying strengths in the child (or parent) in a way that she/he is aware that the problem (and person) is being taken seriously.

- **Stopping things getting worse:** There are occasions when the situation is so deep-seated and serious that the child (and/or parent) cannot accept the idea that she/he can cope. If this is the case and it is evident that progress is not being made then it is important to refer the case to other services such as the educational psychology service or CAMHS of the local Children's Services.

- **Feedback:** All sessions should end with a constructive summary of the session. How the conversation ends is important. Some experienced SFA workers take a five-minute break in order to reflect on the often complex issues discussed, before coming back to reflect back the content of the conversation.

- **Ending:** This is a very important time. The staff-member should try to finish near the allotted time, refer to the goals stated at the start, reminding the child of the indicators of progress and agree to discuss any unforeseen items that might have been raised near the end of this session in the next session.

Readers are also referred to Long and Fogell (1999) or Rees (2001) for fuller accounts of SFBA.

ADDRESSING MENTAL-HEALTH DIFFICULTIES IN CHILDREN WITH BESD

In this section we consider responses to acute anxiety (panic attacks), and mental-health difficulties associated with separation, loss and bereavement before giving brief attention to self-harm and eating disorders.

Responding to panic attacks

Powell (2000) and Long and Fogell (1999) are recommended for their approachable discussions of anxiety issues, including panic attacks. Children who suffer from panic attacks are caught in an increasingly negative behavioural spiral. They usually run away from challenging situations, have difficulty in forming relationships, experience social isolation and have reduced coping skills. The biochemical balance of their bodies is likely to be regularly upset, with stress hormones generated by their limbic system preventing the flow of calming neurotransmitters (see Chapter 3).In order to be able to empathise with the victim of panic attacks, think of a time when you yourself have been particularly frightened. It is likely that your body reacted in some of the following ways: with muscle tension, feeling sick, heart thumping, breathlessness, sweating, trembling, dry mouth, cold clammy hands, an inability to concentrate and a desire to go to the toilet. These are likely to be the very real feelings of the child experiencing a panic attack.

We can try to assist the child in exploring his or her attacks by identifying the triggers that set them off and then exploring the consequences of flight from the situation (or 'freezing'). You might use a four-pronged approach with the child:

- thoughts (what did you *think* about when you were having the attack?)
- feelings (what did you *feel?*)
- actions (what did you *do?*)
- outcomes (what are the *results?*)

You can gradually help the child to build up coping strategies that lessen the impact of the panic attacks. The child's coping strategies could include the following:

- **Control:** Try to help the child to control feelings of panic and build up the speed at which they can do this
- **Confidence:** Help the child build up confidence in his/her ability to control his/her feelings

- **Accuracy of assessment:** Increase the child's ability to recognise the internal 'triggers'/signs of panic and to respond more appropriately
- **Self-talk** (to be discussed in more detail below)
- **Problem solving:** To help pupil choose the most appropriate control (Long and Fogell 1999).

Staff can use imagery as an aid to discussion with the child: Long and Fogell (1999) also suggest comparing the panic attack to a washing machine that has a normal cycle but that is getting its cycle muddled. Can you think of other images that might be useful to the children with whom you work? Another strategy is to identify a place in your school (see 'sanctuary' above) where the child feels safe and she/he can retreat when an attack happens. Rules for the usage of this place should be established and it should be seen as an intermediate step to the child coping with the attacks in the classroom or other situation.

Breathing exercises are useful. Children can be helped by the following:

- **Regular breathing:** The child should place a hand on the stomach and take short calming breaths in through the nose and exhale through the mouth. The breaths should be quite shallow but uninterrupted (avoiding panting). To focus fully, they should say a few words to themselves silently, such as 'relax', 'chill', 'cool down' or 'calm'.
- **Deep breathing linked to thinking of pleasant things:** A place or happening where the child feels comfortable, relaxed – a holiday beach, a favourite meal, etc. where the scene is visualised, sounds are heard and enticing aromas recalled.
- **Deep breathing linked to counting.** As they breathe out through the mouth the first time they should say 10. As they breathe out the second time they say 9, the third 8, and so on down to 0.

Lown (2001) advises imagining one's breathing goes round a square: on side one, breath in to the count of five; on side two, breath out to the count of seven; on side three, breath in to the count of five; then on the last side, breath out again to the count of seven

Self-talk can also help, and you can help the child to develop an internal dialogue. This will remind, encourage, reassure and reward the child after the attack is over. It will probably include 'talking sense into myself' when the 'victim' senses the danger signals. The child can re-assure themselves:

- 'I'm going to be OK'
- 'I can cope with this like I have coped with it before'
- 'There are people who understand and will support me'
- 'I should slow down my thinking, stay calm, let my teacher know I am anxious.'

You can also encourage the child to interrupt his or her negative thoughts:

- First think of a common negative thought.
- When the helping adult says 'Stop!', change to pleasurable, supportive thoughts.
- Think 'Stop, think, do!' – this is useful self-advice when danger signals appear.

After an attack it is important to record the circumstances and details of the incident. Key staff should discuss with the child why it happened when it did in order to help to identify patterns, to discuss better alternatives which could help – perhaps moving seat in the classroom. There are clearly time and resource implications to providing the necessary support, which both specialist and mainstream schools will have to face up to.

Mental-health difficulties following separation, loss and bereavement

Long-lasting anxiety and, indeed, depressed feelings will often accompany experience of separation or divorce, loss and bereavement. It might be helpful to think of children you know who might have shown anger towards other children who were not suffering as they were. They might have become very withdrawn, finding it difficult to cope and being unwilling to trust people. There could have been despair and feelings of 'I am alone and no one likes me'. Sometimes a child seeks revenge by taking it out on other children. There will also be the child who pretends to be 'fine', acting as a 'strong' adult, but suffering intensely beneath this veneer, missing out on the normal enjoyment of childhood.

How parents deal with separation and divorce is the major determinant in how children will cope with it and to what extent they will carry a fear of failed relationships into their adult lives. It is generally accepted that damage to the child's mental health is lessened if:

- the child continues a close relationship with at least one parent
- there is a helpful, supportive adult outside the family

- there is a friendly, flexible atmosphere between the separating parents
- the child is not used as a pawn stuck in the middle
- the legal issues are settled without public 'fighting'.

Although we can do little to influence the above, by working through our close relationships with the child, we can offer support through ensuring the child's normal routines are maintained or are re-established as soon as possible. We can also give the child the chance to talk with staff to whom the child relates well, who can:

- understand the emotions the child is feeling
- encourage the child to show his/her feelings
- be good listeners, to let the child tell his or her story fully and repeatedly.

Crucially do we – or at least one special 'listener' at your school – make quality *time* to devote to the child? However, even if such time can be found it can be very draining to listen in this way and so support from someone else used to such situations (e.g. the school nurse, school counsellor or educational psychologist) should be sought.

Turning to bereavement, there is a need to get away from old taboos which avoid talking about death. Staff might be aware of this but may be worried that in attempting to help they will say the wrong thing. It *can* be easier to say nothing – but this is not wise. Cowie *et al.* (2004) say that open and honest conversations are essential to give young people the opportunity to understand their feelings. Children need a chance to explore their strong emotions around the loss. Age-appropriate and accurate information must be provided at a time when they are ready to absorb it. The child may need to be re-told and have the death re-confirmed many times in order to really understand. Mistaken approaches include lying about what happened or attempting to soften the blow by using ambiguous language, making comments such as 'Your dad went to sleep and won't wake up again'. Sometimes the surviving bereaved parent is too involved in his or her own grief to see that their child is also suffering from grief, thus leaving a greater burden on professionals to provide support.

A child will go through a 'grieving process' as he or she mourns the death of a loved one (this model can also be related to loss through parental separation/divorce). In this process there tends to be an initial 'stunned' or *numb phase* when emotions are blunted. This lasts from a few hours to two weeks. This is usually followed by a *mourning phase*, characterised by intense mourning and distress, sadness, irritability and preoccupation with the person who has died. There are commonly short-lasting hallucinatory experiences, e.g. seeing the dead person; and feelings of guilt or denial. Then there is usually *acceptance and readjustment*, several weeks afterwards. The whole process will commonly take six months but can last much longer. During this process, children might feel anger towards the dead person for 'going away' and leaving them to cope. They might also feel anger at medical staff and others who they think should have saved their loved one. The anger might be accompanied by feelings of guilt for having such feelings of anger.

It is helpful to think of grieving as a 'journey' – sometimes children will go back to where they have already been. If you think for a moment of your own losses, you can appreciate that for most of the time we cope well but then a sudden reminder – for example, a past memory – comes and we find the grief pains flow through us as strongly as ever. We can assist in helping the child go through four stages by helping them to:

- accept the reality of loss
- work through the pain of grief
- adjust to the environment in which the dead or absent person is missing
- relocate the absent person emotionally and begin to 'move on' in life.

(Worden 1991, in Cowie *et al.* 2004)

Useful practical advice for practitioners is offered in Cowie *et al.* (2004), Long and Fogell (1999) and Ratcliffe (2001). We must find the time to give these children the attention they need, and we should discuss with the child how she/he would like to be supported. However, we should not force children on to what we think they should be doing or experiencing – they need to travel on their personal journey at their pace. We need to be sensitive to the child's beliefs, but we must represent reality. We should reassure children that it is natural for them to have intense feelings and we should help them to express these. We should provide quiet 'sanctuaries' to allow them to grieve in private. If possible, we should keep in touch with the family.

We might also:

- involve their special friends
- share experiences with others through a support group
- use literature and/or music

- help the child write stories for, or letters to, the lost loved one
- keep a journal of events and feelings
- do picture stories
- make an audio recording (a spoken 'goodbye')
- create a special photograph album
- be mindful of special days (birthdays, anniversary of death, etc.).

Other suggestions include planting a tree in memorial; sending off balloons, with children writing labels on them; lighting candles or incense sticks; a school memorial service; arranging joint activities with other bereaved children.

However, thinking of Positive Psychology, it can be unhelpful to dwell *too much* on the child's grief. It is also very important to keep the child's established routines going and to continue with the provision of challenging and engrossing activities, particularly those that bring enjoyment, diversion and psychological flow.

Severe depression/depressive illness

Severe depressive syndromes and disorders are clearly the responsibility of doctors and specialist CAMHS. We should refer on children suspected to have these conditions as soon as possible, having already established good links to local services. In these cases doctors and other professionals in CAMHS can offer help through psychological approaches, such as in-depth family and individual therapy and counselling, or appropriate medication.

Responses to self-harm

Understanding and responding to children with BESD who scratch or cut or otherwise injure themselves deliberately (e.g. hitting themselves with heavy objects or banging their heads) can be a highly stressful part of life in some settings. What can we do to prevent or at least minimise the occurrence of self-harm? To start with we need to understand and counter the factors associated with children who self-harm. They feel:

- sad and lonely
- that nobody really understands them or likes them
- trapped and want to escape a situation

- angry but unable to say so
- helpless about their future.

No easy advice can be given here but as staff you should be watchful for signs of distress, and should encourage pupils to tell you if one of their friends or peer group is in trouble or seriously upset and starting to self-harm. You should then ensure the young person feels listened to and offer practical help with solving their problems that might relate to the self-harm.

Self-harm is a safeguarding issue and appropriate links to family, children's services and to CAMHS must be made and regular communication maintained with them, even if this conflicts with the child's wishes. Work with the family could be needed as suicidal teenagers often have great difficulties in communicating with their parents. Are there others in the extended family who might be able to help the child?

Self-wounding is often a habit and help will be needed through a long withdrawal phase. Staff should take a non-judgemental attitude and stay calm and constructive however upsetting self-harm may be. There is also a more general duty to educate other children on the risks so they understand that self-harm, starting in a minor form, does sometimes actually lead to death.

Healthy eating and eating disorders

The massive difficulties in weaning children – and their families – off 'junk' and convenience food make the need for schools to embed the encouragement of healthy eating in curricula and daily school practice very important. The joint DCSF and Department of Health National Healthy Schools programme has healthy eating as one of its core areas. DCSF/DoH (2008b) brings this topic close to BESD in its advice to PRUs ('short stay schools'). Linking good practice to Ofsted self-evaluation criteria, it advises that a member of the senior leadership team should oversee all aspects of food policy and practice. There should be a whole-school policy on diet, food education, delivery of meals on site, and related health and safety issues. Pupils and parents should be involved in creating the policy, which should govern the nutritional aspects of food provision at breakfast club, lunchtimes, and packed lunches, and the contents of vending machines. Pleasant eating areas should be provided and queuing minimised. There should be clear rules about accessing food vendors off-site. The policy should also seek to embed the promotion of healthy eating through aspects of the curriculum (beyond food-technology lessons). Staff should have access to appropriate training.

This general whole-school practice should, as Cowie *et al.* (2004) hoped, help to influence children from their early years – and perhaps impact on the practice of their parents.

The healthy eating policy can give information about helping the obese to lose weight but should also spell out the disadvantages of dieting – that is, its link to eating disorders, which is our major concern here. Research indicates that healthy eating programmes (Cowie *et al.* 2004) can have a useful impact at an appropriate stage of development. In secondary school, they can still be effective for Year 8 and Year 9 pupils but probably not for students in Years 10 and 11, by which time eating habits are largely fixed. Programmes should be interactive more than didactic, making extensive use of discussion and role-play. Pupils should be encouraged to make changes in their eating habits and take more exercise. Case studies can be useful to exemplify issues.

We do, however, have to be wary of how such programmes are delivered to some vulnerable children, who can be *encouraged by them* to indulge in the behaviours being criticised, thereby making existing problems worse (Cowie *et al.* 2004). For instance, encouraging moderate eating can lead to obsessive dieting resulting in anorexia or bulimia. As is the case with other mental-health problems, staff need to be alert to unusual behaviours – that is, children either resisting eating or eating inappropriately. Practitioners need to respond to associated forms of distress in such children and ensure that they obtain specialist help. Dealing with established anorexia or bulimia is clearly beyond the responsibility of staff in educational settings but they will sometimes be involved in the management of 'recovering' children – following, it is to be expected, clear advice from CAMHS or other medical professionals.

REVIEW

In this chapter we have given attention to factors in building relationships; 'active listening' and 'talking' interventions; 'doing' approaches (art, creativity and play; sport and physical activity); using cognitive-behaviourist approaches to promoting more positive thinking (including 'mindfulness' and 'solution-focused brief' approaches). We also examined helpful responses to negative emotions, particularly anger (intervening early to prevent outbursts – or handling the crisis and plateau and recovery phases). We then looked at safeguarding and positive physical handling (including touch/physical contact). We have also considered a range of mental-health problems. Informed and skilful practice in each of these areas can make an important contribution to enhancing the well-being and mental health of children with BESD. We now move on to consider the range of support which should be available to you from beyond your particular workplace.

NOTE

1 The Conservative-Liberal Democrat Coalition government, which came into power in May 2010, is reviewing the area of physical restraint and disciplinary powers of school staff.

2 A more formal way of considering anger outbursts is offered in Breakwell's 'Assault Cycle' (see Faupel, Herrick and Sharp 1998 or Lown 2001), a model which tracks the cognitive, behavioural and emotional cycle through which the child moves – from a normal non-aggressive mood through the explosion back to the post-crisis, passing through a depressed state before regaining normal emotional levels.

CHAPTER 9

SUPPORT FROM BEYOND YOUR WORK SETTING

Michael Fullan (2009) advises educational settings to develop 'permeable connectivity' – that is, two-way communication and mutual influence with other services around them. This notion seems particularly relevant when considering provision for children with BESD. When supporting such children, staff clearly benefit from establishing good relations and having influence with local schools and the range of supporting agencies. If traditions, training and working practices as well as severe resource constraints in these services prove to be barriers, then these must be tackled. Cheminais (2009; 2010) gives detailed advice on how to go about this. In the combined children's services era[1], there are now more examples of good inter-agency practice, although practice overall remains uneven (NFER 2006; 2007).

In this chapter we will consider:

- structures (behaviour partnership working; pastoral support programmes and the Common Assessment Framework)
- the roles of other agencies (children's services, local children's safeguarding boards, youth justice and CAMHS)
- reasonable expectations of social workers and CAMHS
- the dilemmas of confidentiality and information sharing
- building links and trust
- knowing your local services.

BEHAVIOUR PARTNERSHIPS

The government now encourages schools to group together in clusters, federations or other forms of behaviour partnership, in order to share responsibilities, to increase the range of expertise available and to facilitate communication, access to and fair distribution of services from other support agencies. The National Strategies' Behaviour and Attendance strand toolkit units (DfES 2005c) found that schools were at different stages of development in partnership working. Toolkit Unit 10 looks at ways in which schools can move forward. It suggests that schools conduct audits with the aim of creating:

- clear and open lines of communication between the school and all partners (by implication, including other schools) and other agencies that encourage a unified approach
- a key person within the school who ensures continuity and access to information for all involved
- effective support from other agencies for identified pupils
- pupils and parents/carers who are engaged and informed at all stages
- a good balance between access to information and confidentiality (recognising an ongoing obstacle to multi-agency working)
- effective liaison with primary and first schools to manage pupils' transfer.

It encourages schools to

- identify the roles and responsibilities of all partners and other agencies in their localities
- develop a clear understanding of how to access (pathways to) assistance and co-ordinate referrals effectively
- develop their role in co-ordinating multi-agency working. It notes that schools are well placed to co-ordinate multi-agency support and promote the sharing of professional expertise so that resources are efficiently deployed and consistently applied
- nurture and encourage effective jargon-free communication. This includes structures, protocols and the co-ordination of multi-agency working
- fully engage parents/carers in partnership working with the school.

Unit 10 also recognises that partnership working is a two-way process with other agencies having responsibility to 'make the effort' – thus hinting at the experience sometimes reported, that despite schools' ongoing and determined efforts to work in partnership, the response of other agencies can be disappointing.

'PASTORAL SUPPORT PROGRAMMES': ACCESSING SUPPORT FROM OTHER AGENCIES

It could be that your awareness of what is available from behaviour-support service teachers, educational psychologists, CAMHS or social workers has been raised by your involvement in constructing, or monitoring, Pastoral Support Programmes. Brought in by the government in 1999 (DfEE 1999) to counteract a worrying growth of permanent exclusions, a PSP is intended to be a co-ordinated series of interventions to help individual pupils improve their social, emotional and behavioural skills and to lessen the risk of their exclusion from school. PSPs should be drawn up when a pupil's behaviour is deteriorating rapidly as a preventative measure (certainly not as a barrier to clear before using exclusion) (see DCSF undated).

If you play a significant part in the education or support of the child in question, your views should be heard on what additional resources will enhance your ability to help children, particularly for children 'looked after' (such as Stephen in Chapter 1). Any PSP should be developed in conjunction with – possibly integrated into – other existing plans (e.g. a statement for SENs or care plan). This could involve discussions and meetings with representatives of other services and parents or, for the looked-after child, the carers. Undertaking a multi-agency Common Assessment may be appropriate (see below).

As part of the PSP, the LA has to agree with the school precisely what input, support or monitoring it will offer. Children's Services should address home problems that contribute to attendance or behaviour difficulties at school if the child is looked after. Schools are advised to inform the social worker when a looked-after child is failing to achieve the outcomes expected in the PSP. This should include changes to the education targets in his or her care plan. Other LA services such as educational psychology and behaviour support should also contribute to PSPs.

Housing departments could help to resolve accommodation difficulties or to track the whereabouts of children and young people who are regularly truanting. Minority ethnic community groups can provide useful advice and/ or provide specific support such as mentoring programmes. The Youth Service might carry out intensive work with the child, perhaps as part of a group of non-attenders or young offenders. The voluntary sector might have services to offer locally. In relation to further education or career possibilities, 'Connexions' (see below) can help young people make informed decisions about their future and encourage them to continue learning post-16 years of age.

As well as considering using on-site resources such as learning support units,[2] PSPs should look at perhaps jointly registering the child with another school, a 'short stay school' or accessing outreach services from the local BESD school. It should also consider offering the pupil specialist support, e.g. counselling, for bereavement, bullying, alcohol/drug related or mental-health issues. The PSP could refer and specify the need for the professional development of staff, again likely to bring practitioners into contact with professionals from other agencies.

A PSP is time-limited – for example, lasting sixteen working weeks – but should be kept under regular review to see if adjustments are needed. This should involve further meetings with colleagues in school but also partners from other agencies.

THE COMMON ASSESSMENT FRAMEWORK

Where a multi-agency approach is indicated, as will be the case for many children with complex BESD, the Common Assessment Framework (CAF) will probably be used (DfES 2007b). The CAF is a standardised approach to conducting an assessment of a child's needs and deciding how those needs should be met, which can be used by practitioners across children's services in England. It involves the completion of a standardised pre-assessment checklist and a detailed full assessment form. The process involves the appointment of a 'Lead Professional' to implement plans of action and to coordinate inter-agency inputs.

It is worth outlining some of the content of CAF for practitioners not familiar with this procedure. The full assessment form requires details of the current home and family situation; list of services and contact details of those already working with the child; a strengths and needs section asking for information on general health, physical development, SLCN, emotional and social development and behavioural development. This last sub-section gives as prompts: 'Lifestyle, self-control, reckless or impulsive activity; behaviour with peers, substance misuse; anti-social behaviour; sexual behaviour; offending; violence and aggression; restless and overactive; easily distracted, attention span/concentration.'

The form then covers identity, self-esteem, more on family and social relationships; and (for those with severe learning difficulties) self-care skills; aspects of 'learning' and aspirations (including motivation and perseverance). Towards the end there is a page headed 'Conclusions, solutions and actions', a space for 'What needs to change?' and boxes for prioritised points for a short action plan, specifying who will do what and by when. This page concludes with 'How will you know when things have improved?' The form ends with space for comments from the child and/or parent/guardian. In short, CAF asks for a considerable amount of information to inform a holistic multi-agency approach. DfES (2006c) gives further advice on how to complete the form, sub-dividing headings into details on what makes for healthy child development or good parenting.

To avoid duplication and inconsistency, one person, a Lead Professional, will be assigned to the child and family. The Lead Professional should be a single trusted point of contact for the clients, whose role is to ensure that the designated services and interventions are co-ordinated and delivered. This role can be taken on by many different types of practitioners within the range of children's services. The role is defined by the functions and skills required, rather than by particular professional or practitioner groupings (CWDC 2007). Establishing close links with the Lead Professional could be beneficial to you and your colleagues.

DIFFERENT SUPPORTING AGENCIES AND THEIR ROLES

For readers new to multi-agency working, an outline of the roles of different professionals is given below.

Children's Services

- **Educational psychologists** would like to provide assessment, advice, support and training to schools on children and young people who have difficulties with learning and/or behaviour. In practice, they can find much of their time is filled up with meeting statutory SEN assessment, 'statementing' and review duties.

- **Behaviour support services:** Most English LAs still provide behaviour-support services through a dedicated team, which works closely with the educational psychology service. However, recent movements to behaviour partnerships/school clusters or children's trusts could mean that behaviour-support teachers are provided or accessed through other means, e.g. through schools buying in services from staff employed by special schools, PRUs or voluntary agencies. Sometimes behaviour-support teachers will work as part of multi-agency teams, alongside CAMHS and/or SEN specialists. Over the past few decades behaviour-support teachers have often provided an invaluable 'fresh pair of eyes', observing, advising and sometimes modelling particular interventions for very challenging children in mainstream classes.

- **Education Welfare Services (EWS)** (sometimes Education Social Work services) work with schools, pupils and their parents/carers to improve pupils' attendance. In conjunction with school staff, education welfare officers help to identify pupils with attendance problems. They investigate, assess, plan and implement appropriate action. They work with schools in the promotion of good home links; attend court proceedings and conduct truancy sweeps. They often play a key role in supporting children excluded from school.

- **Social workers:** Following the Children Act of 2004, the education (the 'LEA') and children social-services divisions of local authorities were merged into Local Authority Children's Services under a Children Services Director. Within each LA's CS there will still be the social work department and social workers responsible for reviewing all aspects of the care of 'children looked-after' (also referred to as 'children in care'). This will include arranging for and conducting statutory reviews.

- **Youth Service** includes: Youth workers who provide information, advice and counselling; detached and outreach projects; youth clubs and centres; voluntary youth work; and work with disadvantaged youth and specific groups. Again, there are resource and prioritisation issues that may mean that the practical help they can offer to children with BESD is limited.

- **Children's Centres** and **Children's Trusts:** These are geared to provide support to parents in the most acute need, although these services are constrained by limited resources and the need to focus attention on child protection ('safeguarding') work. Crisis situations and legal and administrative procedures can get in the way of the earlier intervention work that might be more widely effective. It is easy for staff working in schools to underestimate the acute pressures under which social workers operate – also how difficult it is in some areas to recruit and retain staff in sufficient numbers and with suitable experience.

Children's Services (and some voluntary bodies) are now devoting more resources to the crucial area of developing the parenting skills of many adults who perhaps did not experience, and therefore did not learn, the best child-rearing practice (see Chapter 10).

Careers and advice on further education

Presently called 'Connexions', the careers service provides advice, guidance and access to personal-development opportunities for thirteen- to nineteen-year-olds. Connexions try to work with the Education Welfare Service to reduce truancy.

Local Children's Safeguarding Boards (LCSBs)

The statutory inquiry into the appalling circumstances surrounding the death of Victoria Climbié in 2003 highlighted the lack of priority given to safeguarding. The Government's response included the Green Paper *Every Child Matters* (DfES 2003b). This led to the Children Act 2004, which stressed the duty on all agencies to make arrangements to safeguard and promote the welfare of children. There was a shared responsibility and a need for effective joint working. The Act led to the setting up of LCSBs, replacing the existing area child-protection committees. The core membership of LCSBs includes representatives from LAs, health bodies and the police. HM Government (2006) saw the LCSB as the key statutory mechanism for agreeing how the relevant organisations in each local area would co-operate on safeguarding and ensure effectiveness.

Regulations governing LCSB include procedures for:

- taking action where there are safeguarding concerns, including thresholds for intervention

- training of people who work with children or in services affecting the safety and welfare of children

- recruitment and supervision of people who work with children

- investigation of allegations concerning people who work with children.

To function effectively, LCSBs needed to be supported by their member organisations with adequate and reliable resources.

An important part of safeguarding is the checking of the past histories of practitioners employed (or sometimes volunteering) or planning to work with children. The Independent Safeguarding Authority is currently the body responsible for carrying out checks under what is presently called the Vetting and Barring Scheme.

Youth Justice

You might also have contact with 'Youth Offending Teams' (YOTs), which exist in every LA. They consist of representatives from the police, probation service, social services, health agencies, education, drugs and alcohol-misuse agencies, and housing officers. YOTs seek in a multi-agency way, to prevent young people offending, and also work with existing young offenders. Given that children with BESD have often been involved in at least minor delinquency (Cole *et al.* 1998), working with YOTs can be an ongoing role for schools and short-stay schools. Further information can be got from the Youth Justice Board website.

Child and Adolescent Mental Health Services

Many children with mental-health difficulties will receive sufficient help from their local family doctor (their general practitioner (GP)), who may prescribe anti-depressants or refer them to a counsellor. If their problems are more complex, they are likely to be referred to the National Health Service's CAMHS. The latter should work in close partnership with local authorities and primary care trusts[3], who in mid-2010 still oversaw the operation of local health services. CAMHS are summarised in the four-tier model shown in Box 9.1 (see also DCSF/DoH 2008a, p.17).

A CAMHS team will have workers from various different professions and will include some or all of the following:

- **Child and adolescent psychiatrists**, particularly consultants, oversee the work of all CAMHS teams. A qualified medical doctor, the consultant will also have completed extensive training, usually in psychotherapy. The consultant is often involved in the first assessment of someone's problems in Tier 3 and Tier 4 services (acute, individualised – see below). If the child needs medication, the consultant will usually be responsible for arranging this. Psychiatrists' work is usually done through out-patient appointments while the child continues to live at home. The referral route to a psychiatrist is usually through a child's GP but is sometimes through a health visitor, school doctor, paediatrician, educational psychologist or specialist CAMHS social worker.

- **Clinical psychologists** are *not* educational psychologists, having received training that is significantly different. Clinical psychologists are trained and experienced in offering psychological treatments (e.g. CBT). They will meet regularly with the child and the child's family for a number of sessions to seek solutions.

Box 9.1: The four-tier CAMHS model

- **Tier 1:** A primary-care level: This refers to everyday 'universal' provision for children and young people, and specialist services that make routine provision, e.g. developmental screening. The workforce delivering Tier 1 includes educational staff and careworkers.

- **Tier 2:** A service provided by specialist individual professionals relating to workers in primary care. People working at this level vary widely in their expertise and training. Within the NHS, it could mean a single practitioner can work effectively with the client and that the practitioner will also be supporting staff working in Tier 1. Tier 2 is sometimes seen as including specialist teachers working with children with BESD.

- **Tier 3:** This is a specialised multi-disciplinary service for more severe, complex or persistent disorders (severe mood disorders, deliberate self-harm, eating disorders, early onset psychiatric disorders, etc).

- **Tier 4:** This covers essential specialist services such as day units, highly specialised out-patient teams and in-patient/residential units.

(HAS 1995)

Note that the national review (DCSF/DoH 2008a) preferred to talk of the three levels of service of CAMHS: *universal, targeted* and *specialist.*

- **Psychotherapists** have had a specialist training in one of the psychotherapies, often called 'talking treatments'. They include qualified **art therapists**, who use art within a therapeutic relationship or group as a means of assisting a child or adult in discovering, exploring and clarifying their thoughts and feelings. **Cognitive therapists** have been trained in CBT.

- **Community psychiatric nurses** work outside hospitals, usually visiting clients in their own homes, out-patient departments or family doctors' surgeries. CPNs can help children and adults to talk through their problems and give them practical advice and support. They can also give medicines and monitor the effects of medication. Some **nurse therapists** have received extra training in particular problems and treatments, such as eating disorders or CBT.

- **Occupational therapists**. OTs help people undergoing treatment, to get back to carrying on their normal lives, through undertaking meaningful occupation which re-builds their self-confidence. This involves doing practical things or talking with other people in groups in a relaxed environment.

- **Social workers** play an important part in CAMHS, sometimes being employed by the LA's children's services. An **Approved Social Worker** (ASW) is a qualified social worker who has undertaken further training in mental health. ASWs play a key part in assessing whether or not someone should be detained in hospital under the Mental Health Act.

If a child with whom you work does receive input from CAMHS, it is likely to be through one nominated CAMHS key worker. After one or two meetings or consultations, the CAMHS team will decide which professional will work with the child – the key worker. Any member of the team can be a key worker, although it is usually a social worker or nurse. The key worker will monitor the child's CAMHS care-plan.

Given demands on limited services, there has to be some rationing and prioritising. It is advisable for your setting to have a lead person for mental health, perhaps a co-ordinator, as well as having access to a community-based, primary mental-health care worker who understands your needs, who can advise on the appropriateness of making a referral and who will have influence with CAMHS when she/he makes requests for help.

FAIR EXPECTATIONS OF SOCIAL WORKERS AND CAMHS

The effect of major high-profile child abuse cases on recruitment and retention of skilled social workers together with chronic funding constraints mean that social work support for educational practitioners with many children with BESD will continue to be limited. Even when funding is not an issue, there are not enough people wishing to undertake or to stick at a career that is stressful, underpaid and sometimes dangerous. Concern about social work prompted the government to undertake a major review of the situation, which included some candid comments:

> Weaknesses in recruitment, retention, frontline resources, training, leadership, public understanding and other factors are compounding one another. They are holding back the profession and making service improvement practice difficult to achieve. Most importantly, people who look to social workers for support are not getting the consistently high quality of service they deserve. (DCSF 2009e, p.2)

Already stretched social-work resources are likely to continue to be targeted on statutory safeguarding and crisis intervention, rather than offering ongoing steady support to most children with BESD and their families. The Steer Report (DfES 2005a) envisaged schools employing their own staff, i.e. not qualified social workers, to engage with families and homes.

The situation with regard to mental-health support was more hopeful before the massive financial crisis that began in 2008. Before then the Government rarely shied away from setting ambitious targets for the public services. One example is the National Services Framework Standard 9, *The Standard for the Mental Health and Well-Being of Children and Young People,* which says:

All children and young people, from birth to their eighteenth birthday, who have mental-health problems and disorders have access to timely, integrated, high-quality, multi-disciplinary mental-health services to ensure effective assessment, treatment and support for them and their families. (DoH 2004b)

(Standard 9 would be achieved through *universal, targeted* and *specialist* individual services encompassed by the four-tier model.)

Extra resources were given to CAMHS in the early years of the 21st century, enabling the training and recruitment of more staff and uneven but, nonetheless real, improvements, which were reported in DCSF/DoH (2008a) and which practitioners working with children with BESD sometimes noted. The National CAMHS Review did identify children with BESD as a vulnerable group. As such their mental-health needs should be assessed, and for those with 'complex, severe and ongoing' needs, 'packages of care' should be 'commisioned by the Children's Trust and delivered, where possible, in the local area' (DCSF/DoH 2008a, p.12). PRUs and behaviour-support services were seen as part of 'early intervention' approaches. Under the heading 'Specialist Help', there are various paragraphs on CAMHS-related issues in connection to BESD, special schools and PRUs. Paragraph 5.22 states:

'It is our view that special schools, PRUs and other alternative education providers need further support with specialist training in order to improve the skills mix within their staff. They also need better access to and involvement of specialist mental-health staff, given the complexity of the needs that they are working with and supporting.'

The report of the National CAMHS Review (DCSF/DoH 2008a) commends alternative-education settings employing specialist teachers 'who are part of the wider community CAMHS team'.

Responses from across England to Cole's (2008) small-scale study heard accounts of both improving and still disappointing practice. Reflecting the findings of the national review and indicating a situation that was getting better were the following points:

- There was improved partnership working between BESD service providers and CAMHS (e.g. CAMHS attend more meetings in the schools – better sharing of relevant information, including supply of timely and more informative reports – the development of local multi-agency teams).

- There were shorter waiting times to access CAMHS and/or streamlined referral pathways (including quicker responses to emergencies).

- The appointment of primary mental-health workers (PMHWs) had helped, particularly in progressing referrals to specialist CAMHS.

- There was more direct input from Tier 2 mental-health service professionals into schools/PRUs. There was one example of a local-authority BESD school having a community psychiatric nurse present on site for two days a week doing direct work with children and staff and aiding quicker referral. One PRU benefited from a full-time NHS nurse on site, as well as a CAMHS nurse for one day a week. A behaviour-support service received regular 'dedicated' support from CAMHS outreach workers.

- Some BESD schools/PRUs and specialist mainstream school settings (e.g. an LSU) were able to make direct referrals to CAMHS. Being respected and accepted by CAMHS as experienced and skilled practitioners able to assess children who may need more specialist assessments and possible interventions from CAMHS is a welcome development.

- Having a specialist teacher with a CAMHS liaison remit helped: where a nominated teacher had this role and was known and respected by local CAMHS, then relations and practice seem to improve.

- There was some skilled training in mental-health issues provided by CAMHS specialists to staff in BESD schools/PRUs.

- Consultant clinical psychologists were occasionally working directly in PRUs.

- Sometimes CAMHS commissioners had specific BESD school remits.

- A large Midland city's Single Point of Access referral to CAMHS system (in place of referral via GPs) helped – although this did not prioritise specialist provision for BESD as it probably should have.
- CAMHS was accepting of the need to persevere in engaging with 'hard to reach' children, with severe needs, who may fail to attend offered appointments, and was creating mechanisms to overcome this problem.
- There was co-location of CAMHS workers and local-authority children' services officers.
- There was access for all children's services staff to CAMHS training.
- There were school-based assessments for ADHD.
- CAMHS was developing outreach teams.
- There were some LA conferences to bring together different professions.

In a less positive vein, the national review (DCSF/DoH 2008a) identified continuing shortcomings, explaining the unhappiness of many educational practitioners with the support available. These shortcomings include:

- resource issues (lack of finance and lack of qualified staff, e.g. clinical psychologists and therapists)
- discrete and conflicting professional histories
- professional preferences (e.g. psychiatrists/GPs following their own areas of interest at the expense of others)
- despite calls to the contrary dating back decades (e.g. DES 1974), CAMHS practitioners remaining clinic-bound and averse to working in schools
- a possible lack of inter-professional awareness
- a lack of clarity about access pathways to CAMHS in some areas.

These shortcomings were developed in Cole (2008), who found some educational practitioners calling for direct access from schools to CAMHS (also requested in Rothi *et al.* 2006). The traditional route, through GPs, was associated with delays and was sometimes seen as inappropriate, given the high level of expertise in mental-health matters of some specialist educational staff in BESD provision/PRUs. CAMHS were sometimes seen as being too quick to close cases, e.g. during brief remissions. 'Brief therapy' could be *too* brief. There was comment on poor feedback from CAMHS to schools and general poor communications (see next section).

THE CHALLENGE OF CONFIDENTIALITY, INFORMATION SHARING AND WORKING TOGETHER

It is a common complaint from educationalists that social workers and CAMHS do not keep them informed. The government is inching forward with protocols for sharing essential information, so that workers in one profession do receive the information they need to know to help them in their work with sometimes very challenging children in school. However, there are no easy answers to sharing information. Medical professionals will often share information within the CAMHS team and with the GP but will not usually share sensitive information about the child with school staff – which is sometimes a matter of deep concern.

Also noteworthy is a National Association of Schoolmasters/Union of Women Teachers report (Rothi *et al.* 2006). In order to improve working relationships, NASUWT wanted the following:

- new mental-health initiatives and services to be communicated to all school staff

- CAMHS to take direct referrals from schools, believing that this would be less time-consuming than the current referral routes available

- a named contact in CAMHS with whom they can build a relationship and obtain information from about appropriate referrals and services available

- access to mental-health professionals and educational psychologists for advice and guidance, particularly on in-class teaching and learning strategies

- a regular, or *ad hoc*, consultation service where they can discuss their concerns about particular issues or children

- mental-health professionals working in schools, providing practical hands-on support to children

- more opportunities for collaboration and joint working between CAMHS, the educational psychology service, behavioural-support services and schools

- greater information-sharing between services and schools. While teachers are aware of data protection/confidentiality issues, they still believe that some middle ground could be found.

BUILDING LINKS AND TRUST

Better or innovative practice seems to happen where there is regular communication and Fullan's 'permeable connectivity' with professionals from the educational, social-care and mental-health settings knowing and trusting each other, and appreciating and empathising with the challenges faced by each service (Cheminais 2009).

There is no substitute for taking the time and effort to build bridges and personal relationships, so that when you pick up a phone you are able to see a face, and to have already shared, one hopes, pleasurable social and professional contact with the professional from the other agency with whom you now wish to discuss an issue. Sharing professional development events, attending face-to-face meetings followed by a chat over a coffee, visiting each other's workplaces, perhaps co-locating offices on the same site have all been found useful. Obviously, if you are a busy class teacher or support worker spending nearly all your working week in classrooms, it can be difficult to find the time and perhaps resources to enable these contacts on a regular basis, but these approaches are, without doubt, helpful.

KNOWING YOUR LOCAL SERVICES

There are probably nominated people on your school staff, through whom requests for assistance or raising concerns should be channelled. Even if there are, it is still worth checking your knowledge of local support services – where their offices are, who key people are and how you would contact them. You might also find it useful to photocopy and complete the table given in Appendix 2 of this book.

Cheminais (2009) also offers a range of forms for analysis of your workplace's needs and performance in what she terms 'Multi Agency Partnership Working'.

REVIEW

In this chapter we have sought to raise awareness of government guidance and the reality of multi-agency working. We considered the potential of behaviour partnerships, using pastoral-support programmes to gain support, the Common Assessment Framework and an outline of the roles of different support agencies. We looked at reasonable expectations to make of social workers and CAMHS, given the constraints under which they work. We highlighted the chronic challenges of professional confidentiality and information sharing, and stressed the importance of making mutually trusting and empathetic relationships with support agencies. Finally, we suggested checking your own knowledge of what is available in your locality to help you in your work.

NOTE

1. The policies of the Conservative-Liberal Democrat coalition government, which came into power in the UK in May 2010, could impact substantially on combined children's services and inter-agency working. We view with some concern the rapid renaming of the Department of Children, Schools and Families with the old name, the Department for Education

2. Children with BESD will sometimes find themselves in LSUs. McSherry (2004) offers sound advice on good practice in these 'on site' units.

3. In July 2010, the Conservative-Liberal Democrat coalition government announced plans to disband primary care trusts in order to give more money and responsibilities for providing health services to GPs (community based family doctors) instead.

CHAPTER 10

WORKING WITH PARENTS AND CARERS

The benefits of establishing a helpful relationship with the parents of children with BESD have long been recognised. In the 1930s, in Leicester, the importance of this was appreciated at the very first State-run school for children called 'maladjusted':

> 'While children are in attendance at the School, their homes are visited with a view to ensuring the co-operation of the parents which in the majority of cases is regularly given.' (cited in Bridgeland 1971, p.299)

DCSF (2008a) echoes these sentiments in the current BESD guidance. If the child is not living at home, then, of course, close relationships must be forged with the child's carers.

The working time of many readers will be dominated by classroom teaching or support work, with specialist responsibilities for working with families given to colleagues, who may or may not be educationalists. Contact may be limited to parent evenings, conversations at a school gate or telephone calls. Nevertheless, it is helpful to outline the issues that surround working with parents and carers, and to look at possible avenues to creating mutually beneficial relationships. There can be times when this can be a daunting challenge. It can be easy to assign blame – sometimes for very understandable reasons – but at other times are we being too hasty in reaching negative judgements?

This chapter will give brief consideration to:

- the government's BESD guidance's advice and expectations
- obstacles to close working with parents and carers
- how people feel when referred to CAMHS or children's services
- strategies for engaging parents/carers
- parent training and support programmes.

GOVERNMENT ADVICE AND EXPECTATIONS

Paragraph 67 of the current BESD Guidance (DCSF 2008a) notes that the SEN Code of Practice (DfEE 2001a) stresses that partnership with parents must play a key role in identifying and addressing children and young people's SEN (including BESD). Schools should promote a culture of co-operation with parents in an atmosphere that is open and welcoming.

The guidance recognises:

Families are a key influence on a child's intellectual and social, emotional and behavioural development. Parents are usually the experts on their own child, and their knowledge about their child can provide a valuable insight about what works and what is needed. Parents can support the school's work in developing emotional, social and behavioural skills by reinforcing them at home and by helping their child develop insight into their difficulties. Schools should therefore work in partnership with parents, sharing respective insights and strategies. (DCSF 2008a, paragraph 68)

Where family dynamics contribute to a child's difficulties, a

parenting education programme may help parents to set clear and appropriate boundaries, provide social and emotional support and manage behaviour. Educational psychologists, behaviour-support specialists, learning mentors, personal advisers or primary mental health workers from child and adolescent mental health service (CAMHS) teams may provide input into such programmes. (DCSF 2008a, paragraph 69)

It claims that family SEAL workshops 'also help to create a positive family atmosphere by encouraging parents to use the SEAL approach to developing children's social and emotional skills'. Evidence is not given of this actually happening, but it does sound a promising approach.

Paragraph 70 covers voluntary parenting contracts where parenting is identified as a factor contributing to a pupil's BESD. There is also scope, it says, for the local authority or school to apply to the local magistrates' court for a parenting order 'if it is judged appropriate to require otherwise reluctant parents to co-operate or to undergo parenting classes' (see DCSF 2007e).

Also if a child with BESD is seen as being *a disabled pupil* (perhaps through his/her ADHD), the Disability Rights Commission Code of Practice, paragraph 7.9, emphasises the importance of positive relationships with parents.

OBSTACLES TO CLOSE WORKING WITH PARENTS AND CARERS

Children with BESD often come from disrupted backgrounds, with fractured family relationships, separations, transient 'uncles', or frequent changes of address. They can be very hard to communicate with – and to 'get on your side'. They might be hard to reach by the usual means, certainly within the time you have available. There may be family- and community-related risks contributing to the child's BESD:

- mental-health problems in parents

- parental reading difficulties making it hard for the parent to give support to their child's learning

- poor living conditions, poverty and unemployment

- inability of the parents to counteract peer pressures (how do you control a teenager out on the streets with his mates starting to get into trouble?).

However, whatever the obstacles, it usually helps to take an empathetic view. The resistant parent may have a long history of past negative experiences with professionals, colouring how she/he sees and interacts with you and your colleagues.

Many parents of children with BESD:

- lack confidence in talking to professionals

- want to hide family difficulties from the outside world

- fear they will 'let down' their child on visits to school

- have had unhappy school days and unsympathetic teachers

- have experienced professionals who talk down to them or make impossible demands

- have no car, and problems with public transport

- have no quiet space at home for the child to do homework

- have difficulties with taking time off work to speak to teachers, or attend meetings

- have difficulty in getting child-care for siblings

- 'fear the worst', expecting only trouble when the school gets in touch.

The experiences listed above were certainly encountered by researchers visiting the homes of some families of children permanently excluded from school (Daniels *et al.* 2003). Parents *may* be trying to work with and support the school but could lack social confidence or the physical means to provide the help requested. What might be commonplace practice for most parents – feeling free to call in for a chat to a teacher, going to parent evenings, attending meetings, phoning in, supporting the school's wishes, seeing homework is done – might genuinely be difficult for the families of Cameron, Ashley, Cheryl and Ryan. Perhaps a new, more pro-active approach by your school would produce benefits? Help could be sought from other professionals employed by other agencies, to make and maintain contact.

Contacting the carers of children who are 'looked after' can be complicated by the movement of such children from one home to another – or perhaps because the carers do not see education as their first priority. Involving local-authority staff with special responsibility for looked-after children could help in this respect.

HOW PEOPLE FEEL WHEN REFERRED TO CAMHS OR CHILDREN'S SERVICES

If you are physically ill, there is usually no shame or feeling of stigma and you will normally welcome a visit to medical services for diagnosis and prescriptions. It can be very different with mental-health or family problems that you may be reluctant to acknowledge. You might admit the problems to yourself and perhaps to close loved ones, but you do not wish to advertise them to the wider world. The prefixes 'mental' and 'psycho' attached to many CAMHS professionals' titles can also be a serious barrier to people seeking help. The stigma of involving social services, using Children's Centre's or Children's Trust facilities, can also be acutely felt – with parents perhaps worrying about children being taken away from them and placed into care.

Both adults and children with mental-health difficulties rarely seek help themselves. They are typically referred for help by concerned others. However, it should not be assumed that because a parent or child is unhappy and desires change to take place that professional intervention will be welcomed or accepted. Many forms of therapy, particularly the psychotherapies, are based on the assumption that the client is a willing participant who actively wishes to change. In practice, many adults and children come to therapists reluctantly and perhaps because they feel they have to give in to more powerful people (Elliott and Place 1998).

While there may be a trend, encouraged by the modern media, for people to be more open about admitting to and discussing emotional problems there apparently remains much resistance and/or uncertainty about seeking help from 'talking therapists': to discuss a difficulty with your close friends or a GP is seen as normal and often desirable, but to seek help from mental-health professionals is a different matter (Anderson, Brownlie and Given 2009).

Once past the hurdle of approaching CAMHS or social services for help, the prospect of meeting a room full of strangers is also an anxiety-inducing experience. The sooner the group of potential helpers is reduced to a key worker whom they know, the easier things are likely to become. This person could act as an advocate who can help the client(s) to make sure that their voice is heard by professionals. He or she could accompany the client to meetings with professionals to help get answers to the questions the client needs answered and to make sure that the child and family's message gets across. Children and their families clearly need support and encouragement from those they already know and trust.

Children's Services (and some voluntary bodies) are now devoting more resources to the key area of developing parenting skills of adults, who perhaps did not experience and therefore did not learn, the best child-rearing practice. It could be that the parents of the children with BESD with whom you work, would benefit from such programmes. However, persuading them of the benefits of this could be challenging, and involve ongoing work helping them to attend classes regularly (see Daniels *et al.* 1999).

STRATEGIES FOR ENGAGING PARENTS

Having outlined some obstacles, we now turn to tested ways of overcoming these. Approaches have, of course, to be highly individualised, taking into account the parents' and the child's needs and preferences. What works for one child and family could be inappropriate or counter-productive for another.

In terms of regularly keeping in touch and maintaining relationships, experienced practitioners have found the following useful:

- informing parents of small successes more than involving them with worries or reports of bad behaviour. You need to break the parent's expectation that every contact from school will be about trouble or difficulty

- establishing regular communication through a simple home–school diary and/or 'good letters', notes, cards or certificates sent home, which celebrate the child doing well

- build trust by not making promises you cannot keep – doing what you say you will do

- making regular phone calls; they could be daily or weekly phone conversations to celebrate things done well, to discuss good and less desirable behaviour, to report plans for weekends, to maintain and develop relationships

- be flexible in how you try to make a relationship with the parents – use the means of communication they find easiest (perhaps texting rather than phoning).

It has been found that hearing positive reports is often a novel experience for parents, and this has been claimed to aid the foundation of later supportive relationships. This created a reservoir of understanding and support for staff when bad behaviour requiring parental support had to be confronted (Daniels *et al.* 2003; Ofsted 2003).

If you are a busy class teacher or support worker it will be helpful to harness the assistance of staff with special responsibility for forming important connections – staff who can work with you, sometimes, acting on yours and school leadership's behalf. Perhaps your school has a home–school liaison officer or access to an educational welfare officer or behaviour-support service worker to make home visits or who can meet the parent on neutral ground away from school.

From the parent's perspective, having a named key worker on the staff who is their special person, who knows their child well, who understands their family situation and who makes regular contact can be invaluable.

Importance was also attached, by senior leaders responding to the national study of Cole *et al.* (1998), to annual reviews and informal meetings and gatherings at the school. One headteacher told how he 'bribed' parents to attend scheduled parents' evenings by offering wine and finger buffets. A welcoming, open-door policy where school leaders would see parents quickly who arrived 'on spec' ahead of official visitors was reported by some schools as paying long-term dividends. Some schools make a point of allowing parents to sit in class or mingle with the school as it goes about its daily routine in order to instil confidence – something that is not always popular with staff but which is beneficial overall, particularly where parents may be dubious about their child's placement. In a few residential schools, there is also attractive accommodation where families can stay overnight.

Turning to the more difficult area of meeting parents beyond the confines of the school, Cole *et al.* (1998) found the leaders of many BESD schools viewed it as beyond their school's task to visit pupils' homes: the parents should and generally did (it was claimed) attend meetings when asked to at the school. At least one Deputy Head reported that it was dangerous to be in a student's house because the parent may make allegations.

However, many other schools discounted such risks and attached great importance to home visiting. The Head, or member of the senior leadership team, who was sometimes personally involved in visiting the child's home, saw it as an important way of building bridges and breaking down parental views of desk-bound professionals who did not understand. Daniels *et al.* (2003) found senior staff in PRUs sometimes setting similar great store by home visits. There was a strong feeling that it was better to sit down and talk, in the parental home over a cup of tea than to use the impersonal and sometimes threatening or misleading medium of communication by letter, text or telephone. This could be a stark and necessary contrast to these parents' previous experience of teachers working in some mainstream schools, who had been seen as being distant, unapproachable and lacking in understanding of their child and their family. Parents could feel respected in a way they had not felt before, making them more receptive to the suggestions and requests of the school. An initial visit might start a pattern of a twice-termly home visit.

Of course, there are families who clearly feel uncomfortable about visits to their home. Also, being realistic, there can be times when visits are unwise on safety grounds. It could be too labour-intensive and beyond your work setting's resources for additional staff 'to ride shotgun' as you or a single colleague make visits in neighbourhoods or individual homes where staff might be in physical jeopardy or at risk of career-threatening, exaggerated or false allegations of malpractice. Clearly making visits in pairs is safer. The school must have protocols in place for assessing the level of risk involved – and balancing these risks against the perceived benefits. Then meetings on neutral territory, e.g. a cafe on a site easily accessed by the parent on a neighbourhood shopping centre, might be the best approach.

Using approaches such as those outlined above can bring about positive changes of attitude, often 'winning over' initially distrustful and apparently obstructive parents, families and carers, making them 'sources of support' rather than people who undermine your work settings' best efforts.

All in all, parents need to be offered a personalised, non-judgemental service that can often be in contrast to the way they have been received by the child's previous schools' staff or treated by representatives of other professions. However, there is a continuing need to be wary of educationalists unqualified in social work or family therapy, getting out of their depth. It is also a task for school leaders to see that less experienced staff understand the pitfalls, do not indulge in well intentioned but potentially harmful family interventions with parents. Further useful discussion on working with parents is given in Porter (2008).

PARENT TRAINING AND SUPPORT PROGRAMMES

It could be that your school links into very promising forms of parent training offered by local Children's Centres, or to schools or CAMHS where staff have received training in well-developed parent-training strategies, such as the two described below.

The Triple P programme or 'Positive Parenting Programme' (Sanders, Markie-Dadds and Turner 2003; Triple P, undated) is delivered at five levels:

- Level 1 offers universal information and is delivered through radio and TV

- Level 2 offers two twenty-minute consultations by a parenting 'expert' such as a nurse in a general practice

- Level 3 is for parents of children with more difficult problems and involves four forty-minute consultations

- Level 4 consists of an eight-week programme of consultations, each lasting an hour or more

- Level 5 intervention is of indeterminate length, involves home visiting and is for parents who have more complex issues such as inter-parent relationship difficulties or depression or who might be at risk of maltreating their children.

It is likely that Levels 4 and 5 will be appropriate for many parents of children with BESD. The Triple P programme is now being offered through Sure Start and Children's Centre in various cities and areas of England, including Birmingham and Cumbria.

Perhaps the best-known approach to working with parents is 'The Incredible Years' (IY) programme associated with Professor Caroline Webster-Stratton from Seattle, which also reaches into social-skills training in schools through 'Dinosaur Schools'.[1] The basic IY parenting programme is designed to promote positive strategies and to assist parents in managing children's behaviour problems. Delivered commonly through detailed group discussion and role play, the parental behaviour that leads to better child behaviour is drawn out and practised. The programmes can be done individually, with or without the children. It includes helping parents to develop skills in playing with their children; assisting their children's learning; positive reinforcement; limit setting; non-physical discipline alternatives; problem solving; effective communication skills; and supporting their children's education. There is also an advanced course for parents whose children have behaviour problems that might merit clinical interventions, e.g. from clinical psychologists.

Webster-Stratton was particularly concerned about engaging 'hard to reach families' who might not attend series of training sessions offered in clinics attached to hospitals. She comments:

> Such families have been described as unmotivated, resistant, unreliable, disengaged, chaotic, in denial, disorganized, uncaring, dysfunctional and unlikely candidates for this kind of treatment – in short, unreachable. However, these families might well describe traditional clinic-based programs as 'unreachable'. Clinical programs may be too far away from home, too expensive, insensitive, distant, inflexible in terms of scheduling and content, foreign in terms of language (literally or figuratively), blaming or critical of their lifestyle. A cost–benefit analysis would, in all likelihood, reveal that the costs to these clients of receiving treatment far outweigh the potential benefits) even though they do genuinely want to do what is best for their children. (Webster-Stratton 1998a, p.184 cited in University of Wales 2006).

Where meals, transport and child-care are laid on then these programmes become much more realistic and attractive. They should be available far more regularly for the parents whose children, aged 2–10 years, are said to have BESD.

REVIEW

In this chapter we have offered a brief outline of an important topic, to which schools respond in different ways. We looked at government expectations in the latest BESD guidance, of the need for an understanding of how parents often feel, and the very real difficulties they can face in forming a mutually beneficial working relationship with educational settings, CAMHS and children's services. We then sketched proven approaches to engaging with parents, before ending with an endorsement of parent-training programmes, now becoming more widespread across the country.

NOTE

1   'Dinosaur School' (DS) consists of 18 weekly, two-hour sessions for groups of about six young primary school children. DS features puppet characters Dina Dinosaur, Detective Wally and Molly Manners. DS teaches social and problem-solving skills, anger management, friendship and academic skills such as concentrating and checking. Desired behaviours are rewarded by labelling the behaviour and awarding 'dinosaur chips' as tokens, which children can exchange for pencils or stickers. For homework, children talk to their parents about their progress.

CHAPTER 11

REVIEW AND CONCLUSIONS

At the start of this book we set ourselves the task of offering an approachable overview of good practice when working with children with BESD. We have been guided by the well-founded premise that increasing knowledge and understanding of social, emotional and sometimes biological/genetic factors in child development is an important step to enhancing practitioner skills, and the first half of the book, in particular, was devoted to this endeavour. In the latter chapters we described interventions that research and experience over many decades indicate are helpful in addressing the wide-ranging needs and building the capacities of children such as Cameron, Ashley, Ryan, Cheryl and Stephen.

There are two parts to this final chapter. First, a review of key points made in the preceding chapters and, second, a brief consideration of the crucial topic of caring for you, the practitioner – without which, effective interventions are nearly impossible to sustain.

REVIEW OF KEY POINTS

In Chapter 1, we expressed our preference for the 'SEBD' ordering of letters, noting the crucial importance of the 'social' and 'emotions' in the construction of children's difficulties. When the 'B' comes first it can lead to an unhelpful focus on a simplistic form of 'behaviour management', which we believe can be counterproductive. However, because 'BESD' is currently used by the English Government, we felt obliged to use it in this book, noting that if the 'B' actually stood for 'biological' then greater accuracy would be achieved – taking the official label closer to the 'bio-psycho-social' perspective that we advocate. We also gave figures suggesting that between 3–6 per cent of children, perhaps more, could be included in a wide and difficult-to-define grouping. We reported the common perception that 'BESD' were now present in more children, linking into changes in childhood and society.

In the second chapter we noted that debates of many decades ago still resonate today: for example, what and how broad an educational curriculum should be required and whether it is better to confront emotional difficulties head-on or to side-step them, trying instead to displace the BESD through giving the child absorbing, successful experience in education or social activity that builds their self-esteem and resilience? We also summarised the types of educational provision made over many decades and continuing today in a five-tiered model – from support within mainstream schools (where the majority of children with BESD are) through to special schools with boarding facilities for a very small percentage of pupils with particular family difficulties. We strongly endorse the creation of a more understanding and inclusive mainstream system but believe that, in an imperfect world, each tier of provision could be the most appropriate option for a particular child.

The third chapter looked in some depth at child development and its links to BESD. Research into neuroscience indicates that the ways in which our bodies react physically and emotionally link to bio-chemical balances in our brain. How young children are nurtured in their early years greatly affects how their nature develops, but we stressed that the child brain remains 'plastic' and educational practitioners can still have a positive impact – particularly during a second flowering and pruning of neural pathways in the teenage brain. We also looked here at attachment and needs theory, the stages of childhood, risk, resilience, play, and the effects of parental separation, before ending the chapter with an outline of mental-health difficulties.

In the fourth chapter we considered some still useful aspects of the psychodynamic perspective and the impact and limitations of behaviourism on school practice. We continued with a consideration of the cognitive-behaviourist approach, and its potential for adjusting the distorted and, sometimes, unduly pessimistic thought processes of children with BESD. Next, we considered the coming together of eastern tradition and modern cognitive psychology in 'Mindfulness'. Finally we looked at the impact of ideas from 'Positive Psychology' on how we should tackle the social and emotional difficulties of children.

In Part Two, 'Helpful Interventions', the different levels of provision that impact on the child with BESD were examined. Whole-school influences, including the importance of distributed and collaborative leadership and the creation of an inclusive ethos, were considered. We described how there needs to be a culture of caring, sharing and responsiveness that encourages children who challenge to participate fully in school life. A deep commitment to the promotion of well-being is also crucial as is an outward-looking attitude that valued connections with other schools and support agencies.

In Chapter 6 we moved to the classroom level. The history of BESD provision, supported by the research, shows that well-delivered teaching and learning approaches that work for pupils without difficulties will *also* help most children with BESD (although flexibility and responsiveness to individual need is of great importance). Therefore the advice of the government on *Quality First Teaching* and *Assessment for Learning* is highly relevant here. So, too, is research and guidance on the importance of establishing routines, general teaching skills and modelling of appropriate behaviours, as well as showing awareness of all the components of the behaviour environment. Further attention was given to building emotional well-being in the classroom. Brief consideration was given to two forms of group intervention felt to be of particular value: Circle of Friends and Nurture Groups.

In Chapter 7 discussion moved to helpful intervention at the level of the individual in and around the classroom. How can a child with BESD be helped to become more receptive to teaching? Strategic planning, involving assessment, implementation, evaluation and review, should always be the backdrop. We considered the advantages and disadvantages of trying to measure achievement and even emotions. Identifying and addressing 'co-morbid' special needs, such as SLCN or difficulties in basic skills, were essential as was a personalised, individual approach to delivering the curriculum. Motivation and control linked to how members of staff spoke to the child with BESD: negative language could inflame difficult moods. Praise or other rewards given had to be given in a way that contributed to a 'growth' mindset. Attention was paid to using school procedures to cope with behaviour difficulties. Finally, the beneficial use of support staff was considered.

The next chapter was concerned with well-being and mental health. Suggestions were made on how to work through relationships. We discussed 'active listening', the when and how of talking to children, suggesting it can be better not to talk but rather to engage or divert or encourage the child through purposeful activities provided by art or sport or other pursuits. We noted how neuroscience supports the appropriate use of physical contact to encourage the flow of helpful body hormones, while recognising the understandable wariness with which touching is now viewed. We considered government guidance on 'use of force', stressing that restrictive physical intervention should be a last resort. 'Safeguarding' issues were sketched before attention was given to the handling of negative emotions, in particular the stages of the 'anger volcano'. Then we considered ways of using cognitive-behaviourist, mindfulness and solution-focused brief approaches. In the final section, we turned to the handling of mental-health conditions.

In Chapter 9 we outlined advice from the government on behaviour partnership working and the potential of Pastoral Support Programmes and the Common Assessment Framework for forging links with support agencies beyond the school. The roles of the different agencies were described before it was suggested a realistic understanding was needed of the constraints under which social workers and CAMHS work.

In the final chapter, we looked at aspects of working with parents and carers, outlining common obstacles to close working – again appealing for an understanding and respectful approach, which, at times, might be hard to offer given the attitudes or resistance that staff can encounter. Strategies for overcoming barriers were suggested before we mentioned the considerable potential of various well-known parent-training programmes for lessening future BESD.

Our remit has been wide, leading at times to only brief consideration of important issues, but further books and resources have been recommended for readers (see also Recommended Resources). In the final section, we move to another crucial topic: caring for staff needs.

CARING FOR THE PRACTITIONER

As one of us wrote recently:

> The most important resources for the effective delivery of education and care for children with SEBD ['BESD'] are people – skilled, energised and committed professionals, with caring yet demanding values and working well together. These practitioners will often be involved in work that is emotionally draining, physically exhausting and occasionally dangerous. A range of stressors, beyond those impacting on professionals working with children who do not have SEBD, will nearly always be present. It is unsurprising that there are often problems in recruiting and retaining 'good' staff. (Cole 2010, p.1)

It should be unnecessary to remind central government or local children's services of this and of the consequent need to attend to the welfare of these staff when calling for a better quality of provision for children with BESD. Yet this topic is neglected in government guidance (DCSF 2008a). Government should be avoiding the imposition of *excessive* and arguably *unnecessary* stresses on practitioners working with pupils with BESD. These stresses can take the form of untested changes to the shape of services or unrealistic and inappropriate expectations of what can achieved. Excessive pressures in England might currently involve expectations relating to 'safeguarding' children and to revised inspection procedures that apparently seek to judge BESD provision in mainstream, special schools and 'short stay schools' (PRUs) essentially by the standards applied to 'mainstream' schools and children without difficulties (Ofsted 2009). Many practitioners fear an altered approach that would be a return to an unfair emphasis (given the chronic barriers to learning of so many of pupils with BESD that we have stressed in earlier chapters) on the importance of raw examination results and national standardised test scores.

These thoughts are in part precipitated by our recent informal communication with school leaders but also, in relation to safeguarding issues, by the English Local Government Association's (LGA 2009) belief that the national inspection body, Ofsted, was 'feeding people's fears' over child safety, with inspectors placing too much emphasis on trivial procedural or organisational weaknesses. The LGA worried that government policy and practice was thereby seriously exacerbating staff recruitment and retention issues to the detriment of troubled children. There have been high-profile cases of appalling child abuse, leading to rightful criticism of children's services and action was required, but there now seems a febrile atmosphere in the UK around 'safeguarding'. Volunteers (ordinary mothers, fathers and neighbours) are reported to be fearful of helping other parents' children for fear of abuse allegations. Professionals supporting children with BESD often work in similar stressful unease, sometimes knowing of the damaged careers of teachers and support staff whose lives have been blighted by false or exaggerated allegations of abuse – allegations sometimes made in the wake of these staff seeking to maintain order in class or carrying out physical restraints for safety reasons (see, for instance, ATL 2009).

Many school leaders fear that instead of the creative, adventurous and committed approaches needed to make learning engaging and accessible to children with BESD, (including trips out, outdoor activities and the like) they are compelled to restrict what they offer. A narrowing of the curriculum is likely, with school leaders ever mindful of 'safeguarding' and – that other contentious issue – an over-zealous application of health and safety guidance.

In short, the stresses on skilled and experienced practitioners in our field could be increasing and could lead to an increasing flow of experienced and talented workers into less arduous work (as Adera and Bullock 2010, find is the norm in parts of the USA). So what can be done in educational settings to protect the well-being of staff and to ensure that their motivation remains high? There are clearly responsibilities for school leaders and colleagues, as well as for individual members of staff to take responsibility for themselves.

With reference to senior staff, we have alluded to the wisdom of a strong but distributed and collegiate type of school leadership, which shares the burden and places trust in emerging talent amongst a team of teachers and other support workers – who feel free to seek help from their fellow workers, who willingly and regularly offer each other support. In specialist settings or in units in mainstream schools, too much responsibility should not rest on any one individual – a likely recipe for bad practice and eventual 'burn-out'.

Senior staff with responsibility for BESD, particularly headteachers of special schools and 'short stay schools' (PRUs), should have access to skilled listeners and advisers from their children's service or governors – perhaps a senior member of behaviour-support or educational-psychology services, or perhaps from a counsellor or therapist from CAMHS. Leadership can be lonely and to have someone respected, trusted, empathetic and non-judgmental in whom to confide when the going gets tough can lower stress levels and help leaders to keep events in perspective.

Within the school or unit, leaders will exercise a supervisory role in relation to their staff's well-being. Thorough, easily accessed support systems should be in place to help colleagues through difficult times, to provide a listening ear and encouragement, to help staff to keep problems in perspective. In relation to continuing professional development (CPD), heads and deputies will appreciate that the greater the skill levels of the staff, the less are likely to be the stressful challenges from pupils with BESD. School leaders have a duty to work with staff to identify needs and then to facilitate appropriate professional development. Observation of teachers' or support workers' practice should be a normal and frequent activity, sometimes by senior staff (perhaps a member of staff such as a behaviour co-ordinator or lead behaviour professional or mentor), sometimes perhaps by peers. In this last respect the co-coaching approach endorsed by the National Strategies (DfES 2005b) can help, and resources should be made available to allow it to happen. Peer observation of teaching is encouraged both for inexperienced and experienced staff. For it to work there is a need for a culture of openness and mutual support for observing, reflecting on and critiquing the classroom practice of colleagues in relation to the whole class or a particular child with BESD, leading to action plans to improve practice. The focus needs to be on a variety of issues but should include enhancing the microteaching and adult–child interpersonal skills outlined in Chapters 6 and 7. To achieve the best results, co-coaching partners should be self-selecting volunteers. The process might also involve the videoing of lessons and later discussion of staff performance. Mentoring and coaching are likely to be of particular importance for new staff, for whom a thorough and extended induction should be organised. The National Strategies' co-coaching is arguably a variation of the Teacher Support Team approach described in Creese, Daniels and Norwich (1997).

Other research (e.g. Hallam and Castle 1999) has suggested the worth of advisory teachers, perhaps working for the behaviour-support service, in developing staff skills in the classroom. The value of development days and longer, accredited courses can also inspire, motivate, reassure and promote reflective practice that lessens staff stress. In short, a variety of ways is likely to be used in effective establishments to develop staff skills. As the Underwood Report noted in 1955, experience, when mixed with the right qualities of character personality, 'is a good instructor' but it does need monitoring and enhancing through continuing professional development.

Finally, there is *you* and the way you yourself, and colleagues, conduct your work and life beyond. We do not wish to end this book in 'preaching' mode – particularly in an area where research data are thin. However, some evidence was given to the national study of BESD special schools in the mid-1990s (Cole *et al.* 1998), to which reference is now made. Our thoughts are also influenced by our extended experience, over some decades, as practitioners and, in recent years, through watching practitioners working with children with BESD. We have seen at first hand the stresses, the illness, and sometimes the resort to comfort eating or alcohol. One school leader in a special school told Cole *et al.* (1998) 'Every experience you don't die from is a good experience', but where these draining situations occur regularly over the years, they contribute to potential burn out. So what can be done to keep staff energetic, enthusiastic and in good health?

The school leaders from over 150 BESD schools told researchers about their ways of reducing stress and relaxing beyond the workplace (Cole *et al.* 1998). Answers included: activities and time with the family, eating out, music, cross-country skiing, rock climbing, amateur dramatics, trips to the theatre, reading, Tai Chi and serving behind the bar in a local pub on a Friday night! We smiled at the London headteacher's antidote to work pressures: 'Regular supplies of beer/wine and cigarettes from France. Humour!' In short, staff in these special schools kept the work worries in perspective and maintained a full and active social and family life. The same is needed for the more numerous practitioners who work with the majority of children with BESD in mainstream schools.

'Mindfulness' might not be for you and Williams *et al.* (2007) recognise that it is very difficult to be mindful when we perhaps need it most. However, other readers could be helped by practising techniques at home or snatching brief moments at work to read their physical barometers through a mini-meditation and body scan, focusing on their breathing, identifying and relaxing places of tension in their bodies – the frown on the face, the tightness in the shoulders. As we outlined in Chapter 8, calm and regular 'breathing into' these areas can help some people to release the body's calming bio-chemicals and to turn your attention away from obsessive and debilitating negative thoughts – if practised and made a part of daily routine (see also Powell 2000). We have also noticed the popularity of physical massage, which has sometimes been offered to practitioners attending 'BESD' conferences.

Advice from another Professor Williams, this time Chris Williams, is relevant for adults working with pupils with BESD as much as for children. The 'Living Life to the Full' programme is being trialled in some Scottish schools. It includes the 'Ten things you can do to feel happier straight away', which link to earlier content in this book (Lyubomirsky 2008) and seems as relevant to staff as to children. Williams and colleagues advise:

- take exercise
- eat fruit as this (particularly bananas) can produce the same 'happy chemical' in the brain as anti-depressants
- see the world for the amazing place it is
- drink 'smoothies', as without fibre your system clogs up and you get sad and sluggish
- eat breakfast – when you do without, your body sulks all day
- work faster when you clean the car or house or do the garden, as that is exercise, but exercise only works properly when you get out of breath and your heart starts pumping
- play music as it cheers you up
- cut out one burger or take-away per week
- do a small kindness for someone else every day
- remember the good things and write them down daily. (Williams 2008)

Gerhardt (2004) underlines the above in her concern about the frequent use of prescription drugs to restore the body's chemical balances. She accepts that the drugs are sometimes necessary and make some people feel better (although the long-term success rate is modest) but for many people, she would advise the alternative approach of changing diet and lifestyle – as exercise stimulates endorphins that are an effective antidepressant. Similarly, body massage can help depression by reducing stress hormones. Meditation acts as a natural tranquilliser, reducing cortisol levels. Diet, she advises, can affect serotonin levels if what you eat is rich in proteins.

There is clearly no magic wand to wave away practitioner stress, but aspects of the above could help staff to do what one headteacher told Cole *et al.* (1998): 'Every time I drive up to school I have to get into smile mode. That's what it is all about'. Another school leader, echoing so many on the need to keep an optimistic outlook, would say to herself regularly: 'It's all a laugh, isn't it!' Display bad humour or regularly show dourness or pessimism and it can spread rapidly to colleagues and to the children, adding to the stress levels of all. Try to keep a balanced view of problems, which for a time can be overwhelming yet a few days later you wonder why you were so concerned. Avoid blaming yourself when actually you know you tried your very best. Sharing problems with trusted colleagues and talking through possible different interventions often helps. Hold to the belief that challenging behaviour in children can and often does change for the better.

We know from our extensive experience that life working with children and young people with complex behaviour difficulties (BESD, SEBD, or EBD or conduct disorders) will never be easy. There are certainly no 'off the shelf' ways of establishing working through relationships, building resilience and well-being, delivering an appropriate curriculum or dealing with acted out or internalised behaviours. However, optimism, a balanced view and self-belief mingled with reliable, empathetic support from colleagues will help to see you through the most stressful times and to highlight the many successes that perhaps you, yourself, sometimes overlook.

We trust that the content of this book has assisted and that we have succeeded in informing, provoking useful reflection and giving practical ideas that either confirm the correctness of what you are already doing or suggest different and better ways of helping.

APPENDIX 1

THE SEBDA ABBREVIATED
POLICY ON INCLUSION
AND SEBD (BESD)

'For children and young people with SEBD inclusion means:

- maximising their access to and engagement with the social and educational settings most appropriate to their present and future needs and aspirations
- providing environments where they experience
  - a personal sense of security
  - respect and being valued
  - supportive relationships
  - sharing their lives with positive adult role models
  - clear, humane and flexible boundary setting
  - successful achievement boosting their self-esteem
  - opportunities to obtain academic and/or vocational qualifications
  - a chance to develop and to exercise personal responsibility
- making available effective support services and facilities whose purpose is to help the young people overcome potential and actual barriers to their healthy social, emotional and educational development.

For many young people with SEBD, inclusion is best promoted by their attendance at mainstream schools with their neighbourhood peers. However inclusion is more than placement in 'ordinary' classes where young people with SEBD can feel isolated or rejected or in on-site provision with little access for the children with SEBD to the social and educational activities of the school. Where occasionally mainstream schools lack the capacity to address the needs of some young people with SEBD and the latter do not *feel* included, then inclusion can be better promoted in special schools, units and other alternative forms of education and training.'

(adopted by governing council of the Social, Emotional and
Behavioural Difficulties Association 2003)

IDENTIFYING SUPPORT FROM LOCAL SERVICES

Complete the following to check your knowledge:

Name(s) of contact(s)	Address(es):	Phone/e-mail – or referral pathway
Behaviour Support Services:		
Educational Psychologists:		
Looked-after children/ social workers:		
Education Welfare Service:		
BESD Schools [LA + voluntary/independent]:		
Pupil Referral Units (short stay schools):		
Special Units/LSUs:		
CAMHS: Tier 2 community services: Tier 3 and 4 services:		
Youth Service:		
Children's Centres:		
Youth Offending Team:		

RECOMMENDED RESOURCES

The following web-sites are recommended for information and sometimes free materials:

Government or government-sponsored sites

A range of resources on children's services, safeguarding, teaching, learning and behaviour available from:

www.behaviour4learning.ac.uk
> wide ranging materials for new teachers and trainers, but of interest to all educationalists.

www.communication.trust.org.uk
> raises awareness of SLCN and provides resources on particular issues such as stammering.

www.dcsf.gov.uk/everychildmatters
> includes materials on Sure Start, children's centres, safeguarding, 'the five outcomes', and much more.

www.healthyschools.gov.uk
> includes anti-bullying materials.

www.nationalstrategies.standards.dcsf.gov.uk
> covers behaviour and attendance, inclusion/SENs, personalised learning, SEAL, AFL, QFT.

www.nice.org.uk
> includes information on mental health (e.g. ADHD).

www.teachernet.gov.uk
> the source for government guidance documents.

INFORMATION ON SCHOOL LEADERSHIP AND WORKFORCE DEVELOPMENT

www.ncsl.org.uk
> the National College for Leadership of Schools and Children's Services site, offering free leadership materials.

www.cwdcouncil.org.uk
 The Children's Workforce Development Council offers free information on the roles of different professionals and on multi-agency working.

INFORMATION ON YOUTH JUSTICE

www.yjb.gov.uk
 free information on the operation of youth justice, including Youth Offending Teams.

Other organisations

SCHOOL-BASED APPROACHES PROMOTING WELL-BEING:

www.nurturegroups.org
 the home of the Nurture Group Network.

www.theplace2be.org.uk
 charity promoting emotional well-being in schools through creative work and play.

www.aquietplace.co.uk
 creates multi-sensory healing environments in schools.

RESIDENTIAL CHILD-CARE

www.ncb.org.uk/ncercc
 the National Centre for Excellence in Residential Child-care, hosted by the National Children's Bureau.

INFORMATION ON MENTAL-HEALTH PROBLEMS AND INTERVENTIONS

www.childbereavement.org.uk.

www.depressionalliance.org.

www.rcpsych.ac.uk/mentalhealthinfoforall.aspx
 free leaflets.

www.winstonswish.org.uk
 resources to support bereaved children.

RESOURCES FOR PROMOTING WELL-BEING AND RESILIENCE

www.brainexplorer.org
 information on the working of the brain.

www.bounceback.com.au
 home of this resilience programme.

www.livinglifetothefull.com
 home of this resilience-building programme.

www.whataboutthechildren.org.uk/research/research-summaries
 free articles on brain development and attachment issues.

SEBD/BESD

www.sebda.org
  assorted information plus description of support and accredited training at master's and
  first degree level and CPD offered by the Social, Emotional and Behavioural Difficulties
  Association, sometimes in partnership with universities.

OTHER SPECIAL EDUCATIONAL NEEDS

www.addiss.co.uk
  for ADHD.

www.bild.org.uk
  for learning disabilities and information on physical interventions.

www.nasen.org.uk
  the national organisation for SENs and inclusion.

INCLUSION ISSUES

www.csie.org.uk/inclusion/legislation.shtml

ASSESSMENT

www.sdqinfo.com
  for the Goodman Strengths and Difficulties Questionnaire.

SUPPORT FOR TEACHERS

www.teachersupport.info
  free confidential support line for teachers.

PARENT TRAINING

www.triplep.net
  Positive Parenting Programme

www.incredibleyears.com
  The Incredible Years programmes.

REFERENCES

Achenbach, T. (1991) *Manual for Teacher's Report Form and 1991 Profile*. Vermont: University of Vermont.

Adera, B. and Bullock, L. (2010) 'Job stressors and teacher job satisfaction in programs serving students with EB/D.' *Emotional and Behavioural Difficulties 15*, 2, 5–14.

Ainsworth, M., Blehar, M.C., Waters, E. and Wall, S. (1978) *Patterns of Attachment: A Psychological Study of the Strange Situation*. Hillsdale: Erlbaum.

American Psychiatric Association (2000) *Diagnostic and Statistical Manual* (4th edn). Washington: APA.

Anderson, S., Brownlie, J. and Given, L. (2009) 'Therapy Culture? Attitudes towards Emotional Support in Britain.' In A. Park, J. Curtic, K. Thomson, M. Phillips and E. Clery (eds) (2009) *British Social Attitudes: the 25th Report*. London: Sage.

Association of Teachers and Lecturers (2009) 'One In Four School Staff Have Faced a False Allegation from a Pupil.' Available at http://www.atl.org.uk/media-office/media-archive/One-in-four-school-staff-have-faced-a-false-allegation-from-a-pupil.asp, accessed on 23/4/10.

Ayers, H., Clarke, D. and Murray, A. (2000) *Perspectives on Behaviour: A Practical Guide to Effective Interventions for Teachers*. London: David Fulton.

Balbernie, R. (2007a) 'Cortisol and The Early Years.' WATCh. Available at http://www.whataboutthechildren.org.uk/images/stories/PDF's/Cortisol%20and%20the%20Early%20Years.pdf, accessed on 23/4/10.

Balbernie, R. (2007b) 'The move to intersubjectivity: A clinical and conceptual shift of perspective.' *Journal of Child Psychotherapy 33*, 3, 308–324.

Barker, P. (1995) *Basic Child Psychiatry*. London: Routledge.

Barker, P. (1996) 'The Psychiatric Treatment of Children with Behaviour Problems.' In V. Varma (ed.) *Managing Children with Problems*. London: Cassell. 13–25.

Baylis, N. (2009) *Happiness*. London: Rough Guides.

Bee, H. (2000) *The Developing Child*. (9th edn) Massachusetts: Allyn and Bacon.

Behaviour For Learning (2009) *A Set of 26 Scenarios*. Available at www.behaviour4learning.ac.uk, accessed on 24/04/10.

Bennathan, M. and Boxall, M. (2000) *Nurture Groups: Effective Intervention in Primary Schools*. (2nd edn). London: David Fulton Publishers.

Bergren, S. (2007) 'Touch Therapy in a School for Children with SEBD in Scotland.' *SEBDA News*, Issue 11, p.16.

Blatchford, P., Bassett, P., Brown, P., Koutsoubou, M. *et al.* (2009) *Deployment and Impact of Support Staff in Schools*. London: University of London.

Boniwell, I. (2006) *Positive Psychology in a Nutshell* (2nd edn). London: PWBC.

Booker, R. and Faupel, A. (2009) 'Social Behaviour.' In N. Frederickson and S. Dunsmuir (2009) *Measures of Children's Mental Health and Psychological Well-being*. London: GL Assessment.

Bowlby, J. (1969) *Attachment and Loss*. Harmondsworth: Penguin Books.

Boxall, M. and Bennathan, M. (1998) *The Boxall Profile*. London: Nurture Group Network.

Bridgeland, M. (1971) *Pioneer Work with Maladjusted Children*. London: Staples.

Bronson, P. and Merryman, A. (2009) *Nurtureshock: Why Everything We Think about Raising our Children is Wrong*. London: Ebury/Random House.

Bush, T. and Glover, D. (2003) *School Leadership: Concepts and Evidence: Summary Report*. Nottingham: NCSL. Available at http://www.nationalcollege.org.uk/docinfo?id=17370&filename=school-leadership-concepts-evidence-summary.pdf, accessed on 23/4/10.

Canter, L. (1990) 'Assertive Discipline.' In M. Scherer, I. Gersch and L. Fry (eds) *Meeting Disruptive Behaviour*. London: Macmillan.

Cefai, C. (2008) *Promoting Resilience in the Classroom*. London: Jessica Kingsley Publishers.

Centre for Confidence and Well-being (2009) *Positive Psychology and Self-esteem*. Available at www.centreforconfidence.co.uk, accessed on 3/2/10.

Centre for Studies in Inclusive Education (2010) *'The Law Supporting Inclusive Education in the UK.'* Available at www.csie.org.uk/inclusion/legislation.shtml, accessed on 4.3.10.

Charlton, T. and David, K. (eds) (1993) *Managing Misbehaviour in Schools*. London: Routledge.

Cheminais, R. (2009) *Effective Multi-Agency Partnerships: Putting Every Child Matters into Practice*. London: Sage.

Cheminais, R. (2010) *Implementing the* Every Child Matters *Strategy*. London: Routledge.

Children's Workforce Development Council (2007) *The Lead Professional Fact Sheet*. IW09/0907. Available at www.cwdcouncil.org.uk, accessed on 15/6/09.

Coffield, F., Moseley, D., Hall, E. and Ecclestone, K. (2004) *Learning Styles and Pedagogy in Post-16 Learning: A Systematic and Critical Review*. Hull: Learning and Skills Research Centre.

Cole, T. (1986) *Residential Special Education*. Milton Keynes: Open University Press.

Cole, T. (1989) *Apart or A Part? Integration and the Growth of British Special Education*. Milton Keynes: Open University Press.

Cole, T. (2005) 'Emotional and Behavioural Difficulties: a Historical Perspective.' In P. Clough, P. Garner, J. Pardeck and F. Yuen (2005) *Handbook of Emotional and Behavioural Difficulties*. London: Sage.

Cole, T. (2008) *Child and Adolescent Mental Health Services: the Views of Professionals Working with Children and Young People with 'BESD': A Survey Conducted in Response to the National CAMHS Review 2008*. Manchester: SEBDA.

Cole, T. (2010) 'Ease practitioner stress to improve services for children and young people with SEBD.' Editorial, *Emotional and Behavioural Difficulties 15*, 1, 1–4.

Cole, T. and Visser, J. (2005) *Young People who Present Challenging Behaviour – a Literature Review.* Commissioned by Ofsted (2005). Birmingham: University of Birmingham.

Cole, T., Daniels, H. and Visser, J. (2003) 'Patterns of provision for pupils with behavioural difficulties in England: A study of government statistics and behaviour support plan data.' *Oxford Review of Education 29*, 2, 187–205.

Cole, T., Visser, J. and Daniels, H. (2000) *An Evaluation of 'In-School Centres,* Report commissioned by Dudley LEA. Birmingham: University of Birmingham.

Cole, T., Visser, J. and Daniels, H. (2001) 'Inclusive Practice for Pupils with EBD in Mainstream Schools.' In J. Visser, H. Daniels and T. Cole (eds) *Emotional and Behavioural Difficulties in Mainstream Schools.* Oxford: JAI/Elsevier.

Cole, T., Visser, J. and Upton, G. (1998) *Effective Schooling for Pupils with Emotional and Behavioural Difficulties.* London: David Fulton Publishers.

Colley, B. (2010) 'ADHD, Science and the Common Man.' *Emotional and Behavioural Difficulties 15*, 2, 83–94.

Cooper, P. (1993) *Effective Schooling for Disaffected Pupils.* London: Routledge.

Cooper, P. (ed.) (1999) *Understanding and Supporting Children with Emotional and Behavioural Difficulties.* London: Jessica Kingsley Publishers.

Cooper, P. (2001) 'Medical Con-trick or New Paradign for EBD? The case of ADHD.' In J. Visser, H. Daniels and T. Cole (eds) *Emotional and Behavioural Difficulties in Mainstream Schools.* Oxford: JAI/Elsevier.

Cooper, P. (2005) 'Biology and Behaviour: The Educational Relevance of a Biopsychosocial Perspective.' In P. Clough *et al.* (2005) *Handbook of Emotional and Behavioural Difficulties.* London: Sage.

Cooper, P. and Cefai, C. (2009) 'Contemporary values and social context: implications for the emotional well-being of children.' *Emotional and Behavioural Difficulties 14*, 2, 91–100.

Cooper, P. and Tiknaz, Y. (2007) *Nurture Groups in School and at Home: Connecting with Children with SEBD.* London: Jessica Kingsley Publishers.

Cooper, P., Smith, C. and Upton, G. (1994) *Emotional and Behavioural Difficulties.* London: Routledge.

Cowie, H. and Jennifer, D. (2008) *New Perspectives on Bullying.* Maidenhead: Open University Press.

Cowie, H., Boardman, C., Dawkins, J. and Jennifer, D. (2004) *Emotional Health and Well-Being: A Practical Guide for Schools.* London: Paul Chapman Publishers.

Cowie, H., Hutson, N., Oztug, O. and Myers, C. (2008) 'The impact of peer support schemes on pupils' perceptions of bullying, aggression and safety at school.' *Emotional and Behavioural Difficulties 13*, 1, 63–72.

Crane, R. (2009) *Mindfulness-based Cognitive Therapy.* London: Routledge.

Creese, A., Daniels, H. and Norwich, B. (1997) *Teacher Support Teams.* London: David Fulton Publishers.

Cross, M. (2004) *Children with Emotional and Behavioural Difficulties and Communication Problems.* London: Jessica Kingsley Publishers.

Csikszentmihalyi, M. (1990) *Flow: the Psychology of Optimal Experience.* New York: Harper Row.

Daniels, A. and Williams, H. (2000) 'Reducing the need for exclusions and statements for behaviour.' *Educational Psychology in Practice 15*, 4, 221–227.

Daniels, H. (2001) *Vygotsky and Pedagogy*. London: Routledge.

Daniels, H., Visser, J., Cole, T. and de Reybekill, N. (1999) *Emotional and Behavioural Difficulties in Mainstream Schools*. Research Report 90. London: DfEE.

Daniels, H., Cole, T., Sellman, E., Sutton, J., Visser, J. with Bedward, J. (2003) *Study of Young People Permanently Excluded from School*. London: DfES.

Delaney, M. (2008) *Teaching the Unteachable*. London: Worth Publishing.

Dennison, B. and Kirk, R. (1990) *Do Review Learn Apply: A Simple Guide to Experiential Learning*. Oxford: Blackwell.

Department for Children, Schools and Families (undated) *Pastoral Support Programme*. Available at http://www.teachernet.gov.uk/_doc/13100/Pastoral%20Support%20Programme%20 Guidance.doc, accessed on 23/4/10.

Department for Children, Schools and Families (2007a) *'Social and Emotional Aspects of Learning for Secondary Schools.'* London: DCSF.

Department for Children, Schools and Families (2007b) *Use of Force to Control or Restrain Pupils*. London: DCSF.

Department for Children, Schools and Families (2007c) *Leading Improvement Using the Primary Framework: Guidance for Headteachers and Senior Leaders*. London: DCSF.

Department for Children, Schools and Families (2007d) *Social and Emotional Aspects of Learning for Secondary Schools*. London: DCSF.

Department for Children, Schools and Families (2007e) *Guidance on Education-Related Parenting Contracts, Parenting Orders and Penalty Notices*. London: DCSF.

Department for Children, Schools and Families (2008a) *The Education of Children and Young People with Behavioural, Emotional and Social Difficulties as a Special Educational Need*. London: DCSF.

Department for Children, Schools and Families (2008b) *Back On Track: A Strategy for Modernising Alternative Provision for Young People*. London: DCSF.

Department for Children, Schools and Families (2008c) *The Assessment for Learning Strategy*. Available at http://publications.teachernet.gov.uk/eOrderingDownload/DCSF-00341-2008.pdf, accessed on 9.6.09.

Department for Children, Schools and Families (2008d) *Inclusion Development Programme (IDP): Dyslexia and speech, language and communication needs (SLCN)*. Available at national-strategies.standards.dcsf.gov.uk/node/165384, accessed on 7/7/09.

Department for Children, Schools and Families (2009a) *Children with Special Educational Needs, 2009: an Analysis*, Chapter 1, Tables 1.1 and 1.4. Available at www.dcsf.gov.uk/rsgateway/DB/STA/t000851/Chapter1.xls, accessed on 10/2/10.

Department for Children, Schools and Families (2009b) *Handling Allegations of Abuse made against Adults who Work with Children and Young People: Practice Guidance*. London: DCSF.

Department for Children, Schools and Families (2009c) *Promoting and Supporting Positive Behaviour in Primary Schools: Developing Social and Emotional Aspects of Learning (SEAL)*. London: DCSF.

Department for Children, Schools and Families (2009d) *Inclusion Development Programme: Supporting Pupil on the Autistic Spectrum e-learning course.* Available at www.nationalstrategies. standards.dcsf.gov.uk/node/165037, accessed on 7/7/09.

Department for Children, Schools and Families (2009e) *Building a Safe, Confident Future: The Final Report of the Social Work Task Force,* Executive Summary. London: DCSF.

Department for Children, Schools and Families (2010) *Inclusion Development Programme: Supporting Pupils with BESD.* Available at nationalstrategies.standards.dcsf.gov.uk/ node/327855?uc=force_uj, accessed on 6/3/10.

Department for Children, Schools and Families/Department of Health (2008a) *With Children and Young People in Mind: the Final Report of the National CAMHS Review.* London: DCSF/ DoH.

Department for Children, Schools and Families/Department of Health (2008b) *PRUs Achieving National Healthy School Status.* London: DCSF/DoH.

Department for Education (1994a) *Pupil Behaviour and Discipline.* Circular 8/94 London: DFE.

Department for Education (1994b) *The Education of Children with Emotional and Behavioural Difficulties.* Circular 9/94. London: DFE.

Department for Education and Employment (1999) *School Inclusion: Pupils Support.* Circular 10/99. London: DfEE.

Department for Education and Employment (2001a) *Code of Practice on the Identification and Assessment of Pupils with Special Educational Needs.* London: DfEE.

Department for Education and Employment (2001b) *Promoting Children's Mental Health within Early Years and School Settings.* London: DfEE.

Department for Education and Employment (2003a) *Report of the Special Schools Working Group.* London: DfES.

Department for Education and Skills (2003b) *Every Child Matters.* Green Paper. London: DfES.

Department for Education and Skills (2004a) *Removing Barriers to Achievement: The Government's Strategy for SEN.* London: DfES.

Department for Education and Skills (2004b) *Improving Behaviour for Learning DVD for Secondary Schools.* London: DfES.

Department for Education and Skills (2005a) *Learning Behaviour: The Report of the Practitioners' Group on School Behaviour and Discipline.* (The Steer Report). London: DfES.

Department for Education and Skills (2005b) *The National Framework for Mentoring and Coaching: Implications for ITE and CPD.* Available at www.nationalstrategies.standards.dcsf.gov. uk/node/83265, accessed on 10/7/09.

Department for Education and Skills (2005c) *Behaviour and Attendance Toolkit Unit 10: Links with Partners and Other Agencies.* Ref. 1266–2005, London: DCSF.

Department for Education and Skills (2006a) *2020 Vision: Report of the Teaching and Learning in 2020 Review Group.* London: DfES.

Department for Education and Skills (2006b) *Learning Behaviour Principles and Behaviour – What Works in Schools.* Part 2 of the report of the Practitioners' on School Behaviour and Discipline chaired by Alan Steer. London: DfES.

Department for Education and Skills (2006c) *Guide to definitions used in CAF Form.* London: DfES.

Department for Education and Skills DfES (2007a) *School Discipline and Pupil Behaviour Policies: Guidance for Schools.* London: DfES.

Department for Education and Skills (2007b) *The Common Assessment Framework for Children and Young People: Practitioners' Guide – Integrated Working to Improve Outcomes for Children and Young People.* London: DfES.

Department for Education and Skills/Department of Health (2007a) *Guidance for Schools on Developing Emotional Health and Well-being.* Available at www.healthyschools.gov.uk, accessed on 12/7/09.

Department for Education and Skills DfES/DoH (2007b) *PSHE Education: Guidance for Schools.* Available at www.healthyschools.gov.uk, accessed on 12/7/09.

Department of Education and Science (1974) *The Health of the School Child, 1971–2, Report of the Chief Medical Officer.* London: HMSO.

Department of Education and Science (1975) *Discovery of Children Requiring Special Education and the Assessment of their Needs,* Circular 2/75. London: DES.

Department of Education and Science (1978) *Report of the Committee of Enquiry into the Education of Handicapped Children and Young People.* [The Warnock Report]. London: HMSO.

Department of Education and Science (1989) *Discipline in Schools: Report of the Committee of Enquiry chaired by Lord Elton.* London: HMSO.

Department of Health (2004a) *At Least Five a Week: Evidence of the Impact of Physical Activity and Its Relationships to Health.* London: The Stationery Office.

Department of Health (2004b) *National Service Framework for Children, Young People and Maternity Services.* London: DoH.

Department of Health and Social Security (1970) *Care and Treatment in a Planned Environment.* Advisory Council on Child-care. London: HMSO.

Dockar-Drysdale, B. (1968) *Therapy in Child-care.* London: Longman.

Dowling, M. (2010) *Young Children's Personal, Social and Emotional Development* (3rd edn). London: Sage.

Duffield, J. (1998) 'Learning experiences, effective schools and social context.' *Support for Learning 13,* 1, 13–16.

Dweck, C. (2006) *Mindset: the New Psychology of Success.* New York: Random House.

Dweck, C. (2009) 'Low-effort success mustn't be praised.' *Times Educational Supplement Scotland,* 18 September, p.21.

Elliott, J. and Place, M. (1998) *Children in Difficulty: A Guide to Understanding and Helping.* London: Routledge.

Fahlberg, V. (2003) *A Child's Journey Through Placement.* London: BAAF.

Farrell, M. (2006a) *Behavioural, Emotional and Social Difficulties: Practical Strategies.* London: Routledge.

Farrell, M. (2006b) *The Effective Teacher's Guide to Moderate, Severe and Profound Learning Difficulties.* London: Routledge.

Farrell, M. (2006c) *The Effective Teacher's Guide to Dyslexia and Other Specific Learning Difficulties.* London: Routledge.

Farrell, M. (2006d) *The Effective Teacher's Guide to Autism and Communication Difficulties.* London: Routledge.

Farrell, M. (2006e) *The Effective Teacher's Guide to Sensory Impairment and Physical Disability.* London: Routledge.

Faupel, A. (2004) (ed.) *Emotional Literacy: Assessment and Intervention.* Southampton Psychology Service SEMERC. London: NfER/Nelson.

Faupel, A., Herrick, E. and Sharp, P. (1998) *Anger Management.* London: David Fulton.

Fletcher, C. (2005) 'Mental Health of Care Leavers.' In A. Wheal (2005) *The Leaving Care Handbook.* Lyme Regis: Russell House Publishing. pp.181–199.

Fox, M. (2001) *The Theory and Practice of Cognitive-Behavioural Management.* Ainsdale: Positive Behaviour Management.

Frederickson, N., Dunsmuir, S. and Baxter, J. (2009) *Measures of Children's Mental Health and Psychological Wellbeing.* London: GL Assessment.

Fullan, M. (2003) *The Moral Imperative of School Leadership.* Thousand Oaks: Corwin Press.

Fullan, M. (2005) 'Professional learning communities writ large.' *On Common Ground,* National Education Service. Available at http://www.michaelfullan.ca/Articles_05/UK_Ireland_preread_final.pdf, accessed on 23/4/10.

Fullan, M. (2009) *The Challenge of Change: Start School Improvement Now* (2nd edn). Thousand Oaks, California: Corwin Press.

Galvin, P. (1999) *Behaviour and Discipline in Schools: Practical Positive and Creative Strategies for the Classroom.* London: David Fulton Publishers. pp.109–111.

Geddes, H. (2006) *Attachment in the Classroom: The Links Between Children's Early Experience, Emotional Well-being and Performance in School.* London: Worth Publishing.

Gerhardt, S. (2004) *Why Love Matters: How Affection Shapes a Baby's Brain.* London: Brunner-Routledge.

Gladwell, M. (2000) *The Tipping Point.* Boston: Little Brown.

Goleman, D. (1996) *Emotional Intelligence.* London: Bloomsbury Press.

Gowers, S.E. and Green, L. (2009) *Eating Disorders: Cognitive Behaviour Therapy with Children and Young People.* London: Routledge.

Goodman, R. (1997) 'The Strengths and Difficulties Questionnaire: A research note.' *Journal of Child Psychology and Psychiatry 38,* 5, 581–586.

Grant, T. and Duthie, L. (2009) 'A circle of support in practice.' *SEBDA News,* Issue 17, p.17.

Green, H., McGinnity, A., Meltzer, H., Ford, T. and Goodman, R. (2005) *Mental Health of Children and Young People in Great Britain, 2004.* London: Office of National Statistics.

Greenhalgh, P. (1994) *Emotional Growth and Learning.* London: Routledge.

Guardian, The (2009) 'Party people: Gregarious types may have more oxytocin receptors.' Available at www.guardian.co.uk/science/blog/2009/aug/13/oxytocin-pair-bonding-social, accessed on 20/4/10.

Hallam, S. and Castle, F. (1999) *Evaluation of the Behaviour and Discipline Pilot Studies (1996–1999).* Research Report RR 163. London: DfEE.

Hanko, G. (1994) 'Discouraged children: When praise does not help.' *British Journal of Special Education 21,* 4, 166–168.

Harris, B. (2007) *Supporting the Emotional Work of School Leaders.* London: Paul Chapman Publishing.

Hay McBer (2000) *A Model of Teacher Effectiveness.* Available at www.teachernet.gov.uk/_ doc/1487/haymcber.doc, accessed on 4/3/10.

Health Advisory Service (1995) *Child and Adolescent Mental Health Services: Together We Stand.* London: HMSO.

Her Majesty's Government (2006) *Working Together to Safeguard Children.* London: The Stationary Office.

Her Majesty's Inspectorate Education (2009) *Developing Successful Learners in Nurturing Schools: The Impact of Nurture Groups in Primary Schools.* Available at www.hmie.gov.uk/documents/publication/ingps.html, accessed on 7/3/10.

Hyland, J. (1993) *Yesterday's Answers: Development and Decline of Schools for Young Offenders.* London: Whiting and Birch/SCA.

James, O. (2007) *Affluenza.* London: Vermilion.

Jones, G. (2002) *Educational Provision for Children with Autism and Asperger's Syndrome.* London: David Fulton Publishers.

Kauffman, J.M. (2001) *Characteristics of Emotional and Behavioural Disorders of Children and Youth.* (7th edn). Merrill Prentice Hall: New Jersey.

Kolb, D.A. (1984) *Experiential Learning.* New Jersey: Prentice Hall.

Kounin, J.S. (1977) *Discipline and Group Management in Classrooms.* New York: Krieger.

Kutscher, M.L. (2008) *ADHD – Living Without Brakes.* London: Jessica Kingsley Publishers.

Laslett, R. (1977) *Educating Maladjusted Children.* London: Granada.

Laslett, R. (1983) *Changing Perceptions of Maladjusted Children.* London: AWMC.

Layard, R. and Dunn, J. (2009) *A Good Childhood: Searching for Values in a Competitive Age. Report for Children's Society.* London: Penguin.

Local Government Association (2009) 'Improvement Agenda Set for Ofsted.' Available at www.lga.gov.uk, accessed on 5/11/09.

Long, R. and Fogell, J. (1999) *Supporting Pupils with Emotional Difficulties.* London: David Fulton Publishers.

Lown, J. (2001) *Anger and Its Management.* Ainsdale: Positive Behaviour Management.

Lyubomirsky, S. (2008) *The How of Happiness: A Scientific Approach to Getting the Life you Want.* New York: Penguin Press.

Maier, H. (1981) 'Essential Components in Treatment Environments for Children.' In F. Ainsworth and C. Fulcher (eds) *Group Care for Children.* London: Tavistock.

Marchant, S. (1995) 'The essential curriculum for pupils exhibiting emotional and behavioural difficulties.' *Therapeutic Care and Education 4,* 2, 36–47.

Maslow, A.H. (1943) 'A theory of human motivation.' *Psychological Review 50,* 370–396.

McCarthy, D. (ed.) (2008) *Speaking about the Unspeakable: Non-verbal Methods and Experiences in Therapy with Children.* London: Jessica Kingsley Publishers.

McCrory, E. and Cameron, R. (2009) 'Resilience.' Part of N. Frederickson and S. Dunsmuir (2009) *Measures of Children's Mental Health and Psychological Well-being: A Portfolio for Education and Health Professionals.* London: GL Assessment.

McGrath, H. and Noble, T. (2010) 'Bounce Back.' Available at www.bounceback.com.au, accessed on 10/1/10.

McLeod, G. (2010) 'Identifying obstacles to a multi-disciplinary understanding of disruptive behaviour.' *Emotional and Behavioural Difficulties 15*, 2, (in print).

McNamara, E. (ed.) (2009) *Motivational Interviewing.* Ainsdale: Positive Behaviour Management.

McSherry, J. (2004) *Learning Support Units: Principles, Practice and Evaluation.* London: David Fulton Publishers.

Mental Health Foundation (1999) *Bright Futures: Promoting Children's and Young People's Mental Health.* London: Mental Health Foundation.

Meyer, W., Reisenzein, R. and Dickhauser, O. (2004) 'Inferring ability from blame: effects of effort versus liking-oriented cognitive schemata.' *Psychology Science 46*, 2, 281–293.

Millham, S., Bullock, R. and Cherrett, P. (1975) *After Grace-Teeth.* London: Chaucer.

Ministry of Education (1955) *Report of the Committee on Maladjusted Children* [The Underwood Report]. London: HMSO.

Montgomery, D. (1999) 'Coping with Children with EBDs in the Primary Classroom.' In P. Cooper (ed.) *Understanding and Supporting Children with Emotional and Behavioural Difficulties.* London: Jessica Kingsley Publishers.

Mosley, J. (2004) 'Can quality circle time support pupils with EBD?' *SEBDA News,* Issue 4, 6–7.

Mosley, J. (2008) 'Setting Up and Running Circles of Support.' *SEBDA News,* Issue 15, Spring 2008, pp.20–23.

Munn, P., Lloyd, G. and Cullen, M. (2000) *Alternatives to School Exclusion.* London: Paul Chapman.

National Foundation for Educational Research (2006) *How Is the* Every Child Matters *Agenda Affecting Schools? Annual Survey of Trends in Education.* Available at http://www.nfer.ac.uk/nfer/publications/AST01/AST01part2.pdf, accessed on 8/3/10.

National Foundation for Educational Research (2007) *How Is the* Every Child Matters *Agenda Affecting Schools? Annual Survey of Trends in Education.* Available at www.nfer.ac.uk/nfer/publications/ASO01/ASO01part5.pdf, accessed on 8/3/10.

National Institute for Health and Clinical Excellence (NICE) (2008) Attention Deficit Hyperactivity Disorder. Guideline 72. Available at www.org.uk/nicemedia/pdf/CG72QRG.pdf, accessed on 8/3/10.

Nurture Group Network (2010) *What is a Nurture Group?* Available at www.nurturegroups.org, accessed on 5/2/10.

Ofsted (1995) *Annual Report of Her Majesty's Chief Inspector for Schools.* London: Ofsted.

Ofsted (1999) *Principles into Practice: Effective Education for Pupils with EBD.* London: Ofsted.

Ofsted (2003) *Pupils with Emotional, Behavioural and Social Difficulties in Mainstream Schools.* HMI 511. London: Ofsted.

Ofsted (2005) *Managing Challenging Behaviour.* London: Ofsted.

Ofsted (2006) *Inclusion: Does It Matter Where Children are Taught?* HMI 2535. London: Ofsted.

Ofsted (2009) *The Annual Report of Her Majesty's Chief Inspector of Schools, Children's Services and Skills, 2008/09.* London: Ofsted.

Palmer, S. (2007) *Toxic Childhood.* London: Orion.

Porter, L. (2000) *Behaviour in Schools: Theory and Practice for Teachers.* Buckingham: Open University Press.

Porter, L. (2008) *Teacher–Parent Collaboration: Early Childhood to Adolescence.* Victoria: Acer.

Postman, N. (1982) *The Disappearance of Childhood: Redefining the Value of School.* New York: Vintage Books.

Powell, T. (2000) *The Mental Health Handbook* (Revised edn). Milton Keynes: Speechmark.

Ratcliffe, L. (2001) *Responding to Pupil Bereavement.* Merseyside: Positive Behaviour Management.

Redl, F. (1966) *When We Deal with Children.* New York: Free Press.

Redl, F. and Wineman, D. (1952) *Controls From Within.* New York: Free Press.

Rees, I.G. (2001) *Pupil Support: A Solution-Focused Approach.* Ainsdale Positive Behaviour Management.

Reinart, H. and Huang, A. (1987) *Children in Conflict* (3rd edn). New York: Merrill.

Reynolds, S., MacKay, T. and Kearney, M. (2009) 'Nurture Groups: A large-scale, controlled study of effects on development and academic attainment.' *British Journal of Special Education 36,* 4, 204–212.

Rogers, B. (1994) *Behaviour Recovery: A Whole-school Programme for Mainstream Schools.* London: Longman.

Rogers, B. (2000) *Behaviour Management: A Whole-school Approach* (2nd edn). London: Paul Chapman Publishing.

Rogers, B. (2009) *How to Manage Children's Challenging Behaviour.* (2nd edn). London: Sage.

Rosoman, C. (2008) *Therapy to Go: Gourmet Fast food Handouts for Working with Child, Adolescent and Family Clients.* London: Jessica Kingsley Publishers.

Rothi, D., Leavey, G., Chamba, R. and Best, R. (2006) *Identification and Management of Pupils with Mental Health Difficulties: A Study of UK Teachers' Experience and Views.* Research report commissioned by NASUWT. London: NASUWT.

Rutter, M. and Smith, D. (1995) *Psychosocial Disorders in Young People.* Chichester: John Wiley.

Rutter, M., Maughan, B., Mortimore, P. and Ouston, J. (1979) *Fifteen Thousand House.* London: Open Books.

Sanders, M.R., Markie-Dadds, C., and Turner, K.M.T. (2003) 'Theoretical, scientific and clinical foundations of the Triple P – Positive Parenting Program: A population approach to the promotion of parenting competence.' *Parenting Research and Practice Monograph 1,* 1–21.

SEBDA News (2009) 'False allegations in the media – the House of Commons Select Committee Inquiry.' *SEBDA News, 19,* Spring/Summer, 12–13.

Sedgewick, J., Jones, N. and Turner, P. (2005) *Short Child and Adolescent Mental Health Programme [SCAMHP].* York: University of York.

Sellman, E. (2009) 'Lessons learned: Student voice at a school for pupils experiencing social, emotional and behavioural difficulties.' *Emotional and Behavioural Difficulties 14,* 1, 33–48.

Seligman, M.E.P. (1993) *Authentic Happiness.* New York: Free Press.

Seligman, M., Steen, T., Park, N. and Peterson, C. 'Positive Psychology progress: Empirical validation of interventions.' *American Psychologist 60,* 5, 410–421.

Smith, C. (1988) 'Working with maladjusted children: There's nothing more practical than a good theory.' Editorial, *Maladjusted and Therapeutic Education 6,* 3, 146–147.

Smith, C. and Laslett, R. (1993) *Effective Classroom Management: A Teacher's Guide.* London: Routledge.

Squires, G. (2002) *Changing Thinking and Feeling to Change Behaviour: Cognitive Interventions.* Ainsdale: Positive Behaviour Management.

Stallard, P. (2009) *Anxiety: Cognitive Behaviour Therapy with Children and Young People.* London: Routledge.

Sunderland, M. (2007) *What Every Parent Needs to Know.* London: Dorling Kindersley.

Swinson, J. (2008) 'The self-esteem of pupils in schools for pupils with SEBD: Myth and reality.' *British Journal of Special Education 35*, 3, 167–172.

Talbot, R. (2002) *Looking After the Mental Health of Looked After Children.* Brighton: Young Minds/Pavilion.

Thomas, G. (2005) 'What Do We Mean by "EBD"?' In P. Clough *et al.* (2005) *Handbook of Emotional and Behavioural Difficulties.* London: Sage.

Thomas, J.B. (1980) *The Self in Education.* Slough: NFER.

Tommerdahl, J. (2009) 'What teachers of students with SEBD need to know about speech and language difficulties.' *Emotional and Behavioural Difficulties 14*, 1, 3–18.

Topping, K. (1983) *Educational Systems for Disruptive Adolescents.* London: Croom Helm.

Triple P (undated) *Triple P for Practitioners.* Available at http://www26.triplep.net/?pid=59, accessed on 8/3/10.

UNICEF (2007) *Child Poverty in Perspective. An Overview of Child Well-being in Rich Countries.* Florence: UNICEF Innocenti Research Centre.

University of Wales (2006) *Update on Conduct Disorder and Parenting Interventions.* School of Psychology, Bangor. Available at www.hm-treasury.gov.uk/d/cypreview2006_universityofwales1.pdf, accessed on 23/4/10.

Verduyn, C., Rogers, J. and Wood, A. (2009) *Depression: Cognitive Behaviour Therapy and Children and Young People.* London: Routledge.

Visser, J. and Jehan, Z. (2009) 'ADHD: A scientific fact or a factual opinion? A critique of the veracity of Attention Deficit Hyperactivity Disorder.' *Emotional and Behavioural Difficulties 14*, 2, 127–140.

Visser, J. and Rayner, S. (eds) (1999) *Emotional and Behavioural Difficulties: A Reader.* Lichfield: QEd.

Warnock, M. (2005) *SENs: A New Look.* London: Philosophy of Education Society of Great Britain.

Werner, E., and Smith, R. (1992) *Overcoming the Odds: High-risk Children from Birth to Adulthood.* New York: Cornell University Press.

Wilding, C. and Milne, A. (2008) *Cognitive Behavioural Therapy.* London: Hodder.

Williams, C. (2008) *10 Things You Can Do To Feel Happier Straight Away.* Five Areas. Available from www.fiveareas.com/resourcearea, accessed on 23/4/10.

Williams, M., Teasdale, J., Segal, Z. and Kabat-Zinn, J. (2007) *The Mindful Way through Depression.* New York: Guilford Press.

Wills, D. (1971) *Spare the Child.* Harmondsworth: Penguin.

Wilson, M. and Evans, M. (1980) *Education of Disturbed Pupils*, Schools Council Working Paper 65. London: Methuen.

SUBJECT INDEX

Page numbers in *italics* refer to figures and tables

3Rs of BESD/SEBD 24, 26
ABC of behaviour 84 *see also* behaviourist approach
AFL *see* assessment for learning
ADHD (attention deficit hyperactivity disorder) 15, 16, 17, 19, 21, 47, 71, 132, 140-141, 188, 197, 221.
ASD *see* autistic spectrum disorders 132, 141
accreditation, importance of 102
acting out *see* behaviour
'active listening' 157, 158, 166, 179, 183, 212
adrenaline *see* noradrenaline
additional needs *see* special educational needs
affluenza/ modern childhood 22
alcohol abuse 75, 78, 164, 188
allegations of abuse 161, 162, 164, 191, 207, 214
amygdala 50, 53, 128
anger management 87, 107, 121, 128, 145, 147, 148, 150, 154, 156, 165-169, 183, 184, 209, 212.
The anger volcano 165
assault cycle 184
anorexia nervosa 76, 183
anxiety 47, 63, 71, 72, 74, 88, 136, 145, 176, 205
arousal-relaxation cycle 54
art and creative activities 154, 158-159, 183, 212.
assessment 42, 101, 103, 104, 105, 125,131, 132-136, 152, 188, 189, 212
assessment for learning (AFL) 103, 106, 111, 136, 142, 212, 221
tools 132-136
see also Common Assessment Framework
Assertive Discipline 148, 153
attachment, development of 52–56, 60, 64, 81, 211, 222
difficulties/disorders 21, 47, 52, 56, 78

attention difficulties 17, 71, 73 *see also* ADHD
autistic spectrum disorders 141

BESD/EBD/SEBD
biological reasons for 17, 18, 19, 210
category of SENs 20
contrasting types of 13,14–16,
definitions/nature of 13, 18, 30, 32, 35
disability and 17, 72, 202
emotional reasons for 18, 19, 21, 202, 210
ethnicity and 18
extent of /identification rates 18, 19–22, 210
gender and 13, 77
history of 29–44
identification of 30
medical diagnosis and 17
patterns of provision for children with 43, 211
SENs and 103, 136–142
social reasons for 17, 18, 19, 64, 202
somatic symptoms 72, 88, 89
youth offending and 192
BESD Guidance, the DCSF (2008) 16–18, 43, 112, 136, 140, 143, 144, 201, 202, 213, 221
Baby P 40, 194, 214
back-up/ 'catcher systems' 150
basic skills, lack of literacy/numeracy 34, 102, 137, 212
behaviour
'acted in' /internalised 16, 17, 21,79
'acted out'/externalised 16, 32, 79, 81, 82, 128, 136, 150, 155, 218
audits 99
management in class 36, 114, 147, 115 -118, 131, 135–136, 137, 147–151, 162
consistency of approach 99
'deviance-provocative'/'insulative' 107, 134
Iceberg of Behaviour 6, 78
individual behaviour plans 148

learning and behaviour policies 98, 147
physical environment 126–127
routines/structures ease BESD 34, 36, 115, 129
school behaviour policies 41
sexualised 15, 78
'behaviour environment', checking the 106, 107, 126, 126–127, 129, 212
behaviour partnerships 134, 185, 199, 212
behaviour support services 134, 135, 152, 187, 189, 195, 198, 202, 215, 216, 220
behaviourist approach/ theory 34, 80, 82–86, 146, 173, 211, 212
observation and recording 83, 146
modelling 83, 212
punishment 83
rewards/positive re-inforcement 83, 146
SMART targets 84
star charts/stickers/tokens 83, 209
time-out 86
bereavement 67, 68, 74, 155, 176, 178–180, 188
'bio-psycho-social' perspective 17, 19, 47, 78, 107, 132, 210
bonding 47, 55, 56, 81
Bounce Back Resilience Programme 122, 222
boundary setting *see* routines/structure
Boxall Profile 134
brain development 48–52, 222
bio-chemicals *see also* neurotransmitters 53, 145, 159, 160, 168, 176, 211, 217
emotional brain (limbic system) 49, 52, 53, 155, 165, 176
plasticity and teenagers 52, 211
pruning synapses 50, 52, 53
three part brain (reptilian, mammalian, rational) 49, 165, 167
breathing (for relaxation) 165, 166, 177, 217 *see also* mindfulness
bulimia nervosa 78, 88
bullying 75, 126, 160, 164, 183, 188

CAMHS (child and adolescent mental
  health services) 15, 33, 46, 77,
  81, 92, 164, 173, 175, 181,
  183, 185, 187, 189, 192–194,
  201, 202, 204, 205, 209, 212,
  215, 220
  access to 197, 198
  Four tier CAMHS model 192, 193
  national review of CAMHS(2008)
    46, 71, 195, 196
careers ('Connexions') 191
carers of children with BESD/SEBD
  24, 52, 54, 55, 64, 201, 204
child abuse see safeguarding
Child Behaviour Checklist (Achenbach)
  132
child development and BESD/SEBD
  46-79, 211
  adolescence 63
  babies 48-58
  protective factors 65
  stages of development 47, 62, 70, 78
  toddlers, pre-school and primary
    62–63
child guidance clinics (CGCs) 32, 33
child protection see safeguarding
  children
Children Act (2004) 39, 190, 191
Children's centres 190, 204, 220
children's trusts 190, 195, 204
children in care see looked after
  children
'circle of friends' 55, 78, 106 123, 212
'circle time' 123
Circular 9/94 (1994 government guidance) 35, 36
'claiming behaviour' 56
classroom practice see also teaching and
  learning
  calm classes in BESD schools 24,107
  group interventions 106–129, 212
  individual interventions 130–153, 212
  seating arrangements 139, 140, 178
  situational-awareness/'withitness' 113
clinical psychologists 192, 196
Climbié, Victoria 40, 191, 194, 214
Coalition Government (2010) 184, 200
Code of Practice, 2001 SENs see SEN
  Code of Practice
cognitive behavioural approaches/
  therapy 34, 47, 78, 80, 86–88,
  154, 169, 171, 183, 192, 193,
  211, 212
  'best beliefs' 170
  cognitive cycle 87
  negative automatic thoughts (NATs)
    89
  thinking, emotions and feelings
    86–87
  self-talk 87
co-coaching 215, 216
co-location 199
Common Assessment Framework (CAF)
  185, 187, 188, 199, 212
communication
  difficulties 79, 102 see also speech,
    language and communication
    needs

skills 64, 65, 125
complain, rights to 162, 164
conduct disorders see BESD/EBD/
  SEBD
confidentiality and information sharing
  185, 186, 197, 198, 199
conflict resolution 112, 121
contamination 31
continuing professional development
  (CPD/training) 41, 97, 99,
  100,101, 104, 107, 140, 182,
  188, 195, 215, 216
copy-cat behaviour 75
cortex (neo-cortex) 50, 51, 53, 155, 165
cortisol (the stress hormone) 48, 50,
  52, 53, 72, 143, 176, 218
counselling 77, 157–158, 170, 173,
  188
curriculum and BESD/SEBD 106–
  153, 158, 159, 211, 214, 218
  behaviour a barrier to 17
  flexible, responsive 42, 130, 142
  practical rather than abstract 32, 37,
    144, 212
  range 32, 34, 37
  style of delivery 25
  work-focused learning (KS4) 144

DSM (Diagnostic and Statistical
  Manual) categories 19, 73
defence mechanisms (denial, transference, regression) 81–82, 155
definitions of BESD/SEBD 18, 30,
  32, 35
depression in children 15, 17, 21, 47,
  59, 63, 71, 72–74, 88, 145,
  159, 168, 169, 173, 181, 184,
  192, 222
Dewhurst, R.A. 31, 42
diet /dieting 23, 76
'Dinosaur Schools' 208, 209
Disability Discrimination Act 21, 103
distorted thought patterns 47, 60, 73,
  170, 173, 211 see also cognitive
  behaviourist approaches.
divorce 69
'do-review-learn-apply' cycle 101, 212
'doing' approaches 154, 183, 212
dopamine 41, 51, 52, 53
drug abuse 75, 78, 164, 188, 192
dyslexia 15, 21, 137

EBD see BESD/SEBD
eating disorders 21, 47, 63, 71, 72,
  76–78, 155, 176, 183
ecosystemic approach/theory 47
Education Acts (1944)31; (1981) 35,
  38; (1988) 37; (1996) 35; (2006)
  104, 162
educational psychologists 33, 135,
  175, 187, 189, 192, 198, 202,
  215, 220
Education Welfare Services 190, 220
effectiveness factors in schools 35, 36
Elton Report (1989) 35, 114
emotional
  intelligence/ literacy 49, 53, 55, 90,
    96, 118, 155

regulation 52, 53, 106, 107, 119,
  147, 150, 165, 184
endorphins 49, 72, 218
ethnicity issues 18, 75, 152, 187
Every Child Matters 39, 57, 58, 100,
  105, 161, 191
  ECM Five Key Outcomes 58, 124, 128
examinations /accredited learning 102
exclusions 38, 187, 203
expectations of CAMHS/ social workers 194–198, 199

families and family difficulties see
  'parents'
feelings, thinking and behaviour 118,
  136, 157, 159, 159, 169 see also
  cognitive behaviourist approaches
  and distorted thought patterns
fight, flight, freeze or flock responses
  49, 50, 100, 121, 167, 176
'flow', psychological 92 see positive
  psychology
force, use of see physical restraint
foster care 31, 67
Functional Behavior Analysis 134

general practitioners (GPs) 192, 197,
  198, 200, 205
genetic inheritance 30, 46, 48, 74, 79
grief / grieving process 68, 179–181

handling negative emotions see anger
  management
happiness, promoting/teaching 39,
  40, 90, 160
health and safety 160, 214
Healthy Schools Programme 104,182,
  221
hearing difficulties see sensory impairments
high expectations of pupils with
  BESD/SEBD 41, 98, 108
home visits 206, 207
hormones 72, 89 see also neurotransmitters
humanist approach/ theory 34, 212 see
  needs theory
hyperactivity see ADHD and attention
  difficulties

Iceberg of behaviour 16, 78, 79,107
Inclusion and BESD/SEBD 29, 35,
  38, 43, 45, 95, 96, 97,105, 124,
  125, 129, 138, 211,   219
  critical mass of staff favouring 97
  Inclusion Development Programme
    138, 141, 173
'Incredible Years' (Webster-Stratton)
  208
individualised teaching and support 31,
  32, 102, 130–183, 131, 136,
  142–144, 153
information technology 41, 142
inspection framework for schools 214
inter-agency/inter- disciplinary working 33, 39, 96, 101, 105, 142,
  185–200, 187, 191, 196, 197,
  198, 219

internal working model (IWM) 47, 60, 78

key stages, National Curriculum –Two: 63; – Four 37, 102, 112
key-worker 205, 206 *see also* lead professional

labelling 25, 26, 71, 98, 131, 133
language
staff use of words/ style of speaking/communicating 113, 114, 131, 144, 168, 212
children's *see* speech, language and communication needs
linguistic elements 138–139
lead professional (CAF) 188, 189
leadership in educational settings 35, 95, 96, 211, 215
'distributed'/'collaborative' style of 97, 101, 104, 105, 211, 215
'learned helplessness' 87, 143
learning difficulties and BESD/SEBD 17, 20, 132, 136–142, 189, 212
learning styles ('active experimentation', 'concrete experience') 41, 143, 159
learning support units (LSUs) 187, 200, 220
listening to children's views 96,103,105, 179 *see also* voice, listening to student
literacy difficulties 137 *see also* basic skills, lack of literacy/numeracy
local authorities (LEAs/children's services) 25, 39, 43, 45, 175, 185, 187, 189, 190, 191, 192, 201, 204, 205, 209
'looked after' children 25, 68, 187, 190, 201, 204, 220

maladjustment 30,31,32,35, 103
Managing Challenging Behaviour (Ofsted 2005) 40, 114
Maslow Hierarchy of Needs 57
massage 173
'medical model' and BESD/SEBD 33, 134
medication 71, 107, 140, 217
meditation 88 *see also* mindfulness
mental health *see also* well-being promotion
definitions 71
difficulties/ disorders 21, 23, 46, 55, 64, 67, 69, 72, 78, 88, 90, 104, 131, 155, 176, 183, 188, 211, 212
promotion 39, 46, 90, 104, 118, 183
mentoring 101,112, 142, 145, 152, 202, 215, 216
mindfulness 88–90, 154, 171–173, 211, 212, 216
body scans 90
breathing and awareness 89, 171, 217
inner calm 89

negative thought avoidance 89, 171, 217
reading your physical barometer 90, 217
rumination 89, 90
mindset 'fixed' and 'growth' 47, 59, 61,107, 131, 146–147, 153, 156, 212
'miracle question' (SFBA) 173, 174
moderate learning difficulties (MLD) 137
multi-agency working *see* inter-agency/ inter-disciplinary working

NATs (negative automatic thoughts) 171, 178
National Curriculum 32, 37, 39, 37, 102, 106, 112, 125, 143, 160
National Strategies 39, 99,102,103, 118, 144, 186, 216
National Survey of EBD Schools (1996–1998) 37
needs of children/needs theory 47, 57, 78, 149, 211
neural pathways 48, 49, 51, 52, 211
neuroscience 46, 48, 52, 61, 88, 155, 211, 212
neurotransmitters 48, 49, 51, 52, 53, 58, 72, 74, 79, 89, 160, 173
non-verbal communication 60, 114, 128, 154, 155
noradrenaline (norepinephrine) 49,53
Nurture Groups 123-125, 212, 222
nurture nature debate 30, 48
nurturing babies and children 51, 52, 58, 60, 211

obesity 47, 160
obsessive compulsive disorder (OCD) 19, 71, 77, 88
'off site' special units *see* PRUs
Ofsted (and HMI) 35, 37, 38, 40, 41, 95, 100, 102, 103, 108, 114, 126, 130, 137, 182, 214
oppositional defiance disorder (ODD) 19, 71
outreach services 188, 197
'outward looking schools' 96, 97, 105, 142, 212 *see also* inter-agency working
oxytocin (the 'love hormone') 48, 51

panic attacks 155, 160
parents
family difficulties 14-16, 18, 23, 36, 51, 53, 55, 56, 60, 63, 65, 67, 76, 77, 78, 88, 203-204
separation and divorce 47, 69-71, 155, 178-181, 203, 211
parenting style 47, 51, 53, 58, 60, 63, 66, 78, 115, 146, 178
parent training programmes 198, 201, 202, 205, 208, 212
staff working with 96, 99,105, 124, 154, 188, 195, 201-210, 212
pastoral care/support 36, 108

'pastoral support programmes' (PSP) 151, 187, 199, 212
personalised learning 37, 102,130–153, 142 *see also* individualised learning
peer group pressures 23, 75, 203
peer mentoring 103
physical contact *see* touch
physical environment/buildings/facilities 99, 126–127, 129, 148, 182
physical exercise/ activities/ outdoor pursuits 143, 154, 159, 170, 183, 212, 214
physical restraint 161, 162–164, 168, 183, 184, 212, 214
placement of pupils with BESD, haphazard 30
play 33, 64–65, 125, 150, 154, 158, 159, 170, 211
policies for schools, *see* behaviour; teaching and learning
integrating different policies 99
positive handling *see* physical restraint
positive psychology 39–40, 59, 80, 90–92, 159, 171, 181, 183, 211
'flow' 92, 171, 181
negative emotions, need for 92
positive reinforcement *see* behaviourist approach
practitioner issues *see* staffing
praise, 85, 98, 141, 146, 156, 212
'over-praise' and 'growth' mindset 146
primary care trusts 192, 200
psychodynamic approach/theory 32, 34, 81, 92
psychological approaches/ theories 80–94
pupil referral units (PRUs) 15, 31, 35, 37, 43, 44, 84, 97, 103, 119, 159, 182, 188, 189, 195, 196, 207, 214, 219, 220
psychotherapists 81, 92, 159, 173, 193, 204
psychiatrists 81, 92, 192
puppets as therapy 159, 209

Quality First Teaching (QFT) 106, 108, 111, 129, 212, 221

reading difficulties and BESD/SEBD 21,102, 137, 212 *see also* basic skills
reformatory; industrial and approved schools 30, 31, 33
relationships 24, 25, 32, 41, 44, 46, 55, 74, 97, 98, 108, 124, 131, 150, 154, 155-157, 160, 176, 176, 183, 199, 200, 212, 215, 218
residential schools/ care 13, 18, 20, 24, 30, 31, 33, 34, 36, 43, 126, 149-150, 169, 173, 206, 211
resilience 24, 47, 55, 63, 65, 78, 91, 122, 211, 218, 222
resignification 24

restrictive physical intervention *see* physical restraint
rewarding behaviour 82, 84, 85, 99, 100, 146, 147, 153, 170 *see also* behaviourist approach/theory
risk factors 47, 65, 74, 75, 78, 79, 211
Ritalin (methylphenidate) 71, 140
roles of different professionals/agencies 189
routines/structures/boundaries, value of 34, 36, 58, 100, 106, 115–117, 141, 146, 181, 212, 219
'rubber boundaries' 100, 156
rumination (over negative thoughts) 89, 90, 130

SATs (Standard Assessment Tasks) 39
SEAL 18, 37, 42, 55, 91, 96, 100, 104, 105, 118–122, 128, 202, 220
Three Wave Model 120
SEBD *see* BESD/EBD/SEBD
SEBDA 17, 38, 219
SENs 30, 102, 103, 131, 132, 136–142, 153, 189, 202
SEN Code of Practice (DfEE 2001) 16, 17, 99, 136, 187, 189, 202, 212
SENCo 102, 103, 137, 139, 142, 163
SLCN 21, 102, 132, 132, 137–140, 141, 188, 212, 220
SMART targets 84
safeguarding children 40, 150, 154, 158, 162, 164, 182, 183, 190, 191, 195, 212, 214
sanctions 99, 115, 117, 118, 131, 147
sanctuaries 131, 148, 180
scaling 173, 174
school action plus (CoP stage) 20, 136
school phobia 17, 71, 88
self- esteem 34, 36, 46, 47, 55, 57, 58–59, 67, 77, 78, 107, 124, 126, 136, 138, 143, 159, 168, 188, 211, 219
self harm 17, 47, 63, 72, 74-76, 78, 155, 176, 181
self talk 87, 91, 128, 177
sensory impairments 21, 132, 137, 141–142
separation and loss 47, 53, 67-68, 69–71, 74, 78, 155, 176, 178
serotonin 49, 50, 52, 53, 72, 218
sexualised behaviour 15, 78
short stay schools *see* pupil referral units
situation-specific behaviours 107, 129, 133
Social, Emotional and Behavioural Difficulties Association *see* SEBDA
social factors explaining BESD/SEBD 17, 18, 19, 65, 67, 131, 188
social skills promotion 55, 112, 118–122, 125, 145, 149, 150, 187, 202
social workers/work departments 34, 173, 187, 190,194–195, 204, 205, 212, 220

solution-focused brief approaches/ therapy 88, 154, 173–175, 183, 212
special educational needs *see* SENs
special schools 35, 38, 103, 137, 159, 188, 189, 195, 214, 214, 216, 219, 220
continuing need for 37–38, 44, 45
speech, language and communication needs *see* SLCN
sport 159 *see* physical exercise
staffing
advocates for children 156
burn-out 215, 216
caring 100 -101, 149
diet and lifestyle 217, 218
induction 100
motivation 25, 53, 108
self-evaluation/ appraisal 120
skills 24, 36, 45, 46, 79, 106, 108, 129 *see also* CPD
stress 13, 90, 128, 162-164, 165, 213
support/care for individual 24, 128, 184, 210, 213–218
support from other agencies 185-200
support staff (TAs etc) 131, 139, 142, 151-152, 205, 212
Standard 9, NSF 195
statements of SENs for BESD 20, 136, 187, 189
Steer Reports 40, 41, 97, 98, 195
Strengths and Difficulties Questionnaire (Goodman) 135
stress hormones *see* cortisol
substance abuse 75, 164, 188, 192
suicide 76
synapses, pruning of *see* brain development

Tai Chi 173, 216
talking and listening to children 34, 88, 92, 154,157-158, 183, 212
talking therapies 88, 205
teacher support teams 101, 128, 216
teaching and learning *see also* Assessment for Learning; curriculum; classroom practice
Quality First Teaching and SENs
assessment and planning 111, 131, 132, 144, 152
collaborative 36, 96, 108. 156
effective 108–110
humour 41, 113, 149, 216
individualised/differentiated/ personalised 111, 130–153, 142, 212
intervention cycle 131
planning/structuring 110, 212
prior learning/strengths, building on 110, 137, 142, 143, 153, 159
questioning 111, 112
readiness to learn 130

responding to BESD/ SEBD 96, 101, 102, 105, 106-129, 130–153, 158–160
small step learning 14, 36, 112, 153, 212
voice tone/vocabulary ('positive language') 113, 114, 128, 131, 144–145, 168, 212
writing skills 143
theories underpinning effective intervention 80-94 *see also* behaviourist; cognitive behaviourist; humanist; mindfulness; needs theory; positive psychology; psychodynamic approach
therapeutic approaches 34, 157
therapy, education as 31, 34, 45.
Tourette's syndrome 17
touch 50, 154, 160–161, 212
'toxic childhoods' 22–23, 35, 211
transitions 99, 131, 152, 153
'Triple P' (Positive Parenting Programme) 208
types/range of provision 24, 29, 43, 45, 211
The Five Tiers of Provision 44, 211

'unconditional love/positive regard' 58, 155
Underwood Report (1955) 30, 32-33, 216
understanding behaviour, importance of 24, 98, 210
units , 'on-site'/resource bases 44 *see also* LSUs
off-site *see* PRUs

values, importance of right 25, 29, 53, 95, 98, 104, 105, 155, 211, 219
vetting staff 191 *see also* safeguarding
voice, listening to student/pupil 96, 103, 105, 156

Waves of Intervention Model 129
well-being and mental health
definitions 71
promotion 39, 90, 91, 96, 104, 106, 118, 123, 153, 159, 183, 202, 212, 218, 222
whole-school issues 35, 95-105, 182, 211 *see also* SEAL
inclusive values/ethos 95, 97, 98, 98
learning and behaviour policies 98
'outward looking schools' 96, 97, 105
wiring of brain *see* neural pathways
'within child' behaviour factors 16, 17, 21 79

youth offending / justice 33, 124, 185, 191, 220, 222
youth service 187, 190, 220

'zone of proximal development' (ZPD) 143, 146, 153

AUTHOR INDEX

Achenbach, T. 132,133,134
Adera, B. 214
American Psychiatric Association 19, 79
Association of Teachers and Lecturers 40, 162, 214
Ayers, H. 80, 82

Balbernie, R. 51, 52, 53, 56
Barker P. 133, 159
Baylis, N. 40, 90
Baxter, J. 135
Bee, H. 61
Behaviour For Learning 113, 115
Bennathan, M. 124, 125, 134
Bergren, S. 160
Blatchford, P. 151
Boniwell, I. 90, 91, 92
Booker, R.135
Bowlby, J. 52, 60
Boxall, M. 124, 125, 134
Bridgeland, M. 31, 201
Bronson, P. 85, 146, 147
Bullock, R. 31, 33
Bullock, L. 214
Bush, T. 97

Cameron, R. 135
Canter, L. 148
Castle, F. 216
Cefai, C. 23, 66
Centre for Studies in Inclusive Education 43
Charlton, T. 35
Cheminais, R. 185, 199
Cherrett, P. 31, 33
Children's Workforce Development Council 189
Clarke, D. 80, 82
Csikszentmihalyi, M. 92
Coffield, F. 143
Cole, T. 13, 19, 20, 21, 24, 26, 29, 30, 31, 32, 33, 34, 35, 36, 37, 38, 39, 42, 43, 67, 87, 95, 96, 97, 98, 100, 102, 103, 107, 108, 109, 113, 116, 122, 126, 130, 131, 133, 137, 143, 148, 149, 150, 152, 155, 160, 192,

196, 197, 204, 205, 206, 207, 213, 216, 218
Colley, B. 19, 21, 133, 140
Cooper, P. 23, 24, 26, 32, 36, 47, 97, 125, 132, 133, 140
Cowie, H. 68, 72, 74, 75, 76, 77, 103, 164, 179, 180, 182, 183
Crane, R.. 88, 90, 171
Creese, A. 101, 128, 216
Cullen, M. 109

Daniels, A. 107
Daniels, H. 13, 26, 35, 36, 39, 42, 43, 67, 95, 96, 97, 98, 100, 101, 102, 103, 107, 108, 113, 122, 128, 131, 137, 143, 148, 150, 152, 153, 204, 205, 206, 207, 216
David, K. 35
Delaney, M. 82, 144, 145
Dennison, B. 101
Department for Children, Schools and Families 16, 17, 18,20, 21, 22, 39, 40, 42, 43, 46, 65, 66, 71, 97, 99, 100, 102, 103, 112, 116, 119, 120, 121, 122, 136, 138, 140, 161, 162, 163, 173, 182, 192, 193, 194, 197, 201, 213
Department for Education 35, 36, 38, 41
Department for Education and Employment 14, 16, 21, 22, 136, 140, 152, 187, 201
Department for Education and Skills 33, 35, 38, 40, 41, 42, 57, 58, 95, 98, 99,101 103, 128, 147, 186, 188, 189, 191, 195, 215
Department of Education and Science 33, 35, 38, 39, 114, 197
Department of Health 21, 22, 46, 65, 66, 71, 159, 182, 192, 193, 195, 197
Department of Health and Social Security 34
Dickhauser O. 146
Dockar-Drysdale, B. 149

Dowling, M. 59
Duffield, J. 143
Dunn, J. 21, 22, 23, 35, 40, 46, 55, 80
Dunsmuir, S. 135
Duthie, L. 152
Dweck, C. 59, 61, 85, 146

Elliott, J. 53, 63, 70, 73, 74, 76, 77, 170, 204

Fahlberg, V. 54
Farrell, M. 123, 137, 141, 142, 184
Faupel, A. 135, 166, 184
Fletcher, C. 68
Fogell, J. 59, 67, 68, 70, 167, 168, 175, 176, 177, 180
Fox, M. 87, 170
Frederickson, N. 135
Fullan, M. 96, 97, 185, 199

Galvin, P. 112, 113, 115
Geddes, H. 53
Gerhardt, S. 22, 40, 46, 48, 49, 50, 51, 53, 60, 63, 217
Gladwell, M. 97
Glover, D. 97
Goleman, D. 90
Goodman, R. 135
Gowers, S.E. 78, 88
Grant, T. 152
Green, L. 78, 88
Greenhalgh, P. 82, 130, 131, 149, 152
Guardian, The 48

Hallam, S. 216
Hanko, G. 85
Harris, B. 25, 36, 37
Hay McBer 108
Health Advisory Service 193
Her Majesty's Inspectorate Education (Scotland) 125
Her Majesty's Government 191
Herrick, E. 184
Huang, A. 109
Hyland, J. 33, 34

James, O. 22
Jennifer, D. 103, 164

Jehan, Z. 21, 133
Jones, G. 141
Jones, N., 158

Kabat-Zinn, J. 88, 89
Kauffman, J.M. 21, 29, 30
Kearney, M. 125
Kirk, R. 101
Kolb, D. A. 143
Kounin, J.S. 109, 113
Kutscher, M.L. 71, 141

Laslett, R. 13, 24, 30, 33, 37, 107,
    109, 113, 149
Layard, R. 21, 22, 23, 35, 40, 46,
    55, 80
Lloyd, G. 109
Local Government Association 214
Lown, J. 167, 168, 177, 184
Long, R. 59, 67, 68, 70, 167, 168,
    175, 176, 177, 180
Lyubomirsky, S. 40, 217

McCarthy, D. 154, 167
MacKay, T. 125
McCrory. E 135
McGrath, H. 122
McLeod, G. 19, 30
McNamara, E. 87
McSherry, J. 200
Maier, H. 57, 126
Marchant, S. 37
Markie-Dadds, C. 208
Maslow, A.H. 57
Mental Health Foundation 71
Merryman, A. 85, 146, 147
Meyer, W. 146
Millham, S. 31, 33
Milne, A. 171
Ministry of Education 19, 30, 32
Montgomery, D. 153
Mosley, J. 123
Munn, P. 109
Murray, A. 80, 82

National Foundation for Educational
    Research 185
National Institute for Health and Clini-
    cal Excellence (NICE) 140
Noble, T. 122
Norwich, B. 101, 128, 216
Nurture Group Network 124, 125

Ofsted 35, 36, 37, 38, 40, 41, 43,
    95, 96, 97, 101, 102, 103, 107,
    108, 109, 111, 112, 114, 126,
    130, 133, 137, 155, 206, 214

Palmer, S. 22, 80
Place, M. 53, 63, 70, 73, 74, 76, 77,
    170, 204
Porter, L. 80, 208
Postman, N. 22
Powell, T. 168, 176, 217

Ratcliffe, L. 180
Rayner, S. 43
Redl, F.100, 116, 144, 145, 168
Rees, I.G. 175
Reinart, H. 109
Reisenzein R. 146
Reynolds, S. 125
Rogers, B. 85, 86, 113, 144
Rogers, J. 73, 88
Rosoman, C.169, 170
Rothi, D., 197, 198
Rutter, M. 35, 54

SEBDA 40, 219
Sanders, M.R., 208
Sedgewick, J., 158
Segal, Z. 88, 89, 90, 171, 172, 216
Seligman, M.E.P. 40, 90
Sellman, E., 103
Sharp, P. 184
Smith, C. 47, 80, 97, 107, 109, 113
Smith, D. 54
Smith, R. 40
Squires, G. 171
Stallard, P. 72, 86, 88
Stean, T. 40, 90
Sunderland, M. 48, 49, 50, 51, 160
Swinson, J. 59

Talbot, R. 53, 54, 65, 74
Teasdale, J. 88
Thomas, G. 19, 30
Thomas, J.B. 46, 59
Tiknaz,Y. 125
Tommerdahl, J. 137, 139
Topping, K. 43
Triple P 208
Turner, K.M.T. 203
Turner, P. 208

University of Wales 209
Upton, G. 20, 47

Verduyn, C. 73, 88
Visser, J. 13, 20, 21, 100, 122, 133

Warnock, M. 38, 39
Werner, E. 40
Wilding, C. 171
Williams, C. 217
Williams, H. 107
Williams, M. 88, 89, 90, 171, 172,
    216
Wills, D. 33
Wineman, D. 144, 145, 168
Wood, A. 73, 88